HARDPRESS.NET
HOME OF HARD-TO-FIND BOOKS

The Life of Rev. Martin Cheney
by George Tiffany Day

Copyright © 2019 by HardPress

Address:
Hardpress
8345 NW 66TH ST #2561
MIAMI FL 33166-2626
USA
Email: info@hardpress.net

PROPERTY
OF
State Historical Society of Wisconsin.

Purchased 187

V. MARION STORY

BY GEORGE ALLAN.

PROVIDENCE.
GEO. H. WHITNEY.
1873.

Entered according to Act of Congress, in 1852,
BY C. S. SWEETLAND,
In the Clerk's Office of the District Court of Rhode-Island.

KNOWLES, ANTHONY & CO. PRINTERS.

PREFACE.

Two years ago last May, Mr. Cheney stated to me that, in answer to the repeatedly expressed wish of his brethren and friends, he was preparing some Auto-biographical sketches of his life, and endeavoring to put his papers into such a state as might somewhat facilitate the preparation of a Memoir, should it be called for after his death; and expressed a strong desire that I would consent to undertake the preparation of the work, unless providentially prevented.

Mr. Cheney was my friend. Though never having enjoyed a very extensive personal intercourse with him, yet, in some sense, he had been my counsellor from the beginning of my christian life; and our acquaintance had ripened into strong confidence and affection. Unfitted therefore as I might have felt for such a task, I could not refuse to comply with his request, when I saw that his heart was strongly set on such an arrangement.

In eighteen months from that time his public labors had closed, before he had completed his intended biographical sketches, or more than partially arranged his papers. He indicated his arrangement for the publication of his Life in his Will, notwithstanding I had in the mean time taken up what was expected to be a permanent residence in a distant State. The Church and Society at Olneyville summoned me to occupy the post which his death had made vacant—a measure which probably grew very much out of his own expressed wishes. That post was finally accepted, and the work, such as it is, has been performed amidst the very scenes which his ministry of nearly thirty years had helped to consecrate.

Though, in some respects, a mournful task, it has still been pleasant to hold such a communion with the departed man as has been afforded by the inspection of his manuscripts, by following him along step by step through his significant life, and by the study and attempted development of his character. Though dead, he has spoken to his biographer, in the midst of these labors, with not less impressiveness than when his form was among us, and his voice was ringing in our ears.

As to the manner in which the biographer's task has been performed, I have no expectation that all will regard it as most wisely or happily executed. It was difficult; not only from its nature, but from the state and character of the manuscripts, from the peculiar character of the man, from the somewhat different views entertained respecting him, and from the rapidity with which, amid the numerous and pressing duties of a large and newly assumed pastoral charge, it has seemed necessary to carry the work forward. It was not undertaken until the middle of August last. These difficulties, however, can only be understood by him who encounters them; and their statement is usually accepted by the reader as a thankless and not wholly unselfish service.

But what is written is written. It has been the aim not to glorify Mr. Cheney, not to say every thing about him that could be recollected or learned, not even to record the whole or the half of the striking things which he may have said or done, or which were otherwise connected with his life; but to present, within a reasonable compass, whatever was essential to give a just and distinct view of the man, in his character and in his life. The facts chosen are selected as much for the purpose of exemplifying the *general* facts of his history, as of presenting, in bold relief, a point in his character. And in culling from his writings, an attempt has only been made to show what he taught *in principle*, rather than what he taught in amount; and to represent *how* he taught *in general*, rather than what his method was in every specific instance of his teaching. From a bushel of manuscripts, and the personal recollection of a thousand friends, it would have been easy to make a larger book, but it would not necessarily have answered the real purpose better than this. A small daguerreotype, true to the original, is better than a life-size portrait, whose chief merit were to consist in its being just as tall as the man.

It has been the steady object to present the man just as he was, without magnifying his excellences or concealing his defects. There are no perfect men, in the usual acceptation of that word; or, if there are, Mr. Cheney was not one of them, at least in his own estimation; and to know that he was to be represented as such, would have tried no heart more sadly than his own. If his defects and excesses were to be studiously kept out of view, his biographer might expect, in case the two should meet in heaven, and Mr. Cheney had not parted with his leading characteristics, that the first greeting would be hardly over before a fraternal but decided reproof would be dealt out to the fond partiality which had shielded him. His faults lay on the surface of his nature, obvious to any candid observer; and they who could not love him for what excellences lay beneath them, he did not wish should love him at all. There is no need of hiding his slight imperfections, as well as no justice in doing so. Men who have no great virtues might fear to have their reputation thus hazarded; but there was enough to admire and venerate in Mr. Cheney, after making the largest allowance for every defect. Biographers have generally seemed over-anxious to make model heroes or demigods of their subjects; thinking, perhaps, that the appeal of unalloyed human goodness will be more powerful than when its voice gives out some earthly tones; but it is to be feared that the course has been no more politic than just. The life has seemed more angelic than human, as it has been pictured; and few think it hardly worth the while to try to be angels and live on ambrosia, while required by circumstances to be men, and while carrying about with them a nature that will be satisfied with nothing less substantial than pork and beef. The Scripture biographers have certainly not set any such example. The majestic ideal of the Poet-King, which seems almost complete, is marred before us in the plain story of David's human vices. The picture of Job's martyr-patience needs only a stroke or two from the pencil of our imagination to make it perfect; but that is anticipated by the hasty and almost cynical words which the plain historian puts into his lips. Jesus of Nazareth alone stands complete; and his biographers are but half aware of the glory they are developing. If it will not do to show but the half of a man, it were better to confess that only the moiety is seen, or keep the whole hidden.

It is possible, after all, that the view here presented of Mr. Cheney may be regarded as dependent more or less on the personal friendship which attached the man and the biographer. If so, this only is to be said—that the biographer is not conscious of having been biassed at all in any direction by any such influence. I have sought to give free and independent expression to my own individual impressions. If they are in any respect unjust, the error is to be charged upon me, for I have not written at all under advisement. Considerable portions of the work have, indeed, been read from the manuscript to a few of Mr. Cheney's friends, but not a single sentence has been modified in consequence.

The analysis of his character, and the estimate of him as a preacher, though somewhat novel features in such a work, it is hoped will prove acceptable. Much, called biography, has been almost solely confined to the statement of outward facts;—leaving the spirit of the subject to be inferred if possible from wholly inadequate data. *To exhibit the man* has been the primary object in the preparation of this volume. It has been desired that the body of the work may do for the inner man, what the engraving seeks to do for the outward.

Probably almost every one of Mr. Cheney's friends will regret that some sermon which impressed them so favorably, or some incident which they remember with peculiar interest, could not have had a place. They will be kind and thoughtful enough to remember that the sermons, as they were preached, are nowhere to be found; that only a small number could be selected; that the same thing is true respecting the personal incidents; that no one else may have been so peculiarly impressed by the sermon or interested in the incident as themselves; and that every one else, and especially the biographer, may be ignorant of the facts to which they attach so much importance. The best has been done that could be under the circumstances, to make judicious selections.

Many sentiments will be found often repeated in the various selections from Mr. Cheney's writings. That could not be avoided, nor would it have been desirable if it were otherwise. Dr. Channing says that minds are distinguished more than in any other way, by the prominence which they give to certain traits and truths. Here their individuality appears. The remark is highly applicable to Mr. Cheney. Certain truths there were which lay uppermost in his mind, and these he made frequently to appear. The repetition, however, will seem less striking, if the circumstances connected with each discourse are distinctly kept in mind.

Mr. Cheney had an important and noble mission while in the flesh. He acted with a strong power on the hearts about him,—kindling up their courage and inspiring the purpose to live worthily in time, by reverencing God and toiling for the redemption of man. And if, by means of this volume, that influence may be perpetuated and extended, the author will feel himself freshly honored in its preparation.

Olneyville, R. I., Dec. 3, 1852.

ERRATA. Page 199; what should have been Chapter XII., is Chapter IX. Page 409; a few copies have Sept. 1852, instead of 1851. A few typographical errors will be found, which the reader's judgment is supposed capable of correcting.

CONTENTS.

CHAPTER I.
Sketches of his early life.................................13

CHAPTER II.
"He was lost and is found.............................27

CHAPTER III.
Entrance upon the work of the the Ministry.........45

CHAPTER IV.
Choosing and entering his field of labor............64

CHAPTER V.
"The Disciple is not above his Master................79

CHAPTER VI.
Moral Positions......................................94

CHAPTER VII.
"Open thy mouth for the dumb." Missions and Moral Reform.......................................110

CHAPTER VIII.
"Remember them that are in bonds as bound with them."..129

CHAPTER IX.
Changes in sentiment. Inviolability of Life........146

CONTENTS.

CHAPTER X.
The Freedom of the Truth........................166

CHAPTER XI.
Comeoutism...................................182

CHAPTER XII.
Sermons......................................199

CHAPTER XIII.
Discourses...................................260

CHAPTER XIV.
Miscellaneous Addresses, Incidents, &c...............300

CHAPTER XV.
Analysis of his character........................323

CHAPTER XVI.
Estimate of him as a Preacher....................371

CHAPTER XVII.
The Pastor and his People.......................395

CHAPTER XVIII.
Sickness and death—Funeral services—Testimonials.407

THE LIFE OF MARTIN CHENEY.

CHAPTER I.

SKETCHES OF HIS EARLY LIFE.

Martin Cheney was born in Dover, Mass. August 29th, 1792. His father, Mr. Joseph Cheney, was in the war connected with the American Revolution; and during the latter portion of his life received a small pension from the Government. He died at the residence of his son,—the subject of this memoir, in Olneyville, R. I., in the 76th year of his age.

His mother's maiden name was Susannah Wadsworth. Her relatives were mostly residents of Maine. She died earlier than her husband,—the precise date is unknown.

Martin was the fourth of six children, of whom three were sons and three daughters. One only of the family survives.

A sketch of his life in the form of an auto-biography, coming down to 1844, is preserved, from which most of the items in his earlier history will be drawn. He closes the succinct account of his ancestry in the following words :—

"It will be perceived that I have not been much a cousining, nor am I much of an antiquarian. In the few inquiries I have made respecting my ancestors, I have found but little of wealth, office or honors,—unless it be honorable to be in the army,—for it seems that my father and one of my grandfathers were in the army of the Revolution ; but in my researches I have never yet found a charge of dishonesty against one of my ancestors or connections. To the best of my knowledge, the coat of arms of my ancestors, was, *Poverty, Honesty, Piety.*"

The religious features of his father's family are thus briefly exhibited :

" My father and mother were both professors of religion, and were members of the Congregational Church in Dover, Mass. They lived and died in the Christian faith. My oldest brother was a member of the Beneficent Congregational Church in Providence. My youngest brother was not a member of any visible church, but died trusting in Jesus. My two sisters now living* are members of Baptist churches.

It may be reasonably supposed that, under such influences, his moral nature was not left without an effort to reach and sanctify it. The religious education of children was at that time held to be a matter of high moment, and was diligently attended to. Of this the auto-biography thus bears witness ;—

" From my parents I received religious and moral instruction, and received it early. I was taught to reverence and keep the Sabbath, to attend public wor-

* One has since died.

ship, and from week to week was taught the questions and answers in the 'Assembly's Catechism,' of the Westminster Divines. In this manner I learned what was the chief end of man, &c. and the reason why I am not a Calvinist is not for want of early instruction in his peculiar sentiments; but from a decided conviction that, as good as Calvin or my parents might be, they had mistaken the will of God on that subject."

There is certainly much to commend in the earnestness with which our New-England ancestry sought to indoctrinate the youth of their charge. They believed the sentiments taught in that catechism to be as fundamental in practical religion, as is education in a popular government. To reject the "Westminster Confession of Faith" seemed to them equivalent to a rejection of God's plan of saving the human soul. That creed they believed was possessed of a divine virtue, wanting to every other series of theological propositions. And their faith was practical. Their conviction expressed itself in action. They felt that their duty was done only when they had securely deposited within the storehouse of their childrens' intellects, that whole digest of theology; and then they waited for religion to spring up from the soil which their training had prepared.

Nor was their labor in vain. It might sometimes have cramped the intellect, by repressing its inquiries, and curtailing its rational freedom. It may sometimes have increased the tendency to fling the charge of heresy at the head of every dissatisfied inquirer, and begotten such a tendency where it was not before.

It may sometimes have helped to bring on a reaction from its almost iron rigidity—a reaction which drove good and discreet men over to licentiousness in both sentiment and life. The doctrines of divine appointment and providence may have sometimes weakened the feeling of individual obligation, and induced a few daring minds,—unable to reconcile the statements with philosophy or consciousness—to plunge boldly into skepticism. After all, that early training operated powerfully as a conservative force in the moral life of that early time; and aided in nurturing and developing elements of character that have done much to make whatever is valuable in American mind and American institutions. It kept alive a solemn reverence for God, for truth, for sacred things, for duty, for moral heroism, for the civil magistracy, for age and for order. If it did not give *polish* to character, it gave, at least, force. If harmony was sometimes wanting in the mental architecture which it developed, it never lacked basis or massive strength. The maturer reason of the young might reject some portions of the theology; but the influence it helped to throw about them still remained, and acted like the discovered presence of God.

With the other children of his native town, Martin was sent to the District School, and enjoyed such educational advantages as the schools of that period afforded. Alluding to this part of his life, he thus writes;—

"Among the recollections of those early school days is that of speaking, at a public exhibition, a piece from the 'Columbian Orator,' commencing thus;—

> "You'd scarce expect one of my age,
> To speak in public on the stage."

I could not have been much above five years of age, and I think I felt something of the spirit of my piece when I uttered the words

> "And where's the boy but three feet high,
> *That's made improvement more than I?*"

This was my first appearance in public. I have often in my subsequent experience had occasion to say, "You'd scarce expect, &c."; for I have been called where I never expected to be called, to fill places and discharge duties unexpected to myself and others.

He found his school privileges operating to create and strengthen a love for reading. The desire to know what was contained in books became so strong as to induce him to lay hold upon nearly evey volume that came in his way; and nearly the whole of quite a respectable village library was laid under contribution to meet the demands of his eager spirit. Had he been put at this period of his life under the direction of a wise teacher, and had adequate means of improvement been afforded him, it is easy to believe that his progress would have been both rapid and delightful. As it was, he read without any regard to order or his own necessities; for he was too young to appreciate either. He read as he found opportunity, and such books and such only as chance threw in his way. This mental exercise, however, was not wholly without benefit. His retentive memory treasured up a multitude of facts which, in after years, furnished not a little food for his reflection. Dim visions of intellectual eminence seem now and then to have floated before his childish eyes;—always, however, accepted as visions bright and brief, to be dissolved in the monotonous stream of his humble and unpromising life. He says:

"When some of my school mates left to prepare for college, I much wished to go too. But my father was poor, and so I was obliged to see them leave with regret. It was perhaps all for the best."

At the age of eleven years he came very near losing his life by means of a fever sore. It was found necessary to perform a severe and painful surgical operation in order to save him. As an illustration of some features in his early character, the following extracts are taken from his own account of the affliction.

"The doctor retired to the fields, where he remained nearly an hour; when he returned, called for pen and ink, and made a mark on the thigh where he was going to cut. My mother and sisters left the room;—all the family, I think, except my father. It was an afflictive time. The other surgeon said I must be held. To my surprise and that of all present, Dr. Miller said, *No, he will bear it, I know he will;*' and such was the confidence and courage he inspired in me, that I did endure it without a groan."

A council of surgeons was subsequently held, who decided that there was no security for his life unless the limb was amputated. It was left to the young and courageous sufferer to decide whether the operation should be performed. The decision was a negative. He was removed to the residence of Dr. Miller in Franklin, and the effort to restore him proved successful; though for a year he was obliged to use crutches in order to walk about. The narrative thus continues;—

"I had the loving attentions of a mother and sister while among strangers. O what a blessing! The kind and gentle treatment of Dr. Miller and Dr. Le Prelate —although his French accent at first alarmed me— won my confidence, and made a deep impression on my young spirit. I could suffer them to cut my flesh without a groan, while the severe and harsh manners of the other surgeon repelled me; and when he threatened to sue my father for his bill, because I had been taken to Franklin, my feelings rose to such a pitch that, when I heard of his death—which occurred during my stay at Franklin—I said 'I was glad of it;'—an expression for which I received a rebuke from my mother. Behold in the conduct of Dr. Miller and its results the magic power of kindness!"

After his recovery, Martin went to reside for a time with a brother in Boston, who kept a grocery with the usual appendages of cider, beer, and whiskey. He says;—"Many gills, pints, and quarts, have I drawn for the customers, of the liquid fire." His father very much desired that he should learn a trade, a mode of life to which the son was strongly averse. If it had been a school to which the father's wishes pointed, the son thinks it would have needed no persuasion to induce him to go. A place was, however, secured in the employment and family of a deacon of the Presbyterian church. His want of sympathy with his position predisposed him to look unfavorably upon every thing about him, and may possibly have done something to create the unfavorable opinion of his employer which he seems to have entertained, and of which he appears never to have rid himself. He calls him one of 'the straitest of his sect.' He says;—"Our clothes must all be of such a make; we apprentices had a table by ourselves; and the provisions were of an inferior quality. I staid two weeks and returned home. In truth I did not *intend* to stay if all had been as it should have been, but, as it was, I had a good excuse." His father soon learned his real position, and finally told him that if he was unwilling to learn a trade he must take some measures to provide for himself. He finally decided to attempt the work of making his way forward by his own energy and skill,—prompted thereto, probably, by much the same feeling as acts on other lads of similar age. He first engaged himself as an apprentice at the business of making nails, at a distance so small from home as to allow of his spending his sabbaths in the bosom of his father's family. The views entertained in his mature life of these early experiences, he thus indicates:

"In looking back at this period of my life, there are two things I would note. 1st. As the leading tendency of my mind was toward reading, books, and the study of letters, this mental bias should have been encouraged more than was done. 2d. I was not kept strictly enough at some employment; hence, my indisposition to a trade, and my tendency to idleness. Children should have something to do, and their employment and recreation should be under the supervision of kind and watchful parents or guardians." Ancient wisdom taught just these sentiments, and all modern experience enforces the same lesson.

After having occupied himself for a season with the duties of his chosen sphere, he went again to Boston to see whether he would answer the requirements made in an advertisement for a boy, which he accidentally discovered in a Boston newspaper. A bundle of clothes, prepared by a mother's love, was swung over his shoulder, and he started for the city, recommended only by his appearance and, as he says, his "awkwardness," which was probably accepted as the index to honesty. He found the place and the man, and hired himself out at nine dollars per month. The introduction to his new post, and the picture of the post itself shall be presented in his own words.

"What I was to do I knew not, only that it was to be work about the house. When dinner time arrived, my employer took me to his residence in Atkinson street, led me into his kitchen and introduced me to his kitchen maid, who, he informed me, would tell me what I had to do. My work I found to be as follows : 1st. In the morning to build the kitchen and parlor fires. 2nd. To sweep the parlor, and set the breakfast table. 3d. When breakfast was prepared to take it to the parlor and wait upon the table ; and when breakfast was over to take the dishes to the kitchen, where the maid and myself breakfasted. 4th. When my employer went to his store he took me with him, to bring home for dinner what he purchased from the market on his way to the store. After this I had little to do ;

sometimes a pair of boots or handirons to clean, or a note to carry a few rods, and I was left mostly to myself till dinner time. I then went through the same service as at breakfast, and repeated the service at tea time. I had plenty of newspapers to read, and plenty of time to read them. Here, for the first and last time I had the disease called *Home-sickness*, which, though not often fatal, is still extremely disagreeable. O, how I longed for *Home!* Home with its many privations, still it was '*Home, Home*, SWEET HOME,' to me. I could have embraced even its dust. My father found where I was and called to see me, but I could not see him with the feelings which I then had, and so absented myself. After a few weeks I recovered from this difficulty, and could then talk of home and see my father calmly. The people with whom I lived were church going people, yet they visited the Theatre occasionally, and gave and attended large parties; which, when they had or attended them, kept me and the maid up late at night, a thing we often scolded about, behind their backs of course.

"While here, a circumstance transpired which had some effect, I think, on my subsequent life. This was the hearing of a sermon by a Universalist. I had been warned by the people where I lived not to go to hear them, but curiosity prevailed and I went. The text was, 'He that believeth not shall be damned.' Well, thought I, if he can make that agree with the salvation of all men, the doctrine must be true; for it then seemed to my untutored mind that these words were absolutely irreconcilable with the sentiment that all will be saved. However, with my wishes and hopes on his side, he made out, as I thought, a plausible case. Damnation, he said, meant condemnation, and this was in the conscience, and did not extend beyond the grave. Christ had died and brought life and immortality to light, and as in Adam all die, so in Christ all would be made alive. I received the teaching greedily. I was glad there was no punishment beyond the grave. I feared not the punishment on this side. I did not then perceive, as I have since done, that Universalism, as well as its parent, Calvinism, leave out or make of no effective account *the conditions of the Gospel.* Alas! if I mistake not, moral responsibility, human accountability, with the freedom of the human will, are crushed between the upper and nether millstones of Calvinism and Universalism. At all events, the effect on me was such, that I felt less restrained in the indulgence of my propensities."

After remaining in this family about a year, Martin decided to leave; not on account of any dissatisfaction felt toward his employer or family, nor from any want of sympathy on their part toward him. He was urged to remain, and larger wages were offered as an inducement, but without avail. He encountered reproach on account of his position as a servant, and his proud spirit could not brook the taunt of servility. Another year was spent on a farm, where the same wages were received for constant and severe physical labor, and where his relation to a master was not less close or obvious than before. Dissatisfied with such a mode of life, he determined to accept an invitation from an elder brother to leave Massachusetts, and live with him in Rhode-Island. This brother resided in Olneyville, then called "Tarbridge," "The Hollow," &c. He accordingly started for this latter place in June, 1810, and after a short journey, mostly performed on foot, he arrived in what was to be his future home and field of influence. The place differed much, both in character and appearance, from the Olneyville of the present day. It contained some twenty dwelling houses, one small cotton mill,—the third built in this country; some six rum-shops; one Distillery; no Meeting House; no Sunday School; no Public School: and not a few of the inhabitants were irreligious, intemperate, and profane. "The Hollow" was regarded as a special seat of almost every form of individual and social iniquity, and though, as in most cases, the people were probably less inhuman than they were supposed to be, there was abundant room for moral improvement. Through this place Mr. Cheney passed at the time above specified, on his way to Triptown, North Providence, a short distance up the stream from Olneyville, where his brother was temporarily occupied. In November following, he formally took up his abode in Olneyville. The inferences which he drew from his observations at this time, were not very creditable to the people, among whom he found a subsequent home. His advent among the descendants of Roger Williams, is best exhibited in his own language.

"My first impressions of Rhode-Island, when I made my first visit in June, before I came to reside in November, were unpleasant and unfavorable. The people seemed awkward, uncouth, uncivilized. But there were peculiar reasons for these impressions. I was somewhat an ignorant, uncouth lad myself. I was weary and foot-sore when I entered Pawtucket, and not less so as I approached Providence, Olneyville and Triptown. Some one or more persons gave me incorrect directions, which vexed me. The first and only person to whom I spoke in Olneyville, was a colored man, known as Wat Walmsley. I inquired of him the way and the distance to Triptown. He replied,— '*Over Tarbridge, and about a mile.*' Of Tarbridge, I was as ignorant as I was of the Koran, and at a Rhode-Island mile—with my sore feet—I shuddered; having been told before, about a mile back, it was a mile; and when about half a mile farther on I was told by a woman, who, by her voice and size, I thought might have descended from the Amazonians and done honor to her ancestry, that it was *about a mile* to Triptown, my patience was well nigh exhausted; and I inwardly exclaimed,—' O, these Rhode-Island miles!' Surely, I have got among the natives!' But after it became my adopted home, I found reasons for changing my earlier opinions. At that time there was much of the *free, generous, independent* spirit of their renowned ancestor, Roger Williams, among the people, mingled with the jealous cautiousness which marks those who have been the objects of persecution.

"I had come from Massachusetts, where the law laid its hand on religious observances. There, if a man labored on the Sabbath, or went on a journey for pleasure, he might expect to be visited by a minister of the law; thus, the real religious character was not developed; many were outwardly religious by constraint. Not so in Rhode-Island. Nearly every man, woman and child did religiously what was right in their own eyes. It did not affect the reputation of a man whether he kept the Sabbath or not, whether he went to meeting or not. It was, indeed, from the beginning, 'a receptacle for all kinds of consciences.' So that *first impressions* of Rhode-Island would be likely to be unfavorable. In short, at that time, to say the least, there was but small temptation to pretend to be religious in Rhode-Island; hence, more intimate acquaintance always resulted in a higher estimate of her character."

CHAPTER II.

"HE WAS LOST AND IS FOUND."

THE state of society into which Mr. Cheney found himself thrown, has been partially set forth in the extracts from his auto-biography presented in the preceding chapter. A view of his character as it was when, at the susceptible age of eighteen, he came into the world of temptation found at Olneyville, may aid us in apprehending the results appearing in his subsequent life.

Mr. Cheney at this time, had all the ardor, the buoyancy and hopefulness of spirit, which are wont to attach to that period of life. His temperament was nervous and active; and his energy of character, when roused into action, was such as to give him influence in every circle where he acted. As always afterward, so then, he was respected or feared in proportion as he was surrounded by friends or foes. He was, by nature, joyous. Whatever contributed to human merriment, was almost sure to meet more or less sympathy from him; the moral character of the mirth was something which seldom came in to interfere with his enjoyment of it. In the circles of pleasure and laughter, he generally found a place; for his own inclinations, and the wishes of others, combined to carry him there. Even practised jesters not unfrequently made him the centre of their circle, and became the convulsed spectators of his comic drollery, and the victims of his mischievous, but not malicious fun. Even at this early age, he was beginning to develope that firmness and self-reliance, that impatience of dictation, that iron sternness of will in carrying out his plans, which appeared so prominently in subsequent life. An effort was not abandoned because it had once met defeat. He might appear quiet and forgetful; but he only waited his opportunity, and when it appeared he bounded with a sudden and decisive energy forward to the object which he had always kept in his eye. These characteristics had appeared early, and they grew with his years. He was highly impulsive; and yet the movements which betrayed suddenness and strength of feeling, seemed guarded with forethought and sagacity. He was disposed to be wilful; a tendency which he attributes, in part, to the indulgence which his early illness purchased at the hands of his parents. The religious influences which had acted on him, had temporarily repressed his mirth and his fire, but they had not taken such a hold upon his understanding, or his heart, as to control their action. His spirit was the dwelling place of strong forces, some of them just waking into life, and others pent up by outward pressure, but all waiting to leap out on to the field of action, to do a good or an evil work, according as they were summoned by worldly passion, or religious principle.

He had but little acquaintance with the world, for he had seen it in but few of its phases. Of what he was to meet in his intercourse with it, he was ignorant; and so he had laid down no definite principles of action when he went forth to enconnter its successive experiences. Though possessing such definite and marked features of character, still, the life he was afterward to lead was to depend very much upon the moulding influences which were to act upon him. Martin Cheney he would always be, but he might become the efficient leader among the irreligious hosts of the world, or the inspiring standard-bearer in the ranks of righteousness. So, Saul of Tarsus, volunteering at Jerusalem to aid in crushing the heresy of the Nazarene, and Paul the Apostle, stirred by what he saw at Athens, to raise it to a recognition of the authority of Christ, are one and the same person. It is a mental giant giving his strength to the bigotry of the Pharisees, and then consecrating his energy to the philanthropy of Christ.

The business in which Mr. Cheney was engaged, was that of preparing and vending meat; a business which he regarded as having very little tendency, either in itself, or in its associations, to improve his morals or manners. He lived in the family of his brother who made no profession of religion, and so enjoyed no influence there adapted to restrain either his passions or his conduct. He did not feel it to be at all a *home* to him, but simply a stopping place, where very little real interest was felt in his moral welfare. Moreover, he had brought with him the sentiment—if a mere careless acquiescence in such a notion, can be called a sentiment,—that all men would be happy after death; and so both the love of virtue and the fear of vice were wanting as motives to his heart. The result he thus states :

"My moral feeling and habits began rapidly to decline. I could play ball, pitch quoits, or play cards on Sunday, as boldly as any of the Rhode-Island youth. I commenced spending my evenings at shops where liquors were sold, and where gambling was often practised. Profane language, corrupting songs, and the free use of liquors abounded in those places; and from a looker on, I soon became a partaker. O, how terrible in its influence upon me, was the want of an attractive home, where I might spend my evenings! O, could my voice be heard by parents and guardians, I would say earnestly, strongly, 'make home attractive to your children; spare no pains to accomplish this. Let not the shops, taverns, stables, and streets educate your children. I have had a sad experience in this species of instruction.'"

In the year 1813, he was married to Miss Anna Brown, daughter of Mr. Fleet Brown, of Foster, and commenced keeping house in an humble chamber, but which, to him, was full of sunshine, for *home* influences were acting afresh on his longing heart. In the rousing of his domestic sympathies and feelings which had lain dormant for years, he seemed to be living a new life. Better voices whispered to him, and, for a time, he listened with gratitude and pleasure. The attractions of home were sometimes sufficient to overcome the influences that sought to draw him abroad, at evening, to the haunts of vice. He says—"I was industrious and economical, and prospered."

But trial was before him in a new form. The story of his misfortunes is best told in his own words—

"In the winter of 1815 and 1816, I removed, with my oldest brother, to Brooklyn, L. I., and went into the grocery business in New-York city. We engaged also in the Mackerel Fishery. We were unsuccessful in both. My brother, while on a journey of business to Rhode-Island, was taken very sick, and after many weeks of suffering, recovered only so far as to be able to walk about, and was in a confirmed consumption. We were obliged to sell our small property, which was left, at a great sacrifice. My brother broke up housekeeping—his wife, with her children, went to her father's in Lincoln, Mass.; while he, accompanied by my youngest brother, went to his father's in Newport, N. H. These events left me in the great city of New-York, whither I had removed from Brooklyn, among almost entire strangers, and in a state of almost entire destitution. All my money was expended in the removal of my brother and his family,—or, rather, all *his* money,—for mine was already gone in the losses we had sustained. All that remained was an old sloop, bought for the Mackerel Fishery, which was the joint property of myself and my brother. Finding no way to pay my rent, I removed into a hut or hovel, not much larger than an Indian wigwam, a little above Hoboken, on the North River. There, with my wife and child, and youngest brother, I spent the winter of 1816 and 1817. *And such a winter!* It was the winter following what was called the 'cold summer,' when the crops were so extensively destroyed by the frost. Thirty thousand were supplied with soup, daily, in the city of New-York, that winter; hundreds were flocking into the county offering to work for their food, the farmers refusing to employ them on account of the scarcity of provisions. And there were we, wife, child, brother and myself, without funds, without work, among strangers, a cold winter upon us, and starvation in the land. We were willing to dig if digging could be had; from begging we revolted. We had fresh meat *once* during that winter. We lived on Potatoes while we could get them, then on Turnips, to save what little bread we could get for the child. We freighted a little with the old sloop, until she became frozen up in the river, then a little chopping of wood in the New Jersey woods. It was a winter long to be remembered. O, how I wished to be where I could get to Providence River, then I could, at least, get a few clams. I then thought that if I could get bread for myself and family, I would never again complain. Well, the dreary winter at last passed away, and selling the old sloop for a trifle, I was able to get back to Rhode-Island, stripped of all the property I had when I left, except a few dollars; my furniture pretty much a wreck, and, what is to be more lamented than all, my heart made no better by all these trials."

Previous to the departure for New-York, the brother with whom Mr. Cheney was living in Olneyville, was converted, and united with the Beneficent Congregational Church in Providence, then under the pastoral care of Rev. James Wilson. The voice of prayer in that dwelling, where religion had been a stranger, was an unpleasant surprise to Mr. Cheney, and he carefully avoided the influence of that new spiritual life. Still it acted upon him. But during the absence from Christian sympathy, occasioned by the removal to New-York, the religious interest of the convert obviously declined, and the moral restraint which his faithfulness had thrown about the younger brother almost entirely ceased to operate; and on his return to Rhode-Island the same associations were renewed, and the work of moral corruption went on. Home lost its power to keep him from the resorts of the vicious. Before going to New-York he had felt desirous to accumulate property; but on his return this desire departed, and he speaks of being likewise indifferent in regard to his reputation. The temporary check laid on his passions by his brother's religion, his own home, and his pecuniary distresses, was now removed; and he went rapidly downward at the bidding of his impulses. Then was written what he calls " the darkest chapter of his history." He became an acknowledged leader among the associates who had been his instructors in the school of sensual indulgence and passionate gratification. Their circles became incomplete without him, their gatherings lacked spirit in his absence, and their wild plots of mischief were deemed imperfect, until he had endorsed them, and pledged himself to their execution. He frequented the taverns and grog-shops; drank freely, though seldom became insensibly intoxicated; was an habitual attendant upon the theatre; and became more and more averse to moral associations. This period of his life finds its record in detail by his own hand, and, for the same reasons that induced him to recall it, is an outline of it presented here. It shows how "evil communications corrupt good manners," and pervert high powers; and it will show the glory and power of that grace which could redeem and consecrate that sin-seared, but powerful nature, to high and holy ends. From the records of human folly and guilt, as well as from the high illustrations of moral excellence, may be drawn lessons of practical wisdom and motives to purity. The Bible has its Ahab and its Herod, as well as its Abraham and its John.

In the autumn of 1817 his wife died. She had trusted in God while living, and she passed away in peace and hope. Her death seemed to produce no lasting or serious impression upon his mind. It was impossible for him to be the subject of any serious experiences while pursuing such a round of sensual gratification; and he seemed disinclined to break away from his associations. The voice that would have spoken to him from the lips of that Faith which had just disappeared from his dwelling, was drowned in his thoughtlessness and dissipation. He had never intentionally wronged her; and so repentance for the neglect of his home and the disregard of her religious influence was not awakened. He found a good boarding place for his child, and went on less restrained than before. He says:

"I plunged still deeper and more greedily into scenes of folly and wickedness. I had now no parents, brother or sisters near,—no wife or home to restrain, and on I went, madly, in the road to death. From the period of my wife's death till the time that

I experienced a great change in my views and feelings in 1820, I fairly revelled in the indulgence of sensual gratifications. And the consequences I now feel to my sorrow. Not only are the sins of the fathers visited upon the children unto the third and fourth generation, but the sins of *youth* are visited upon *age*, and it is wise and just that it should be so. O when will young men be wise and understand this?"

His Universalist prepossessions still remained; for how could he look forward to the future as a scene of moral and just retribution with satisfaction? He would sometimes attend, with one or more of his companions, upon the ministry of some preacher of that sect, and would then go home seeking to strengthen each other's confidence in the doctrine they were so anxious to believe.

In October 1819 he was married to Miss Nancy Wilbour, and commenced housekeeping; but the home influence could not, as before, overcome the tendencies which wedded him to his companions and gratifications abroad. His heart was becoming more and more the servant of his passions, less and less under the dominion of moral and domestic obligation. The impulsions of duty were feeble; inclination acted on him like the pressure of a tempest. A very remarkable dream which he had during the winter following his marriage produced some serious impression upon his mind, but was inadequate to change the current of his life.

The year 1820 was distinguished for an extensive religious interest in Providence and vicinity, in connection with which large numbers professed to pass from death nnto life. Meetings were held every evening in almost every neighborhood, but Mr. Cheney felt little interest in them. His heart was elsewhere. He attended on one occasion at the baptism of a large number of persons in Providence, and felt somewhat impressed by the scene. Subsequently at a Methodist meeting, when an invitation was extended to any who might desire it, to go forward to the altar for prayers, he felt prompted to go forward with others, but the suggestion of his better nature was scornfully repelled. Thus God left himself not without witnesses of his desire that the sinner might be brought to repentance and life.

The whole account of his mental exercises connected with his conversion, as found recorded by his own hand, is so interesting and instructive as to demand an insertion. No apology for introducing it entire will be needed. It will be likely to suggest its own lessons better than a foreign hand could present them. The occurrences related took place during the same year as the events above specified.

"At that time in the village of Olneyville there was no meeting-house, no church, no Sunday school, no stated religious meetings. There were but few who professed to be the disciples of Jesus. These few, with some from the city, would occasionally hold conference meetings. One of these meetings I attended ; the why I cannot tell. I can only recollect that the man of the house where the meeting was held was one with whom I had often played cards ; this might have induced my attendance. His wife professed to be a Christian. I went to this meeting as careless and thoughtless as I had previously been, as far as my recollection extends. After sitting in an adjoining room a little time, I thought I would step into the entry and look into the room where most of the people were, and see what the meeting folks were doing. I did so. There was a man exhorting, who I afterwards learned was Mr. Peter Place. None of his words were impressed on my mind. I know not what he said, but I received *one* distinct impression ;—*The man is sincere.* O that all speakers might beget this conviction within their hearers! The first thing of which I was conscious after this, was the breaking up of the meeting; and I had been standing in that entry as near as I could afterwards judge, *about an hour.* It seemed to me that I had somehow been strongly, unconsciously interested,—as it were, spell-bound. How it was or why it was I know not, God knoweth. "The wind bloweth where it listeth;" so are God's influences as universal and incomprehensible as the air we breathe or the wind that bloweth around us. At the close of the meeting my principles I suppose remained the same, but my feelings were wonderfully changed. I felt disposed to converse on religious topics, and did so on my return from the meeting. For a number of weeks my mind was more or less powerfully exercised on religious subjects. I felt disposed to attend religious meetings, and did so frequently. I wished to hear prayer. There was a meeting held occasionally in the village to practice singing, which I was told was opened or closed with prayer. I thought I would attend one of them, as I had been invited to do so. I went, my object being to hear prayer; but to my disappointment no prayer was offered. I afterwards learned that it was omitted on my account, lest it should drive me away. What an admonition to Christians to be faithful! So anxious was I to hear prayer that I had a singing meeting appointed at my house to secure the object. As they were about leaving without prayer, I ventured to request Mr. Peter Place to pray. A clap of thunder in a clear day would not have surprised them more. Mr. Place told me afterwards that he was confounded; that he did not know whether the question was asked in earnest or in mockery. To have a leader among the wildest and most reckless ask him to pray, was so unexpected as exceedingly to perplex him. However he prayed, *how* he hardly knew. The meeting closed, and all retired to ponder upon and talk over the wonder. About this time I remember being in a barber's shop on a Sunday morning, where was one of my neighbors, a professor of religion. I asked him if he was going to Fruit Hill to meeting that day. He replied that he was. I told him I thought I would go with him, and accordingly I did so. Elder Zalmon Tobey preached. As I was in the habit of singing sometimes, I was invited to a seat in the choir. I declined, for I did not feel like singing. The text was; "They that are whole have no need of a physician, but they that are sick." I was much affected under the preaching. I recollect also of being at a meeting one evening at the Merino Factory. Elder Tobey and Williams

Thayer were present and spoke in the meeting. I was deeply impressed and wept through nearly the whole exercises. I remember too of Elder Potter's calling one day to see me, but my feelings were such that I could not converse, and I left the room.

About this time I discovered that the mind of my wife was deeply interested on religious subjects. One night after returning from meeting under deep feeling, being troubled, distressed, and anxious, I knelt down by the bedside and tried to pray. I know not how I prayed, and hardly know for what I prayed. I knew that I was a sinner, I was in trouble and wanted mercy. I suppose, therefore, that I expressed those feelings in some way, but in what words I know not. I wept much. I was thus exercised for a long time; at last I fell asleep. I think I was thus exercised a large portion of the night. The morning following was Sunday. I arose as usual, built a fire, &c., and, what has always appeared singular to me, I have no recollection of my attention's being directed to my exercises of mind the past night. I was cheerful and buoyant in spirits without seeming to be conscious of it. While passing about the house, doing the chores of the morning, I commenced singing:

"Come listening angels, assist me to sing
The love of my Jesus, my crucified King."

I had formerly sung this hymn with others from a book. It surprised me on reflection afterwards, that I had sung the hymn that morning without a book. The first *distinct thought* that seemed to arrest my attention was: *It is Sunday*, and I shall have nothing to do but read the bible and attend meeting; and I shall be very happy. And as a matter of fact I was happy. I had delightful feelings. The man who lived in the house with me, who was a professor of religion, hearing me singing, came in to see me. He had known my previous exercises of mind. He asked how I felt. I told him. He replied: 'You have experienced religion.' What that meant I did not know definitely. I only knew that I felt calm and happy, and that there was a wonderful change in my feelings. One thing I soon noticed, viz: that I could converse on religious subjects without being agitated; whereas, for weeks previous, when anything was said on religious topics it would affect me to tears; I would be convulsed with emotion. The expression of my neighbor rung in my ears: 'You have experienced religion;' and although I knew not *what* experiencing religion was, yet I had the idea that they who had experienced religion were Christians, and in the favor of God, that their sins were forgiven and they were prepared to meet God.

"The question soon came up in my mind, Have you experienced religion? This I could not answer. I asked those who professed to have passed through this experience how they felt; but none of their relations agreed precisely with mine. For weeks I continued this search, but in vain. It was indeed, as I have since learned, 'seeking the living among the dead.' When I had nearly decided that my friend was mistaken, and that I had not experienced religion, *all at once*, while at a neighbor's shop where I used to converse on religious things, the thought entered my mind ; "How foolish you have been, *you have a Bible ;* if you had consulted that you would have had your questions solved." Wondering that I had not thought of this before, I immediately started for home to consult the bible on this question.

"I had an old bible which, by the merest chance, I had bought at auction among other books, but which I think I had never read. However I went, confident that my question would be settled by consulting that book. As I was on my way home, these words came into my mind, or I found them on opening my bible, (and which it was, my recollection will not positively say,) 'We know that we have passed from death unto life because we love the brethren.' It seemed to me that these words were written for the purpose of solving the question. Thus I reasoned ;—passing from death unto life means what my neighbor called 'experiencing religion.' It means 'becoming a new creature,' or being a Christian. Well, then, the question returned ; Have I passed from 'death unto life ?' How am I to know whether I have or not? The words decided this plainly ; 'because ye love the brethren.' Yes, I replied to myself, that is it. If you love the brethren, you have 'passed from death unto life ;' you are a Christian. But another question arose, viz. Who are meant by brethren ? My judgment at once decided that they must be the disciples of Jesus, or Christians. Another question arose; Do you love the brethren? I felt conscious that I did ; for while I formerly avoided associating with them, I now desired it. I was conscious of a great change in my feelings towards them. Another question still followed ; Do you love them because they are brethren, because they are Christians? This I found on reflection to be the case. It was not wealth, nor reputation, nor color, nor because they showed attention to me, nor association, nor because they were kindred that made me love them, but because they loved Jesus, loved the truth, loved the right ; in a word because they were Christians. Then it was that the conviction rolled into my mind with great sweetness and power, *I have* 'passed from death unto life,' I am a Christian. 'Bless the Lord, O my soul, and all that is within me bless his holy name.' I had much peace and joy in believing. From such a source sprang up a *hope*, which was and is and I trust will ever be 'as an anchor of the soul, sure and steadfast,' 'a hope that maketh not ashamed.' It will be observed that my conclusion, and the joy resulting from it, had reference to the *fact* that I had passed from death unto life, not to the *how* or *when* the change took place;— that I *was* a Christian, not *how* or *when* I became such.

"In analyzing this change in my views and feelings subsequenly, I discovered, first, that I was surrounded and had been surrounded with the divine goodness all my days, and that this goodness was urging, leading me to repentence. Second, that this goodness flowing to me and the world in such abundance, came from *God's great heart of love*, and through the appointed medium. his only begotten Son. Third, that this goodness operated first, on my perceptive faculties, showing me what I was, what I ought to be, what I might be if obedient, and what I should be if disobedient;

secondly, it operated on my emotional nature, my sympathies, and thus I was affected even to tears. In this way was I brought to the 'valley of decision,' and the cry was heard:—' How long halt ye between two opinions?' 'Choose ye this day whom ye will serve;' 'If any man will be my disciple let him deny himself and take up his cross and follow me.' Thus divine goodness brought me, thirdly, to exercise my *choosing* faculties or my *willing* nature, or that Power found in all moral beings and which determines moral character, usually described as the 'Freedom of the will'—the freedom to choose between good and evil, to obey or disobey the commands of God. Now I perceived that I 'passed from death unto life,' or became a disciple of Christ, a son of God, not when my understanding was enlightened to *see* the truth, nor when my emotional nature was deeply affected *by* the truth, but when my willing or choosing nature chose or preferred *to submit to or obey*, the truth. It is when the sinner chooses to obey God in all things rather than man or any other power, that he 'passes from death unto life,' is 'born again,' becomes 'a new creature,' 'old things pass away and all things become new.' And it was when I perceived that I did thus choose God and his Son, God's truth and his people, that peace and joy filled my soul. I do not say this process was realized *at the time*, but in analyzing it afterwards, I found that this was the way in which I was led to embrace Christ."

Through such a path of darkness, and out from such "an horrible pit" of sin, was the soul led forth into "a large place," where the light of life shone gloriously ground it. The cords of sin were broken, and the spirit clapped its hands joyously in its new freedom. With scarcely less of wonder than was displayed when Saul of Tarsus knelt before the Saviour he had persecuted, did Olneyville gaze at the miracle of grace in its midst, and exclaim;—" Behold he prayeth!" The leader in vice had broken his covenant with iniquity, and laid his strong earnest spirit as a willing offering at the feet of him who is the Captain of our salvation. Henceforward we shall find him leading another host, clad in new panoply, maintaining another and a better warfare. We have seen his power in the flesh making the holds of iniquity strong; henceforward we are to watch for the waking of his spiritual energy, mighty through God for their overthrow.

CHAPTER III.

ENTRANCE UPON THE WORK OF THE MINISTRY.

The best proof of the genuineness of conversion is to be found in its fruits. These afford vital testimony; the details of the process are of comparatively little moment. The night of conviction may be more or less dark; its hours may pass away more or less tardily; spiritual light may break forth like the sudden flash of noonday on the newly opened eyes of blindness, or the dawn of hope may be so gradual as to make it impossible to separate clearly the new life from the old; one class of truths or another may have been employed to bring us to God; our experience may be common or peculiar; it matters not very much. He who finds his heart turning itself to God in submission, and faith, and love, and turning to the world in earnest solicitude for its spiritual redemption, discovers a better evidence of his membership in the family of God, than any form or degree of religious emotion can afford. Not past feeling, but present obedience is to settle the question whether we be Christ's. Following the written word we are safe; to lean on anything else is to be in danger of having the staff of our confidence fail us just when we most need it.

It was well, perhaps, for Mr. Cheney, that his earliest religious developments took on so rational a phase. The method adopted to settle the question touching his own conversion, is simple and unusual, but most natural and efficient. He laid hold upon a definite principle which God had revealed, and by it he tested some definite obvious facts furnished by his own consciousness. It was one of the simplest exercises of the judgment to compare the facts with the principle, and decide respecting their agreement or disagreement. And the more simple it was, so much the more confident could he be that the conclusion was correct. He knew the facts, and he firmly believed the principle. That he loved the brethren his own soul told him; that this was a proof of his being a Christian his Bible told him, and so doubt was at an end, while the assurance of faith had begun. This first step in his religious career, indicates the logical feature of his mind, and its success strongly disposed him to prosecute every subsequent religious inquiry in a reverent, yet rational spirit. Had it not been so, his ardent nature might have driven him into many and grievous excesses. His impulses were easily stirred, and, when roused, acted with a fiery force; and it was well that he accepted the new influence which was to wake them into life, with watchfulness and discretion. His understanding endorsed his position; he could give a reason for his hope, and for his new mode of life. Hand in hand had his judgment and his heart walked up and bent themselves before the Cross, and now hand in hand they had come down girded for the work set before them. Each leaned on the other in its weakness; each inspired the other with its own strength.

It was no slight task which Mr. Cheney had assumed,

that of walking as a christian, day after day, through the temples of sin he had himself aided to erect. Many would, perhaps, have left the place where everything was setting so strongly against the soul. Here he was surrounded by the former associates he had aided to corrupt; here were the temptations before which he would be most likely to fall; here were the suspicious ones who would hesitate to trust him even when he was most earnestly sincere; here were a host of things adapted to dishearten him, by reminding him of his former shame; and here he would be singled out by all who hated God, as one to be decoyed back to his old associations by every possible artifice. But his courage was equal to the emergency, as it was equal to every emergency into which life threw him; or, perhaps, it might be said that emergencies acted on such a nature as his, to develope its courage and multiply its power of resistance. He knew the trial, but he would not shrink from it. He knew his weakness, but he had learned where to look for strength. Here he had shown the power of sin, and here he determined, under the pressure of duty, to display the power of the gospel which had come to redeem from it. Here his life had been a cord drawing others along the "broad way," and here he felt it was fitting that it should become a magnet attracting them to "the strait and narrow path." And who can doubt that he chose wisely?

Mr. Cheney *was* a changed man. *That* was not to be doubted even by those who feared or wished the change might be superficial or temporary. It was a mystery to all who had not themselves felt the power of the gospel; and these, as they looked upon him day after day, firm, faithful and joyous, could only exclaim,—" What hath God wrought!" On the third Sabbath in June, 1821, he was baptized by the Rev. Zalmon Tobey, and united with the Second Baptist Church in North Providence. Not a few of his old associates were present, and predicting, in his own hearing, that the Christmas and New Year's Holidays would find him again at " Esek's ;" this being the usual appellation of a low grog-shop where he and his companions had been wont to revel. In reference to this, he says:—

"But Christmas and New Year's came and went, and came and went, and yet *Esek's* found me not. True, they might have found me at Esek's, had they watched me closely many years after their prediction. Yes, I was there to speak a word to a sick and dying man. Yes, I was there, on the very spot where I had gambled, and drank, and spent whole nights, to speak to the people on a funeral occasion. That dying man was *Esek;* that funeral service was *Esek's*, the keeper of that shop who had said, before my change of views, that he dreaded my coming to his house more than any other man. Wonderful change!"

" The world beheld the glorious change,
And did thy hand confess."

On the third Sabbath in July following, his wife, having consecrated herself to God, was baptized, and united with the same church, and his home became a temple of Faith and Love, a place for mutual counsel and encouragement.

The year following his conversion, the few Christians in Olneyville established a meeting for mutual improvement, somewhat like a Methodist class meeting, which was held from place to place weekly. In these meetings Mr. Cheney was accustomed to speak, sing and pray, led on by his own feelings and the wishes of his Christian friends,—nearly all of whom regarded him as called to preach the gospel. This conviction was not unfrequently expressed in such forms as to find its way to Mr. Cheney's ear, and did something, doubtless, to turn his thoughts in that direction. He says of this:

"How much the influence of my friends had to do in turning my attention to preaching, and how much *divine influence* was exerted in the matter, I have been unable to tell; or whether the influence of my friends was a means which God used to bring me to think on this topic."

He was selected, by the Christian friends who had united in the meeting above noticed, to act as their leader, and was frequently called on to attend and conduct conference meetings in other places. On attending a meeting in the neighborhood of some friends in New-Hampshire, and speaking as he was wont, a deacon present sent him a message, to the effect, that if he did not preach God would punish him. Several aged and experienced Christians used to express to him the conviction that he was called to preach. One of these used frequently to say to him;—"They will yet build a meeting house in Olneyville, and you will preach in it." Rev. Mr. Tobey, who had baptized him, also expressed to him plainly his conviction, that he ought to be

5

preaching the gospel. Such things as these, together with his own experiences, directed his attention more and more frequently and strongly toward the work of the ministry. He speaks of being present at a meeting in the Chestnut Street Church, Providence, and heard read a hymn containing these lines:—

> " His only righteousness I'll know,
> His saving truth proclaim;
> 'Tis all my business here below,
> To cry, ' Behold the Lamb;'
> Happy if with my latest breath,
> I might but gasp his name;
> Preach him to all, and cry in death,—
> ' Behold, behold the Lamb.'"

His heart was very deeply moved, and in his tears he felt peculiarly attracted toward the work of preaching the unsearchable riches of Christ. He found, however, similar difficulties to those urged by most who feel summoned to this sphere. He says,—

"But *who* was I, and *what* was I, and *where* was I, that I should think of preaching? Only a limited school education, in a business that seemed inappropriate to such a work, poor in the things of this world, a family to maintain, my former character,—all these things seemed to forbid the attempt. Then there was no Church, no Meeting House, no Society in the place to aid. Alas! the future seemed as dark as darkness itself should I attempt it; yet it seemed, on many accounts, to be duty; and at times I had a desire for the work. Thus I was tossed to and fro in my mind."

A severe fit of sickness which he suffered at about this time, and which some Christian friends regarded as a punishment from the Lord, sent because he had not gone about his work, operated to induce him to promise inwardly that, if his life was spared, he would devote himself to the work of the ministry. Some time after his recovery, he related his mental exercises to the Church of which he was a member, and a meeting was appointed to be held on the evening of Thanksgiving Day, in the month of November, 1823, for the purpose of hearing him preach. He preached on the occasion, from 2d Peter, 3 : 9 ; " For the Lord is not slack concerning his promise," &c. The auto-biography thus continues :—

"After preaching, I was examined as to my sentiments on doctrine and ordinances, &c. Finding me Anti-Calvinistic, and a Free Communionist, they informed me that it would be useless for them to approbate me as a preacher, as the ministers of that order would not ordain me with the sentiments I then held; and advised me to take a letter of dismission and unite with a church holding sentiments similar to my own. They, however, decided unanimously that they thought I was called of God to preach the gospel. The remark of the man who then preached for them, Rev. Nicholas Branch, impressed itself deeply on my mind. When asked his opinion of my call to preach, he replied : '*If he was a Calvinist, I should think he was called to preach ; and I don't know but he is as it is.*'"

Mr. Cheney explains his connection with a Calvinist Baptist Church, by the remark, that he did not know as these sentiments were held by the Church at the time of his uniting there, as the Articles of Faith were not shown him; and that Mr. Tobey, who was then pastor, did not hold to these views. The advice of the Church was complied with, and his membership was removed to the Fourth Baptist Church in Providence, which was then under the care of his former pastor.

On the 5th of February, 1824, he preached before this Church on trial. Text, Jonah, 3: 1. 2. "The preaching that I bid thee," was the clause to which his attention was particularly directed. Expressive of his feelings at this time, the following little record was made,—"It is my heart's desire and prayer to God that I may be ready and willing to declare the whole counsel of God, whether men will hear or forbear. O Lord help, for from thee is all my strength." After examination by the Church, he was furnished with a certificate, setting forth their hearty approbation of him as a brother and minister, and commending him earnestly to the confidence and fellowship of all Christians.

A little time previous to these last related occurrences, Mr. Cheney commenced holding meetings in a hall in Olneyville, connected with the tavern, having been earnestly solicited to do so by the little band of disciples with whom he had been associated in the weekly meeting. This hall was ordinarily used for far different purposes. It was the gathering place for the wildest youth, who occupied it for parties, dances, &c. These were frequently held on Saturday night, and it would be late on Sunday morning before it was vacated. At 10 o'clock A. M. Mr. Cheney would go to the spot,— having sometimes to build his fire and prepare the room previously—take what the fiddler had occupied for a stand as a pulpit, and speak to those who came to hear of the great things of the gospel. Among his auditors were often found those who had joined him there previously in the work of noisy mirth; and he who had been their leader, stood up boldly before them, to tell of his own redemption through Christ, and to beseech them to go in penitence and give themselves to God. Many were attracted by curiosity to see and hear, and some there were who went for better reasons; but to them all did he speak in the earnestness of his nature, roused by his new faith, and from the fullness of his own sad experiences in the life of sin, from which he sought to rescue them. That hall stands yet, almost in the shadow of the temple of worship in which he afterwards preached to crowds gathered from every circle of life, and from which his body was borne to the tomb amid the tears of thousands; the one speaking of the humility and faith of his ministerial advent, and the other of the glory of his triumphant exit.

In August of this year, (1824) he made a tour eastward as an Evangelist, with Rev. Abner Jones of the Christian Denomination. He was absent some two weeks,—preached on the average about once each day, attended some conference meetings, and received some five dollars above his expenses. He preached during his absence in Salem, Haverhill, New Rowley, &c. No events of particular importance appear to have been connected with this tour. He sowed the seed of truth in faith and sincerity, and of its springing up and its fruit God knoweth the history.

At about this time he became associated with several brethren in the ministry, in what was termed a "Union

Conference," organized for the purpose of mutual improvement. Z. Tobey, Allen Brown, John Prentice, Ray Potter, Henry Tatem, and others, had a membership in this body; the association embraced also a few churches. Mr. Cheney preached several times before this Conference, and at the instance of its members wrote and read an Essay on "Qualifications for the Christian Ministry," which appears to have been among the first, if not *the* first production of the kind. It will be read with interest, both on account of its character, and its historical associations. His educational privileges, it will be remembered, had been small, his habits had been unfriendly to mental growth, his secular business still claimed nearly the whole of his attention through the week, and the Sabbath was spent in preaching. The following is a copy of the Essay as found among his papers.

ESSAY.

"BRETHREN: In offering a few thoughts upon the qualifications of a Christian minister, the great, the important work he has to perform meets our view. To announce God's will, to be an ambassador of Christ, to proclaim the terms of reconciliation to guilty sinners, to warn the unruly and comfort the feeble minded, to point penitents to the Lamb of God, to feed the Church of God and to watch for souls as they that must give account, are some of the duties that belong to the minister of Jesus. Our inquiry at this time is: What are the qualifications requisite to perform these and all other duties which are connected with the gospel ministry? and,

First. We conceive that no one is or can be qualified for this work without having the love of God shed abroad in his heart. He must be born again, not of the will of man but of God. The eyes of his understanding must be opened ;—for if the blind lead the blind both shall fall into the ditch. However, God may overrule the preaching of unconverted persons for the good of his people, or even for the conviction of sinners; yet as they were not called, so neither are they qualified to preach the truth as it is in Jesus. As soon shall you find a blind man who is fitted to be a judge of colors, as an unconverted man who is qualified to preach the gospel. For the natural man receiveth not the things of the spirit of God, neither can he know them; and if he do not know them neither can he communicate them to others: and if he be not able to do this he is not qualified to preach the gospel which is spirit and life. Indeed, nothing is more absurd than for one to attempt to teach and instruct others in those things concerning which he is himself ignorant. Such an one can only darken counsel by words without knowledge. How can he open, explain, and apply the law, which is a schoolmaster to bring us to Christ, if he has not been slain by the law? And how can he, who has never felt the sun of Righteousness arise in his own soul, cry, 'Behold, behold the Lamb?' However different views may be taken of those who preached the kingdom of God before the resurrection of Christ, yet after this event they were commanded to tarry at Jerusalem till they were endued with power from on high. Reason, and Scripture which points out to us the practice of the primitive disciples, decide, as we conceive, that to be qualified to preach Christ we must experimentally know him.

But farther. All who are the children of God know him as we have mentioned. But all who thus know him are not qualified to preach. To be qualified, therefore, one must not only know Christ in his own heart, but must be able to communicate this knowledge to others; or, in other words, he must be able to preach that gospel which to his own soul has become the power of God unto salvation. To do this he should be well acquainted with the Scriptures. As by these the child of God is made wise unto salvation, so by these the minister should be furnished for his work. This is is the magazine from whence he is to draw his supplies. This is his sword with which he is to fight. He should be intimately acquainted with all the truths which the scriptures contain. The doctrines, precepts, promises, warnings, threatenings, judgments, and mercies which are revealed in the Bible, should be well understood and thoroughly digested. That scripture should dwell in him richly; and as this is the word of truth which he is to divide, he should, if he would be a workman that needeth not to be ashamed, be well acquainted with all its parts. In order to this it will be perceived that he must possess a good natural understanding. This is not, indeed, necessary to the receiving of the truth into our hearts to the saving of the soul, but it is so to him who is commanded to bring forth from the word of God things new and old. He should understand the doctrines, precepts, and promises of the bible in their importance and connection with each other. Connected with a good understanding he should have a solid judgment; for he who is destitute of these, which may be termed natural abilities, is in danger of being carried about with divers and strange doctrines; but possessing these he will be enabled to become settled and grounded. Another danger to which, as a preacher, he may be exposed, is the condemnation of the devil; but possessing a solid judgment, by the grace of God he may escape this. A preacher should be no novice, nor think of himself more highly than he ought to think; and this he may do either through a defect in his judgment, or too superficial an acquaintance with the scriptures or his own heart. But to a good natural capacity for receiving the truth, joined to a solid and discriminating judgment of men and things, connected with a deep and extensive acquaintance with the holy scriptures and the love of God shed abroad in the heart, must be added the gift of utterance. He must not only be *able* but *apt* to teach. Without this, all his knowledge and judgment can never qualify him to be a good minister of Jesus. His heart must indite good matter, but his tongue must also be as the pen of a ready writer, so that he may communicate to others that knowledge which he has received, with ease if not with high propriety—a propriety founded upon the grammatical construction of words and sentences. A sound mind, good judgment, clear understanding and ready utterance, appear to be the natural abilities suitable to a good minister of Christ; and to these must be added a change of heart, a thorough conversion to God, with an acquaintance with the gospel scheme of salvation as contained in the scriptures, and a hearty desire to this work. Having these, the man of God appears to be furnished with every qualification which is absolutely and essentially necessary for the work of the ministry.

But while these are the only, and perhaps some might say more than the only qualifications which are absolutely and essentially necessary to a gospel minister, there are yet other qualifications which are highly important and exceedingly useful. Such, we would observe, is a knowledge of the rise and fall of kingdoms, of the different orders and classes of men in the world; in a word, a general knowledge as derived from ancient as well as modern history. A knowledge of the Church, from its commencement to the present time, is of much, though not of essential, importance to the minister of Jesus. Indeed, learning, in all its branches, although despised and ridiculed by some, and overrated by others, is, in subserviency to the will of God, of much use to an ambassador of Christ. The more we know of nature, the sooner we ascend to nature's God. The more we know of ourselves, the more ready are we to learn of Christ. Indeed a knowledge of past ages and of the present condition of mankind, while on the one hand it teaches the ambassador of Christ his duty or discovers to him his work, and presents to him the fields all white to the harvest, on the other presents him with strong proofs of the truth and certainty of the holy scriptures, while ancient and modern historians have presented him a picture so truly agreeing with that of the bible, of a whole world lying in wickedness. If to these should be added a lively and brilliant imagination, it will add to the preacher's usefulness, if chastened and corrected by a sound judgment. By the aid of this faculty, truth appears more lovely, and virtue more charming, while vice of all kinds shrinks from before it into its native darkness.

Shall we proceed to mention that a Christian preacher should possess courage? He is called to endure hardness as a good soldier of Jesus; and not a soldier simply, but one who is placed in the *forlorn hope*, to clear the way, and to gather out the stones. Says the Apostle, we are made a spectacle to the world, to angels, and to men. He needs invincible courage to meet the Lion and the Bear, as well as the proud and boasting Philistine. A frowning world is in his path; Principalities and Powers oppose his march, and the grand foe of God and man would desire to sift him as wheat. The waves of ungodliness rise high and threaten to destroy the Church; iniquity abounds, and the love of many waxes cold; friends forsake, and false brethren deceive; but amidst all this and more, let the language of the heart be that of the bold and resolute Nehemiah; Should such a man as I flee? or of an Apostle as bold,—None of these things move me. But let this noble principle be tempered by meekness and humility. In meekness, the servant of the Lord is to instruct those that oppose themselves; and although he should never shrink from declaring the whole counsel of God, yet he should always remember that it ought to be done in a gentle, meek, and humble spirit. The servant of the Lord must not strive, but beseech sinners to be reconciled to God. A proud, haughty, and imperious spirit, manifested in a minister of Christ, is not only an inconsistency, but will inevitably destroy his usefulness. Let the minister of Jesus, then, while he declares the day of vengeance of our God, beware that he do not take vengeance into his own hands. Let him rather clothe himself with meekness, which, in the sight of God, is of great price. Let him use the sword of the spirit as the skilful surgeon does his lancet, not to kill but to cure. And this heavenly temper is also of great importance to the servant of Christ in reproof. He is to reprove and rebuke with all long-suffering and doctrine. But let every one take heed in what spirit he reproves, considering himself lest he also be tempted. We would further observe, that the laborer in God's vineyard has need of *patience*. In him, in a special manner, should patience have its perfect work. He will have numerous occasions for the exercise of this grace. His friends, his brethren, perhaps, will call for the exercise of patience. His work, especially when he sees but little fruit of his labors, calls for patience. As the husbandman waiteth for the early and the latter rain, so the minister of Jesus should, in the morning sow his seed, and in the evening not withhold his hand, waiting patiently to see whether God will prosper this or that. In much patience he should possess his soul,— patiently endure and suffer persecution and reproach in the cause of the blessed Redeemer, knowing that hereunto he is called.

Further. A preacher of the gospel should be a man of the strictest integrity. No consideration should tempt him to swerve from the strictest regard to truth. He should abhor even the smallest approach toward dissimulation; truth, sacred truth, should dwell forever on his lips. As the priest's lips should keep knowledge, so also they should keep truth. Of him it should be said—

"No slanders dwell upon his tongue,
He hates to do his neighbor wrong."

He should also be a peace-maker! never should he be found encouraging, much less *sowing*, discord among brethren. Let him ever maintain the spirit of his first salutation,—Peace be to this house.

To all of which we have spoken, should be added wisdom. This wisdom which, if any man lack, he is to ask of God, is of the greatest importance; it is, as it were, a regulator, to enable the man of God to bring into exercise all the combined powers of body and soul in the most proper and efficient manner. It is by this wisdom, which is from above, that he is taught when, where and how to wield the sword of the spirit. It is this that must teach the minister of Christ how, without sin, he may become all things to all men. It is this that must teach him of those things which are lawful, but not expedient. It is this that must teach when to speak a word in season, and when to answer a fool according to his folly. It is this which will show the time, the place, and the circumstances, that aid in gaining access to the sinner's heart, with the greatest prospect of success. It is this which will regulate and direct his courage and his zeal, so that success will attend his labors."

This essay will not bear the test of a nice rhetorical criticism; and, in itself considered, is not a very remarkable production. It indicates a lack of finish, both in the mental culture and compositional taste of the author; but it bespeaks quite as plainly a power of close thought and careful discrimination. It is marked by a clear direct simplicity, an acquaintance with the Bible, and a felicity in the use of scripture quotations and allusions, adapted to excite surprise. That " old Bible" had evidently been diligently studied, from the time it was appealed to with so much success, to decide the question of his conversion. The effort surprised the Conference. He says:

"I was asked where I got those thoughts; if they came from 'Solitary Hill;' (the name of a hill in the place of my residence.) I had a suspicion that the Conference thought I had pilfered some of them from others, and called them mine. They were, however, the result of what I had heard, and read, and thought, all of which had passed through my own *thinking machine.*"

In the spring of 1825, after being examined by several of the members of this Conference, and others, it was decided that he should be set apart to the work of the ministry, by the laying on of hands.

His ordination took place in the old Johnston Meeting House, near the village of Olneyville, on the 28th of April, in this same year, at 2 o'clock, P. M. The order of exercises were as follows, as appears from a record kept by Mr. Cheney:

1. Hymn;—"Go preach my gospel," &c.

2. Introductory Prayer ;—by Rev. Mr. Kenney, of Bristol.
3. Hymn ;—" How beauteous are their feet," &c.
4. Reading of Scriptures ;—by Rev. Ray Potter.
5. Sermon ;—by Rev. Zalmon Tobey. Text, John, 13 : 15, 16. "For I have given you an example," &c. Topic,—*Christ, the Preacher's Example.*
6. Ordaining Prayer ;—by Rev. Henry Tatem.
7. Charge ;—by Rev. Ray Potter.
8. Right Hand of Fellowship ;—by Rev. Allen Brown.
9. Prayer and Benediction ;—by Mr. Cheney.

A large concourse of people assembled on the occasion to witness the exercises, which were full of interest and impressiveness. The work of the ministry had now been fully assumed, the consecration had been publicly made, and henceforward Mr. Cheney was to be known as a herald of the cross, a leader among the hosts of righteousness. His former companions, who had looked for his backslidings, were now compelled to feel that their haunts of sin were to be visited by him again only in his rebukes, and disclosures, and warnings. He preached the faith he had before labored to destroy. And it is in this work, chiefly, that we are hereafter to follow him.

CHAPTER IV.

CHOOSING AND ENTERING HIS FIELD OF LABOR.

It is well that the future is hidden from human view, and especially from those who enter upon the life of Christian faith and obedience. "Sufficient unto the day is the evil thereof." To be obliged to add to this evil the dread of that other evil, awaiting us in the days to come, would be often to overpower faith and destroy hope. And especially is this so of those who consent to take the lead in religious duty. Christ in Gethsemane, tells us how terrible is the cup of suffering which the prophetic eye sees moving slowly, but surely, forward to the lip of human weakness. The sustaining power of his divinity did not keep him from struggling with resignation, till he was baptized with the sweat of blood. Moses had hardly faith enough to walk forward and meet the anticipated difficulties created by his tardy tongue; what would he have done if he had foreseen the wrath of Pharoah, the blind, thankless stubbornness of his nation, the forty years pilgrimage in the desert, the punishment which buried the whole generation of his people, and his own tomb hidden from view in a land of strangers by the rebuke of God! But for narrowing the sphere of vision to the present day's trials, there might have been no Daniel resting in state among the Lions, and no Hebrew worthies marching in triumph over the flaming pavement of the tyrant's furnace. "Sufficient unto the day *is* the evil thereof."

Mr. Cheney entered upon his ministerial work, not without forethought and decision. He endeavored to count the cost; but it was well that *he could not count it;* that the price was kept out of his view. Not that he had a bitterer cup, or more terrible hardships than others have had, but there was abundant to try his spirit. Of some of these experiences account will be taken as his life is developed. What effect would be produced by laying bare the vices about him, he knew not; what friendships he must sacrifice, what losses encounter, and what sorrows of heart endure, were matters to be learned only in the school of coming experience. And his pecuniary circumstances, too, were such as to awaken distrust. He had no assurance of being provided for, given by any man or body of men; for no one or ones had become chargeable with his support. Of this matter, twenty-five years afterward, he thus speaks:—

"I wonder, even now, that I ventured to attempt preaching. I do, indeed wonder, with what willingness I arranged to meet poverty; for although I was poor, I saw, if I preached, I must be poorer still. I wonder how, with willingness, I received second-hand clothing for myself and family. I remember, when I had reduced my rent one half, paying but twenty dollars per year, that a minister from Boston called upon me and tarried over night. He was dressed fashionably. But such a lodging place as he had I cannot describe.

A garret of the poorest kind, and as poorly furnished. But," he adds, " it was the best I had, and I thought good enough for him, or it might do him good, for I fear he was a ministerial dandy."

But he went forward, and through privation and trial, grew strong and prospered. When most depressed, and questioning whether it was really his duty to attempt to preach, the singing of the words which stirred him in his anxiety—

> " 'Tis all my business here below,
> To cry, ' Behold the Lamb !' "

would rouse his spirit, and consecrate him with a new faith and courage to his chosen work.

Soon after his ordination, he was invited to preach to the Church and Society at Fruit Hill, North Providence, some four miles from Olneyville. He accepted the invitation, and went, on Sabbath, P. M., after the close of his service in the hall at Olneyville, where he still preached in the morning, to his appointment at that place. While thus engaged, the work of erecting a meeting house in Olneyville had commenced, and, on the completion of the Vestry, the meetings were removed to that place from the hall where they had been formerly held. He continued to preach thus till the meeting house was completed, or nearly three years from the time of his engagement at Fruit Hill. During this time his preaching had attracted not a little attention, both on account of the character of the preacher, and of the character of the preaching.

Among the hearers, assembling from week to week in that little unimposing hall, were found men of talent, and influence, and station, who attended on his ministrations with not a little interest. Of these was Dr. Messer, then President of Brown University, who explained his attendance there by saying that he always carried away from that humble spot most profitable instruction. And the fact that, in two years from the time that the hall was opened for religious service, there had been sufficient interest awakened in Olneyville to erect a good house of worship in the very suburbs of the city, indicates that he was doing not a little to arrest and control attention.

On the 2d of July, 1827, the House, having been completed, was dedicated by a public service to the worship of God. Services as follows :
1. Reading Scriptures ; by Rev. Z. Tobey.
2. Singing.
3. Dedicatory Prayer ; by Rev. Mr. Seamons.
4. Singing.
5. Sermon ; by Rev. Martin Cheney.
6. Prayer; by Rev. Z. Tobey.
7. Singing an Anthem. Benediction.

A large assembly convened on the occasion, and the services were full of interest.

The written sketches of the Sermon preached on this occasion,—prepared merely to give definiteness to the thoughts and something of precision to the language—are found among Mr. Cheney's early papers. They are scattered over several pieces of paper, in beautiful confusion ; indicating that he wrote just *when* and just *as* the spirit of writing came upon him, and opportunities were secured. It was evidently closely studied; for some portions of it are written two or three times. It is not easy ro pick out his connected thoughts; but the following copy is probably very much like what he delivered, in substance, though it was doubtless much amplified in the delivery. For other reasons than because it appears to have been his first effort of this kind, will it be read with interest. The Introduction, (written two or three times over,) is omitted, because it is not necessary to the discourse, and because it has too much of apology and explanation—a feature in which his efforts of this kind were quite apt to abound.

SERMON.

"How amiable are thy Tabernacles, O Lord of Hosts!" *Psalms* lxxxiv: 1.

We have assembled this day to set apart or dedicate this building to the worship and service of the true and living God; in doing which we hope to meet not only the approbation of every candid and pious mind, but that which is of infinitely higher importance, the approbation of the great and blessed God.

It is true that the New Testament affords no positive precepts upon this subject, to guide and direct our steps; yet, to us, there seems to be a peculiar fitness and propriety, when opening a house erected professedly for religious worship, in those services, the tendency of which is to make all present feel, "This is none other than the house of God!" That the exercises on this occasion may, by the divine blessing, have this effect, is, by your speaker, earnestly desired.

The beautiful Psalm from which our text is selected, is, by some, supposed to have been written during the Babylonian captivity, and by one whose language gives abundant proof that he had not only seen, but felt and enjoyed the presence of God in his holy temple. Reflecting upon these happy privileges which he had once enjoyed, he exclaims ;—" How amiable are thy Tabernacles, O Lord of hosts!"

The word Tabernacle, which, in the text, is in the plural number, literally signifies a tent or dwelling place ; and in the text doubtless refers to those places where the power and presence of God had been seen, and where his name was adored. The word has been used in a figurative sense by the inspired writers to signify the human body, the humanity of Christ, and even Heaven itself. The first building which was expressly designed for the worship of God, of which we have a distinct and particular account, was erected in the wilderness and called a Tabernacle. The scriptures inform us of three structures called by this name. The first was built by Moses, and was called the Tabernacle of the Congregation. The second was also built by Moses, and the third by David, for the reception of the Ark when he received it from the house of Obed-Edom. Of the second of these we have, in the scriptures, a particular and very interesting account. It was built according to the pattern given by God himself unto Moses in the Mount ; was composed of the most precious and costly materials, and within were placed, besides other significant emblems, the Ark of the Covenant, which contained those wonderful tokens of God's power and goodness—the two Tables of Stone, the Pot of Manna, and Aaron's Rod that budded. The weight of brass, silver and gold used in the erection of the Tabernacle and its furniture, is said to be upwards of *fourteen tons*, and its cost more than half a million of dollars. Here the Israelites brought their rich and costly offerings. Here was spilt that blood which, though of itself it was unable to reach the conscience, yet pointed to that which *was* sufficient. Here were offered those lambs which were emblematical of the Lamb of God who taketh away the sins of the world; and here, amid these expressive types and shadows, was to be seen the pious Israelite in humble prostration, his prayer ascending with the morning and evening incense all fragrant to the skies. Well might a pious Hebrew exclaim, while reflecting upon scenes like these;—" How amiable are thy Tabernacles, O Lord of Hosts!" We might notice the Temple, which has also been called the Tabernacle; but as it was erected on the same plan as the Tabernacle already described, we forbear, and proceed to the main object of this discourse, which is to point out in a few particulars, *the beauty and excellence of God's house*, or in other words. the place which is appropriated to social and religious worship.—And,

1st. *It is the Lord's house.*

It is not the house of a mighty prince, it is not the palace of an earthly monarch, it is not a house built for the worship of saints or angels, but it is an house erected expressly for the worship and service of the Lord of Hosts. This it is that gives peculiar attractiveness to the building set apart for religious purposes. The ignorant and unenlightened may behold with astonishment, mingled with superstitious awe, those mighty structures which have been reared by pride and vanity to perpetuate the name of some idol god or mighty conqueror; but the true believer, while viewing the sanctuary of the Most High, passes by the splendor and pomp of outward show to the contemplation of that Being for whose worship and service it was erected. And when he beholds the name of Him who is not only the Father of the spirits of all flesh, but Him whom also by the spirit of adoption he can call Abba Father, written upon it, he cries with the man of God; "How amiable are thy Tabernacles, O Lord of Hosts."

2. The *services* of God's house point out its beauty and excellence.

These, under the Mosaic dispensation, were numerous and expensive, but withal glorious; but under the gospel, the burdensome and expensive parts being removed, the glory is greater. Those under the gospel we shall proceed to notice.

The first is *Prayer*. This is one of the most important parts of that service which is performed in the house of worship;—so important that it has given name to the house. For thus saith the Saviour "My house shall be called an house of prayer," &c.; and likewise the prophet; "I will make them joyful in my house of prayer." It is when the disciples are gathered together in one place, and with one accord make supplication to

God, that the Holy Ghost descends, an awful solemnity rests on the mind, and all feel to exclaim;—"Surely God is in this place." Here, while beholding the servant of God pleading for the grace power and spirit of Christ to be poured out upon the world, when we behold him wrestling like Jacob of old for mourning backsliders, penitent sinners and trembling saints, carrying their cares and wants to the throne of grace, we exclaim; "How amiable are thy Tabernacles, O Lord of Hosts!"

The second is *Singing*. This in ancient as well as in modern times has been considered an interesting and important part of divine worship; and when hearts and voices in sweet union join in offering up the grateful emotions of the soul in praise and thanksgiving to God, the scriptures teach us that such offerings ascend like fragrant incense to the skies, and will not be forgotten amid the loud hallelujahs in the courts above. While joining in this delightful employment, how often has the saint of God been led to break forth in the language of the Psalmist;—"How amiable are thy Tabernacles O Lord of Hosts!"

The third is *Preaching the word*. The reading, explaining and enforcing the Holy Scriptures are essential parts of divine service; and when this has been neglected the house of God has lost its holy and beautiful character, and become a cage for every unclean and hateful bird. But when this fountain of truth is exhibited in its native purity; when the servant of Christ applies these truths to the heart and conscience, the sinner, cut to the heart, exclaims;—"This is none other than the house of God!" When we hear the minister of Jesus, in the light of the scriptures, point out the character of the holy and blessed God, his mighty work, his unbounded goodness; when we see him directing us to the Lamb of God, and saying;—Behold him living, dying, rising, ascending, able to save to the uttermost; when we hear him directing us to that spirit which is to lead into all truth, and be a holy comforter even in death; when, like Moses the man of God, he ascends Mount Sinai's awful summit, and there points out the fitness and propriety of the Law of God; when, with his eyes a fountain of tears, he shows the sinner his awful danger; and when with love beaming in his countenance, we behold him crying, "Ho every one that thirsteth, come ye to the waters," we exclaim with the Psalmist; "There will I dwell for I have desired it."

The fourth is *the administration of the Gospel Ordinances.* While the table of the Lord has been spread, many have experienced the truth of that saying "Truly our fellowship is with the Father, and with his son Jesus Christ;" and they have enjoyed fellowship one with another.

3. The beauty and excellence of the house of God is seen *in the happy influence which it exerts.*

There are few, if any, in this highly favored country, but are enjoying directly or indirectly, the blessings which flow from the the house of God. Many of the sons and daughters of our land, might I call as witnesses to this fact. Pointing to the place where prayer is wont to be made—to the house of the Lord, to the temple of Jehovah,—they exclaim, There were my eyes opened, there did I first learn of myself, and there was mine ear opened to hear the joyful sound of sins forgiven and pardon bought with blood. Its happy influence has been felt by those who, awakened by the spirit, were laboring and heavy laden. Like Noah's dove they have found no rest in the world for the sole of the foot; and, fleeing to the house of God, they have found it an Ark of safety. The saint as well as the sinner experiences the happy influence of the house of God. They are instructed, they are strengthened, they are made exceeding joyful in the house of prayer, and are led to exclaim:—' How amiable are thy Tabernacles, O Lord of Hosts!' It exerts a happy influence upon the morals of society. We have only to contrast those places where the house of God is deserted, or where there is none, with those where the house of God is honored. In the first instance we find the day and name of God profaned; in the latter we behold parents early directing the steps of their children to the house of God, there to be taught their duty to God and man; and at the hour of prayer we behold aged, middle aged and youth, wending their way to the house of God. And when we perceive that the house of God exerts a happy influence in promoting peace, harmony and love in cities, towns and villages, our feelings again break forth in the expressive words of the text.

4. We would lastly notice the peculiar beauty and excellence of the house of God, when viewed in connection with *that rest that remains for the people of God.*

The true believer reads of the Tabernacle erected by Moses in the wilderness; he admires its form and beauty; beholds with delight those mysterious emblems which it contains—the Ark, the Tables of Stone, and the Rod that budded. The Temple of Solomon passes in review. Its astonishing magnificence and splendor, its rich and costly furniture, and the numerous offerings made at the altar, are inspected; he beholds the Priests and Levites, the High Priests, their order and service, but he stops not here. He looks forward to a greater Priest and a greater Temple. He looks for a Priest after the order of Melchisidec, and a house not made with hands, eternal in the heavens. So will the true believer, while in the house of God, enjoying the consolations of religion, have his mind upon that house to which our Saviour alludes, when he says: " In my Father's House are many mansions." When, in holy contemplation, he is lifted in the visions of God to the throne of the Great Eternal, and in anticipation walks those golden streets; when filled with holy joy he beholds, in the house of God below, some glimpses of that glory which fills the house of God above, like Simeon in the temple, with Christ in his arms, he exclaims; "Now lettest thou thy servant depart in peace, for mine eyes have seen thy salvation;" or with David;—"I had rather be a door-keeper in the house of my God than dwell in the tents of wickedness."

In closing these remarks, permit me to express my feelings with regard to this house and this people. We dedicate, this day, this house to the service of Almighy God. May it ever be devoted to his service, and may the doctrines and precepts here inculcated be in strict accordance with his Holy Word. May the sinner who, in the Providence of God, may pass the threshold of this sanctuary, be faithfully warned. May the Star of Bethlehem direct the poor wanderer to the fold of Christ. And may the Sun of Righteousness here rise upon all with healing in his wings.

At the expiration of the time for which Mr. Cheney was engaged at North Providence, he was urged, by the Society which had built the house at Olneyville, to occupy its pulpit regularly. The Church at North Providence sought earnestly to retain him in their service, but he finally concluded that his highest usefulness required that he should be principally devoted to the moral and religious welfare of the place of his residence. There was, as yet, no Church in the place; and the pews in the Meeting House were to be rented for five years to pay the debts incurred by the Society in its erection. There was no aid received from any Missionary Society, and the Freewill Baptists were held low in the public estimation. But, satisfied that this was the sphere of labor for him, he accepted it in the faith that, by some means, he should be sustained. And thus commenced the relations between the Pastor and the People unbroken for twenty-five years, and broken up at last by death when the cords of union had become almost as dear as life. His compensation was very small for a few years, and he never allowed himself to receive but a very moderate salary, even after the society had come to embrace numbers and wealth.

But he says, "Bread has been given me, and my waters have been sure."

On the 7th of November, 1828, a church was organized in the vestry of the Olneyville Meeting-House, called the "First Baptist Church of Christ, in Olneyville." At its organization it consisted of eleven members,—five males and six females. Rev. Zalmon Tobey was present, and gave the little band the right hand of fellowship. A Covenant was written by Mr. Cheney and adopted by the little company, as they knelt hand in hand before God. That covenant is still retained, unmodified save in the change of a single word. There were additions to their number every month for the first sixteen months from the organization. His preaching was attended with saving influences, and he was fast rising up to influence, and the Society increased in ability and social and moral force. He preached regularly twice on the Sabbath in the meeting-house; but this was only a small part of his ministerial labor. He had been known in his career of sin beyond the limits of his residence; and he was solicited to counteract the evil influences he had aided to create abroad, as he was engaged in doing it at home; and his heart was too warm to allow him to withhold the service, which promised to save others, so long as he was able to render it. In meeting-houses, halls and private dwellings, did he proclaim that gospel of whose saving, quickening power he was himself so striking a monument. Many, at first, went to hear him from curiosity, wondering scarcely less than did the astonished querists, of old who asked;—"Is Saul also among the prophets?" and they went again and yet again, attracted by the earnest sincerity and impressive views of truth which they had not expected to find.

He had entered upon the work of preaching the gospel with his whole heart, laying cheerfully and gratefully the entire energies of his ardent nature on the altar of that work; and the mental power, which had been crushed and hidden by the life of sensuality, now sprang up beneath the touch of that grace to which it had been yielded. And so he grew in grace, in knowledge, and in real intellectual strength. Life had now a purpose, worthy of all the heart's devotion; and, in the concentration of his powers on the great end set before him, it could not be otherwise than that the spirit should wax strong. Most deeply, too, did he feel the want of early systematic culture; but instead of sitting down despairingly over his loss, it only roused him to do what he might to repair it by earnest, present effort. The greatness and responsibility of his work were ever in his eye; and he made them mighty motives, forever urging him to fit himself to honor it. It was not in him to be contented to occupy a subordinate and dependant place in the ranks of the ministry; it was opposed to his tendencies of mind, to his sense of duty, and to the responsible sphere he had consented to occupy. He had always been a leader,—he believed the pulpit should be filled with leaders, and Olneyville especially demanded a leader. And so with a modest, humble, but firm self-reliance, he grasped the banner of his new faith, and dashed into the heat of the moral conflict, gathering courage and strength as he swept on to victory.

CHAPTER V.

"THE DISCIPLE IS NOT ABOVE HIS MASTER."

It must not be supposed that the marked change in Mr. Cheney's character and life, attracted all hearts to him, even from among the professedly religious; nor that his first sudden and decisive onsets upon the hosts of evil, saved him from all future conflict. The warfare of faith lasts as long as life, and no one act of goodness or courage, establishes forever, in all minds, an unimpeachable character. Not a few of the heroes of history,—the highest examples of merit and faithfulness, have found life a perpetual running of the gauntlet—a skilful warding off the blows of malice, the darts of opposition, and the feathery shafts of secret dislike. Toward the highest virtue, and its mission on earth, the world has generally conceived a dislike; and on one or another pretence has sought to justify it. It quarrelled with John's abstinence, and curled its lip at Christ's gluttony. It execrates the memory of one of its prophets for a trait of character, whose absence warranted the stoning of his predecessor. He who goes resolutely about the work of rebuking prevalent sins, and reforming society, has no just ground for hoping an entire freedom from difficulty and opposition. If there be not courage sufficient to meet him on the real issue, false ones can be created according to the demand. When the witnesses failed to agree together in their accusations against the Savior, in the Sanhedrim, a fresh charge was ready. If he had not profaned the temple, he had perverted the nation. If his character and abilities were above suspicion, still it was certain he had come from Nazareth! Ten years since, Elihu Burritt sent a few peace documents, with a notice of a lecture which he intended to deliver on war in the city, to a Boston Clergyman; requesting that the notice might be read from his pulpit. The package, with the unread notice, was returned to the philanthropist; and the coarse, brown wrapper, superscribed something as follows: "*Elihu, put on your leather apron and go back to your anvil!*" Still, as in the days of the Great Teacher, may it be said;—"It is impossible but that offences should come."

Mr. Cheney's experiences in intemperance had opened his eyes to the evils of drinking to any degree; and so at an early day he planted himself firmly on the ground of total abstinence. The custom of drinking prevailed all about him. In the hall where he preached, the very walls were sometimes perfumed with alcoholic odors—the fruit of the previous night's excesses—when he entered to commence his Sabbath service, and members of his audience found it sometimes difficult to retain an upright position and keep from stupor, in consequence of their indulgences at the adjoining tavern.

What was to be done? The evil was there. He saw it; he felt it. The bible spoke plainly against this evil; God had given solemn warnings against tarrying at the wine, and against putting the bottle to the lips of a neighbor. He was set for the defence of the gospel,—to be the mouth-piece of God.

True, custom sanctioned the sale and use of intoxicating drinks every where. The grocers would as soon think of being without molasses as without alcohol; and an evening party or a wedding feast, without spirits of some kind, would have been deemed a breach of courtesy, for which there could scarcely be offered a satisfactory apology. The advent and exit of life were alike celebrated by a free use of the bottle of whiskey, or the decanters of choicer mixtures. Drinking alcohol was deemed almost a necessity of life. These were so many facts calculated to lessen the enormity in the eyes of men, and increase the hazard of openly denouncing the indulgence. Custom, wealth, office, power, influence, and worth, all lent their support to the indulgence; and he who set himself against it, had flung the gauntlet at the feet of no ordinary foe. It is not strange that many who saw the evil, and mourned over it in secret, should still deem it prudent to be silent. With such expediency, however, Mr. Cheney seemed to have no sympathy. In his sin he had never been a coward, or a hypocrite, and he had little inclination now to become either. To him, the question,— what was to be done? was plain and simple. Sin was in his presence, and he was set to rebuke and remove sin. And so the work commenced. The hall, which had rung but a few hours before with the shouts of Bacchanals, echoed to the voice that, in clear and earnest tones, set forth the prohibiting law of God. He analyzed the traffic, and the indulgence, as he was able, and disclosed the immoralities they involved. He was not driven from the hall as might have been supposed, but he did awaken some severe opposition, not only from those actively engaged in the traffic, and those who largely indulged in the use of alcohol, but not a few of those who had been his friends deemed him rash and unwise. After the Society was organized, and the meeting house erected, he was assured that his course would disorganize and break up the Society; and some of his supporters did actually forsake him on this ground. But he spoke on not less earnestly for the opposition excited, and the support withdrawn. These were just the influences that served to confirm him in his course, and fire his spirit with a new fervor.

He was early and frequently called to attend funerals, as was the case through his whole ministerial life. And not a few of those over whose coffins he stood, were the victims of intemperance; some of them having been his companions in his wild career. Among the very first of those whose funerals he attended, was a man of this character, and one, moreover, with whom he had gambled and drank. It was a place no one would covet to occupy. But he stood there and spoke what he believed the circumstances demanded. These were terrible scenes, coming up now and then, and standing in the path of his ministerial faithfulness. Not unfrequently has it been said by those who listened to him on such occasions, in reproach and hostility, *" he preached the poor man straight to hell."* The auto-biography thus speaks of some of his labors in this cause :—

"I recollect two brothers, at whose funerals I preached. They were both picked up nearly frozen to death, on their way home from one of those places which Dr. Beecher calls the "breathing holes of hell,"—a grog-shop. They were found at two different times, months apart. The awful death of one did not deter the other from visiting the same place. They lived but a little time after they were brought home. At the funeral of the last one, I obtained leave of the afflicted widow to speak all I wished on the subject, and the wrath of the tavern-keeper and grog-seller was aroused. Homily after homily has been given me on my want of wisdom. I went too fast, and too far. I was an ultra; I injured a good cause; for they—*dear souls!*—were for temperance. And then the church records began to tell a story about this fearful, desolating curse, and this was trying. And then came trials when the temperance pledge was raised to *total abstinence;* brethren differed, and this was a trial. I lectured on temperance in most of the towns in Rhode-Island; in the city of Providence, in almost all the churches and halls, in school houses and meeting houses; ten, twelve or fourteen times a year, for years. Side by side with a Tew, a Jewett, and a Pierpont, have I labored in this cause, and urged it in quarterly meeting, and the churches, and have seen its principles and practice obtain a mighty triumph."

So, too, did Mr. Cheney find trial in the neglect of courtesy on the part of older and influential ministers. Young, timid, hesitating, and unknown as a minister, he felt that he needed and was entitled to the sympathy of those who had been long laboring, professedly, for just such transformations in character as he was exhibiting. But the sympathy was seldom found. "He went unto his own, and his own received him not." The following is a specimen fact, indicating the treatment he was wont to receive:

"A venerable preacher, pastor of one of the largest churches in the city, once preached, by invitation, in the hall where I was statedly preaching. I was present, but he did not notice me, not even so much as to speak to me."

From the circumstances, it was evident that the oversight was intentional. He might have been somewhat related to the clerical dignitary of another city, who sent back the documents to the "Learned Blacksmith."

While the battle was thus raging without, bereavement came to his house. His second wife was removed from the circle of his home and the pressure of her own pleasant cares, to her rest. She died December 23, 1831, in the peace and faith of a Christian, leaving her husband to carry on the moral warfare uncheered by her sympathy and aid. He unbent himself long enough to weep over his affliction, and bind up his bruised heart with the tenderness of past recollections and the consolations of the gospel, and then he was back again at his post, with an earnestness and zeal which seemed to be inspired by the new lesson taught him, of the speedy coming of the night when no man can work. He was married a third time, to Miss Lydia Sheldon, on the 4th of March, 1833, who still survives to sorrow over her loss.

A still fiercer conflict was endured a few years later in the great struggle of freedom, when mob law prevailed in some of the cities, and a formal effort was made to suppress the discussion of Slavery. The path of reflection through which he went forward to the post of duty and peril, is worthy of inspection; and is presented more or less clearly in the light of his own account. He says:

"My attention was called to the condition of millions in bonds in this country. It amazes me that my attention was not called to it before. It was about the time of the formation of the American Anti-Slavery Society,—probably a little earlier. I soon arrived at the conclusion that the church and pulpit should speak out fully, plainly, boldly, lovingly. Well, I was the Pastor of a church, and the occupant of a pulpit. I was fully aware that no ordinary storm was approaching. Governors had recommended legislative enactments to suppress Abolition meetings. A bill was then before the Rhode-Island Legislature to that effect. I had decided that the attention of the people in the place where I preached, ought to be directed to this great question. But who was to do it. It was suggested,—exchange with some one, and let him do it. But the response within was,—will that do your work? will that clear your conscience? I was forced to reply in the negative. Besides, a voice within, as well as circumstances without, told me that no one could meet the storm of unpopularity as well as myself. I felt an assurance that if the people would listen to any one on this subject, they would listen to me. The conviction became strong ;—' Thou art the man.' O, that all who minister at God's altar had come to the same conclusion and carried it out! We should then have had no Texas annexation, no Mexican war, no Slavery extension, no Fugitive Slave Bill. I had settled it in my own mind that the cause of the slave must be advocated before the people, and that I must do it. The only remaining questions were—*when, and how* is this to be done? The first was decided thus: As soon as you can do it. *Now* is the time. Thy brother is among the thieves. *Now* is the time to 'lift up thy voice like a trumpet,' to 'cry aloud.' *Now* it is no time to pass by on the other side. The second question I answered thus,—I had been pondering for some months upon the propriety of lecturing upon the Ten Commandments. I had been deterred only by a feeling of inability to do justice to so mighty a subject. I was resolved to do what I could ; and announced to the congregation that I should deliver a discourse on each succeeding Sabbath on the Ten Commandments, commencing with the first. I stated that if it had not seemed like an insult to the audience, I should have asked if they were willing I should lecture on the Ten Commandments, without omitting any of them; but that, on reflection, I had taken it for granted that a Christian audience, in a land of freedom, would not only be willing, but anxious, to hear God's commands explained and enforced. I commenced; the congregation increased as I proceeded, till the house was crowded. On the sixth commandment, Rumselling in its moral character, effects, &c., was examined, and offence was taken, and influence withdrawn from the Society, of which I was not aware till afterwards. But the lectures went on. On the seventh and eighth commandments the Slave System underwent a searching examination. Its blasphemous and God-insulting claim of property in man, its setting the image of God on the auction block, its trampling on inalienable human rights, its entire disregard of the command, 'Love thy neighbor as thyself;' and of the Golden Rule,—'all things whatsoever ye would,' &c., were set forth with what ability I possessed, and with the zeal of a newly awakened attention to a mighty wrong. Its woes and its wrongs were commented on, its fetters, its whips, its gags, its thumbscrews. The scarred and bleeding forms of its victims were held up to view. The licentiousness of the system was unveiled, and its indescribable pollutions unmasked; and it was my aim to make the wail of the bondman heard in all the large assemblies. Our country's guilt and danger were described, the black spot in her Constitution pointed out,—that compromise with sin which our fathers made in an evil hour, and which has brought forth its legitimate fruit—Texas annexation, Mexican war, Fugitive Slave Bill, and, what is worse, *a drugged and stupified church and national conscience.* Our duty as individuals, and as a nation, was attempted to be shown, the work of the pulpit, the press, &c. &c. There were sincerity and zeal in these lectures, whatever they may have lacked in wisdom— of this last feature, others are, perhaps, the better judges."

Some of the results were just what might have been

predicted. Intense excitement prevailed, which drew in many who wished to see and to hear, and drove away a few who could not bear such teaching. About seventy dollars, pledged on a subscription of three hundred dollars, were withheld; but this difficulty was disposed of by the enthusiastic efforts of the ladies, who raised one hundred dollars to meet the deficiency. Mr. Cheney's comment upon this and similar experiences is laconic and characteristic. He says: "*So the bread and cheese argument failed.*" He was told that such preaching would not be tolerated; that it was treasonable; and that he would be dismissed from the pastorate if he persisted; and he was once informed that a week's time would be allowed him to consider the matter. He says:

"I replied, in substance, that I had not consulted the Church or Society whether I should speak from the pulpit in behalf of the slave, but had consulted a higher authority than Church or Society, Court or Constitution; that on my knees before God, I had settled that question, and therefore did not need a week to decide upon my course; that I should speak upon the sin of slaveholding, just as I should on all other sins, whenever and wherever I might deem it duty thus to do; that if the Society were opposed to my course, they had only to dismiss me at their next meeting."

So spoke the man; and all who knew him understood him perfectly. But he was not dismissed. The great mass of the members of the Society, though, perhaps, not ready to go with him in the endorsement of all his positions, still stood by him in that dark hour, resolved that his rights should be guarded, and *their pulpit should be free.* The effort to remove him was confined to a small number, and it seemed to bind him more strongly to his post. Some few left the meeting, and he was hailed more or less as a rabid Abolitionist abroad; but the public controversy was over. Difficulties and trials he still met, many and fierce ones, in his advocacy of the cause of the slave; but all were welcomed, and made the occasion of fresh effort and fearless speech. His narrative of these events contains also the following:

"About these days, a singular phenomenon appeared in the Olneyville meeting house. A pew, nearly in the centre of the house, was occupied Sabbath after Sabbath, for a number of weeks, by colored people. Their advent no one in the congregation knew, that I am aware of. The *why* of their departure was, I believe, also unknown. Their advent and exodus were as mysterious as the pedigree of Melchisedec. They came, no one knew from whence, they went no one knew where. The pew occupied was owned by one who had ceased attending the meeting. Many conjectures were raised by the phenomenon. Some thought it was intended to test the Anti-Slavery feeling of the congregation. No little curiosity was excited, but no offence seemed to be taken or suffered. There was no sneering, no one left his seat on account of it. The colored people were treated with great courtesy, and a practical demonstration was given of different colors mingling in a congregation without harm. Of this demonstration it might be said, '*none killed; none wounded!*'"

Up to the time of this controversy, Mr. Cheney had been acquiring general influence and popularity as a preacher among all denominations—that word popularity being used in a good sense. His preaching seemed to find its way to the hearts of the people wherever he spoke. Though not the idol or the pet of aristocracy, yet it was true of him as of his Great Master, that "the common people heard him gladly;" and worthy men of learning and influence sat with pleasure and profit under his ministry. He was invited to preach on exchange and otherwise before the largest and wealthiest congregations of the city. But, after his avowal of anti-slavery sentiments and his public avowal of sympathy with the objects and efforts of the abolitionists, these courtesies grew less frequent; and after he had pleaded the cause of the slave in other pulpits as he did in his own on a few occasions, they nearly ceased altogether; and he incurred not a little of the odium attaching to abolitionists in those days of tyrannizing public opinion, and silent servility. The effect on him was to make him feel that the reasons for crying aloud and rebuking strongly were now numerous and strong. And so his words grew more fiery as his heart grew more heated; and seldom did he let an opportunity to utter rebuke that should reach them pass unimproved. Their repulsion roused his fire, and his fire drove them still farther away; until some of them regarded him as a rash and severe enthusiast, and he in turn regarded them as criminal and cowardly time-servers. Comment on these facts and experiences is designedly omitted here, with a view of presenting, in a subsequent chapter, an analysis of his character, and an estimate of him as a preacher and general public speaker.

Thus fairly committed to these great moral causes in their infancy, and wielding a power which everywhere commanded respect, he was often summoned abroad to fight over the battles which had sprung up at Olneyville, and which had made him accept a life of open conflict as something never to be shunned. Controversy had developed his logic and his cutting sharpness of speech, and given him no disrelish for the work of openly and formally fighting with a moral evil. He had no such aspirations for peace and repose as made him willing to find it by shutting his eyes to peril, or stopping his ears against the clamor of injustice. And so he was still bearing the standard elsewhere, before those who coveted his leadership. He shrank from before no reproach which came in consequence of his quarrel with Rum-selling, or his active sympathy for the Slave. He went abroad and lectured and discussed these great questions; and his name and reputation and reported speeches went where he could not go; went sometimes to inspire gratitude and courage; but went also to create suspicion and rouse enmity. And so, sometimes, in going abroad simply to preach the gospel, in a place strange to him, he would find that rumor had been there before him, sowing the seeds of prejudice and building up barriers between him and the hearts of those whom he would fain have led to the cross. The Jewish bigots dismissed the whole question of Christ's authority and Messiahship by the sneering query,—" Can any good thing come out of Nazareth?" and not a few turned sullenly away from the place of concourse, uttering bitter words when they knew only that the speaker hailed from Olneyville.

There was one thing which did not a little to keep alive the sympathy of the people for Mr. Cheney; and that was his high and obvious sincerity, his lofty conscientiousness, his fidelity to his moral convictions. That he possessed this trait of character, few, if any, could doubt, after knowing him for a brief period. He had sacrificed popularity too much and too freely for the sake of principle, to leave room for a charge of selfishness. He grieved too many of his warm friends in the courses which he adopted, to justify any other supposition than that he held his convictions more sacred than he did the approbation of those whose smiles were most grateful to his eye, and whose commendation was sweetest to his ear. Integrity was, with him, a cardinal virtue; injustice was something from which his whole nature revolted. On no pretence would he voluntarily wrong even an enemy. To him, nothing was more real than rights; and his reverence for his own rights made him scrupulous in respect to his dealing with the prerogatives of others. Whatever else might be thought of him, his *honesty* was admitted on all hands. Every business transaction displayed his care and accuracy in making an engagement, and his promptness in meeting it.

Blended with this, or constituting a part of it, was his *frankness*. So far as his public policy was concerned, he had nothing apparently to conceal. He approached no man with a mask. He never made a mere profession of friendship. He never assented to a sentiment or a piece of policy when his judgment opposed it. He hated ambiguous language, and hated still more ambiguous lives. He practically believed with Solomon, that open rebuke was better than secret love. His dissent from an opinion was just as decided and just as certain, if he deemed it called for, in the circles where dissent purchased reproach, as in those where it invited applause. He nailed his colors to the mast, and sailed over the sea of life in the clear light of noon.

The result was, everybody trusted, though some failed to like him. And so, too, everybody's conscience proclaimed the wrong of forbidding to speak such an honest, earnest, sincere, frank, and christianly conscientious man. All felt as he did when he was arrested in the hour of his conviction, "*The man is sincere;*" and though some gave no more heed to his words than he gave to the exhortation of his earnest neighbor, still they listened with reverence. But for this he must have been crushed by the influences arrayed against him; for he would have found less to sustain him within, and his foes would not have found him so well guarded by the sense of public justice. But he lived long enough to silence every tongue disposed to asperse his character, and lay every suspicion against his integrity to rest, within the circles where he was known. Though there might be disagreements respecting the *fittest* epitaph for his monument, all would have conceded the fitness of inscribing it: "HERE LIES AN HONEST MAN."

CHAPTER VI.

MORAL POSITIONS.

The influences which had been acting on Mr. Cheney were just such as not only to rouse his heroism, but to quicken his intellect. He was thrown on the defensive; and he was not to yield without an earnest resistance. He attached importance to his public efforts; for he knew they were to be criticised and attacked. He had taken positions hostile to the sentiment which more or less prevailed about him; and so he was interested, not only to defend them, but to commend them to the confidence and acceptance of others. They made him think; and in thought does the mind find the condition of its growing power.

Those lectures on the Commandments would be full of interest, both as a history of the time, and as an index to his own mental progress; but a few of the brief sketches which he took into the pulpit as a guide, are all that remain. The following, on the Sixth Commandment, will somewhat illustrate his methods, and indicate the discrimination and love of system which, at that early day, began to appear, and which were so prominent in later life. The sentiments differ somewhat from those adopted at a later day. He would not have endorsed the *"limitations"* upon which he here insists, fifteen years later.

LECTURE.

" Thou shalt not kill."—Ex. 20: 13.

1. This command, as it stands, is universal. In its letter, it forbids the taking of life in all cases and in all times; human, animal, and, for aught I can perceive, even vegetable. Some there are who will not take animal life; they strain the water which they drink to avoid it.

2. This Command, then, has no limits, except as God has limited it.

3. This Command differs from, " Thou shalt love," &c.

4. This Command will have no place when and where immortality reigns.

What are the limitations to this command? for God can explain his own Law, or, if he please, annul it.

1. The life of animals may be taken in cases where they are necessary for food, and when hostile to us. The ox that gored was to be stoned. This right arises from God's grant. We know not whether this grant existed before the time of Noah, but it was made to him; animals were offered to God by his direction in sacrifice; and Christ made use of animal food. The *blood* however was, and still is, absolutely forbidden.

2. The life of *man* may be taken under certain circumstances. First; under the Patriarchal dispensation. Gen. ix. 6: " Whoso sheddeth man's blood, by man shall his blood be shed." That man's life may be taken for murder, has been believed by almost all nations.

Second; under the Mosaic dispensation the same grant continued. Life could be taken for murder, and for other crimes.

Third; under the gospel the same grant exists. Says an apostle,—" The law was not made for a righteous man but for murderers." Now if it was morally right under the patriarchs and under the law to take life by the magistrate, and if Christ did not repeal the moral law, it must be lawful for the magistrates to do it now.

Fourth; Life may be taken in Self Defence; which includes the right of Defensive War.

To this view, objections are sometimes urged by the Friends and others. But,

1. No one disputes that, under the Jewish institutions, life might be taken. The same people who had the Ark, the Tables of Stone, on which was written,—" Thou shalt not kill," were commanded to take the life of the murderer, and destroy the nations of Canaan.

2. If the words,—" Whoso sheddeth," &c. be not a prediction, life was to be taken at that time; and if the commandment still stands, then human life may—ought to be taken.

3. The support of Civil Government implies that life may be taken. Christ paid taxes, used physical force, told the disciples to buy swords, not to propagate the gospel, but for self defence. Paul says that the ruler " beareth not the sword in vain." Mr. Dymond says,—" It is the duty of the magistrate to repress the violence of one man upon another." But how is he to do this without physical force?"

It is said, however, that the precepts of the gospel forbid it; that its injunctions are,—"Love your enemies;" "Resist not evil;" and that no man can take life and obey these precepts. But were not the Jews required to love their neighbor? Christ did not alter but explain the moral law which had always been in force. Well, then, when Samuel hewed Agag in pieces, was he obliged to hate him? When the Jews destroyed the nations of Canaan, were they obliged to hate them? And is that man who takes the life of another in the defence of his own life, or of his family or of his country, obliged to hate the assailant? Is the executioner obliged to hate him who is hanged? Does Christianity require us to extinguish the instincts of nature? What would be the result if nations were to abandon the use of physical force? Where would they find protection?

We allow the permanent authority of the Christian Law; but we maintain that the Christian law is the *Moral* law; that the Christian law recognizes the use of the sword; that the Christian law does not take away man's natural rights. That God may authorize man to take life is clear; that he has done it we contend in the recognition of Civil Government.

This command is violated,

1. When life is taken for any other cause than those above specified. All laws which make any crime punishable with death except murder, violate this command.

2. Willingly endangering another's life, or neglecting to save it when it might be done.

3. Duelling violates it, under aggravating circumstances. There is a deliberately formed design to kill;

and, in the spirit of revenge, every element of success is sought. He acts without just cause; the pretence is poorer than that set up by the assassin or highwayman. For, suppose he gets killed, what then! suppose he kills, what then! What has he gained? what good done? It has not made wrong right, or falsehood truth, or cowardice bravery. It has only exhibited two guilty fools violating the law of God.—He acts against the strongest reasons: 1. His own life; 2. The duties he owes to his friends; 3. Injures his country and the world.

4. Aggressive wars violate this law.

REMARKS.

1. What evidence of human depravity is here!

2. Governments should punish duelling—make it infamous.

3. No man should give his vote to a duellist, till he has disavowed it, and pledges himself to refrain from it.

4. See the duty of cultivating in children the spirit of forgiveness. From whence comes the spirit of murder? From your lusts, &c.

5. See the wisdom and benevolence of the Lawgiver, in laying a prohibition where it is so much needed.

This discourse is, doubtless, liable to criticism; and few would probably criticise it more severely, than would the author in his subsequent life. But it shows a thoughtful, inquiring, critical mind, struggling to classify facts, to eliminate and apply principles. It shows a dissatisfaction with resting on superficial views, a struggle to systematize the truths scattered over the pages of God's book.

Wider and more comprehensive grew the views of Christian truth and ministerial duty which found utterance from the Olneyville pulpit. As the field of study was explored, as the inspection of the world grew closer, as the experiences of the heart were modified by time, the preaching of Mr. Cheney increased in compass, directness, and force. His work grew more and more significant in his eye, and he applied himself to do it with the zeal and fidelity which gave success to his ministry. The house of worship was enlarged, and not a few were added to the church, who, it seemed, had been added to the Lord. A public discourse, preached not far from this time, indicates both the views of the gospel which he was holding, and the rational grounds on which they rested. No apology is needed for introducing it here. The question to which the discourse is intended as a reply is as follows;—

"Does the preaching of the whole gospel require the discussion of such topics as Intemperance, Slavery, &c."

DISCOURSE.

"Wherefore, I take you to record this day, that I am pure from the blood of all men. For I have not shunned to declare unto you all the counsel of God."—*Acts* xx.; 26, 27.

To answer this question, it is necessary that we understand what the gospel is, and what is implied in preaching it. This question is full of interest and importance in itself; and especially so in view of the fact that there exists a wide diversity of opinion respecting it, among the professed ambassadors of Christ. The decision has a practical bearing upon the work of the ministry, and is so vital as to require that it be examined without prejudice, and in a serious and prayerful spirit.

1. The term Gospel signifies *Good News.* It is called the gospel of the Kingdom of God; it is a message of mercy to a ruined world. It is contrasted with the Law; " The law came by Moses, but grace and truth by Jesus Christ." It is the announcement of God's purposes and plans of mercy, and was preached to Abraham, yea, even to Adam in the garden.

2. It is applied to the history of Jesus Christ by the four Evangelists; also to the discourses of Christ and his Apostles.

3. The term *preach* signifies to proclaim, to announce, to declare.

4. It is addressed to every creature; and so may be supposed to be suited to the wants of every creature. Now man is a moral agent; the gospel approaches him as such, and must, therefore, we think, solve every moral question concerning him.

If these statements be correct, then it follows;

1. That the preaching of the gospel, is making known God's plans and purposes of mercy to the world. This will include the Being and Perfections of God; his existence as Father, Son and Holy Ghost; his unlimited and illimitable Power, his inflexible justice, his unfathomable Wisdom; his Love, so deep, so high, so wide, shoreless, fathomless, boundless, unspeakable.

God, Christ, Angels, Ministers, and all other agencies employed in carrying these purposes and plans into effect, should be declared.

2. It is revealing the condition of man; as originally upright and innocent, and as now guilty; why he now needs the gospel; his guilt, weakness, danger; his powers, agency, and relations.

3. Making known God's Law; its length, breadth, purity, spirituality, perfection, its claims, and penalties.

That the law must be preached is clear: for by it is the knowledge of sin; by it the character of God is seen; by it man's duty is made known.

4. Revealing Christ. His incarnation, his birth, his teaching, sufferings, death, resurrection, ascension, and advocacy; his wonderful character, as God manifest in the flesh; as our Wisdom, Righteousness, Sanctification, and Redemption; our Prophet, Priest, King, and Example.

5. Exhibiting Man's Duties; as a sinner, as a christian; in all his relations,—to God, to his neighbor, to the Church, and to Society.

Man's obligations arise from the powers he possesses, from the relations he sustains, and the opportunities given him; hence those powers are to be described, those relations defined, and those opportunities pointed out, that he may feel the force of obligation.

These powers are of body and of mind; of the understanding, will, and affections. These relations connect him with God, as a subject of his government, requiring love and obedience; show him a sinner, deserving and receiving punishment, as required to repent, believe, and obey. They connect him to Christ, as Redeemer, Saviour, Judge; to his race, as citizen, neighbor, parent or child. All these relations, in connection with his powers and opportunities, create obligations, and determine their nature, extent, and authority.

Now, if this be the gospel, and this what is implied in preaching the gospel, what moral question can arise which is out of the pale of gospel examination? We are most intimately related to, and most deeply interested in, whatever concerns sin, its nature, power and results; in knowing what the law is, its claims, and penalties; what we are, our condition, duty, and dangers; what God, Christ, heaven, and hell are;—and so to preach the whole gospel, seems to me to imply the examination of every moral question arising from all these inquiries in all their branches; in short, it implies the pointing out and rebuking all sin, describing and enforcing God's law, and describing and enforcing man's duty. So preached Christ and his apostles, giving principles applicable to all times and circumstances.

We conclude, therefore, that the whole gospel cannot be preached, without discussing these moral subjects. This does not imply that any one man is obligated to preach the whole gospel in one life; nor that all moral questions are of equal importance.

To this view, objections have been urged; some of which will be noticed.

1. Paul determined to know nothing save Christ and him crucified.

But Christ and him crucified, are only other terms for the gospel.

Note how Paul preached, and on how many topics he dilated. On God, man, angels, devils, sins, duties, relations; he preached in words of exhortation, warning, rebuke.

2. The example of Christ is cited as opposed to this mode of preaching. Christ says that he sends his disciples as he was sent of his Father. And when asked to render a decision in relation to a secular matter, he replies;—" Who made me a judge or a divider over you?" "My kingdom is not of this world," &c. Great stress is, by some, laid upon this.

In reply to this, we observe,

First. That we mistake if we look for a complete personal example in Christ. That Christ's personal example is supreme where we have it, will be admitted; but there are some points in which there is no pattern. In relations, there are many we sustain in human life which never attached to him.

Secondly. That, as a preacher, his example is supreme only in his spirit, and in the great truths which he uttered. The truths which were to be brought forth on the different occasions were determined by the character and condition of those whom he addressed; and we follow Christ, not when we use the same words, or utter the same truths simply, but when we utter them under like circumstances.

Thirdly. That we do not know how pointedly and specifically Jesus might have dealt in rebuke with the institutions about him. We have but an outline of his history. " There are many other things which Jesus did," &c.

Fourthly. That an unction was given to his disciples. They were to do greater works than he. Principles are unchangeable, but their application may vary as the condition of man varies.

Fifthly. He did preach on many just such subjects. Examples.

3. It is preaching politics.

But if we have any political duty, it should be done right; and it is the gospel that points out the principles, rules, and spirit that should direct in this duty. " Whether ye eat or drink, or whatsoever ye do, do all to the glory of God." And a man is as much bound to vote as to eat to the glory of God.

4. It is unconstitutional.

If this be admitted, still it must be remembered that *God has a constitution.*

5. It produces strife and contention.

That there is strife, &c. is admitted; but who are the guilty cause? Christ was the occasion of division; so were the apostles; so was Luther; so Wesley. But why? If all had been right there would have been no strife. Peace is not to be purchased with purity. No wonder there is strife; and if the nation were not nearly dead to truth and liberty, there would be more strife. Gag laws, Lynch laws, mails robbed, Freedom's temple in flames, the soil of a free State drinking the blood of her martyred son, laws trampled on by magistrates, men not allowed to speak in their own temples of worship! No wonder there is strife. There ought to be, there must be more.

6. A hobby is made of these subjects.

To this we reply, by asking the objector,—Have you seriously examined these evils? If not, how can you judge whether too much is said? If you have, are you prepared to say, at the present time, that these are not among the weightier matters? Do not some dwell much and long, without rebuke, on the evidences of Christianity? others on Missions? others on Sunday Schools? These are weighty matters; but are the others less so? Besides, some are set for the defence of the gospel; to raise up some neglected doctrine or practice from the dust. Why did Luther dwell on the doctrine of justification by faith, or Wesley on holiness, or the Baptists on immersion, or the Friends on plainness, or Christ on the self-righteousness of the Pharisees? Surely, because these things were sadly neglected by the masters in Israel, who held the key of knowledge.

What does Christ term the weightier matters? Is it names, sects, or ordinances? No, but judgment, mercy, faith. True, there is need of wisdom, the wisdom of the serpent; but there is need also of fidelity and courage.

To preach the whole gospel, then, is to hold forth all its full, free, rich, and varied invitations; to utter all its solemn warnings; to administer all its pointed rebukes; clearly to point out and accurately define man's duty to his God, his neighbor, and himself, in all the multiplied relations which he sustains; and to set before him, in all their thrilling importance, motives—motives wide as the earth, broad as the sea, high as heaven, and deep as hell.

If there is any moral question touching man, which is not included in such a gospel as this, we confess our vision is not keen enough to discern it. We should as soon expect to find rays of light which had no relation to the sun, a river which did not find its outlet in the ocean, as to find a moral question not connected with the gospel of Christ. Why, sirs, the gospel is the great central truth, from which all truths emanate, and where they find their termination; the great central fountain from which go forth those streams that fertilize and make glad the whole moral field of man; the grand catholicon or panacea which is to cure all the moral maladies of the world.

Thus from the nature and design of the gospel, we see that it must embrace every moral question, unless we may suppose the gospel will destroy all moral evil without being applied to it; which would be about as wise as to suppose a remedy to be effectual without being taken or applied. The design of the gospel is to remove all moral evils, and it must then have to do with them all.

Now, friends, if slavery, intemperance, and licentiousness are not sins, then has the gospel nothing to do with them. But if they are sins, then has the gospel something to do with them, or there are some sins for which the gospel makes no provision, and in view of which there is no call in the gospel to repentance. And it is interesting to ask how our opponents expect the jubilee to come.

APPLICATION.

1. We see what a glorious scheme is the gospel. It is worthy of its great author; worthy, too, of all acceptance by those to whom it comes.

2. We may learn who are the real disturbers of the peace, the dividers of churches, the troublers of Israel. Not those who declare *all*, but a *part* of the counsel of God; who keep back part of the price; who cry *peace*, when there is no peace.

3. This subject is of thrilling interest to the ministry. O, brethren, we are to make full proof of our ministry; to give account, to answer for souls. We are watchmen, stewards, servants; to reprove, rebuke, &c. Let us see to it, that we can say with Paul; I have not shunned to declare the whole counsel of God; I have kept back nothing; I am clear from the blood of souls. Let us see that, in preaching, we lay stress on the weightier matters. If the making and vending of intoxicating drinks be a sin, then should the minister of Jesus point it out, and apply the gospel power for its removal. Surely, he may reason on temperance with Paul, or warn with Moses. If no drunkard shall inherit the kingdom of God, surely, he may describe drunkenness, its causes, and effects, and warn against it.

So, if the young man is in danger of entering the house of the strange woman, shall not the man of God raise the alarm?

Again. Shall oppression fill the land with groans and anguish, and tears, and blood; shall theft and robbery, and lust and pollution, roll in streams over the moral field; shall mischief like this be framed into a law, and the ministers of purity and righteousness, of mercy and love, be silent? Shall truth be trampled in the streets, and ministers of truth not cry aloud?

4. The spirit in which we preach should be closely watched. The truth should be spoken, but spoken always in love.

5. Christians should learn that the gospel rule, the gospel spirit, and the gospel motive, should be with them always,—in the family, in the shop, at the ballot box,—cover the whole field of action. So will Zion "arise and shine, her light being come, and the glory of the Lord being risen upon her."

These views of the gospel were not held as a mere theory. As *such*, they would have been generally accepted in the churches and pulpits, where these evils were seldom named. But, at Olneyville, they were often urged from the pulpit, the more earnestly and frequently perhaps, because they were kept back elsewhere. To raise up these weighty, but neglected truths, Mr. Cheney counted himself specially called; and he gave himself to the work. Men of heterodox creeds, and men of no creeds, took hold of these causes, under the guidance of interest, sometimes, perhaps, and sometimes impelled forward by their own anxiety to relieve the suffering, and save the perilled. Many shrunk back from laboring with such associates, as if fearing to be laid under suspicion of unsoundness in the faith; but Mr. Cheney was at his post, ready to incur false charges, if need be, in the work of humanity and religion. He would sometimes say, in explanation of his course, that he was willing to labor with wicked men to overthrow wickedness; that he would have no objection to carrying one side of a basket of provisions to relieve a starving family, though Satan himself should take the other half of the burden. He did not, however, escape censure and suspicion. Still he went on, using his influence wherever he could bring it to bear, to secure a higher prominence for these features of the gospel. Chiefly through his influence, the church at Olneyville, in 1837, made total abstinence from ardent spirits a condition of securing membership in that body; and the Society had become united in their stern opposition to slavery, and in their active sympathy for the slave.

CHAPTER VII.

"Open thy mouth for the dumb."

MISSIONS AND MORAL REFORM.

A Pastor's life is more or less hidden, in its most striking and important features, from the public eye. When it appears quiet and even to the ordinary observer, it may be the theatre of the severest conflicts; and what would be set down to inefficiency by most men, may be scattering the choicest seed, and reaping the richest harvests. The sermon, which is listened to with pleasure and attention, and then forgotten, in the ordinary course of Sabbath exercises, may have borne witness to the most earnest activity of the intellect, and the almost agonizing anxiety of the heart. The inner history is generally unwritten; and human language is all too meagre to give it expression. The study of the characters with which he has to do; the fear that he shall fail to affect them favorably through the want of wisdom; the scrutiny given to his motives, his methods, his spirit, and his teaching; the struggles to keep his own heart consecrated to his work; the hopes, fears, elevations, depressions; these are phases presented to no human eyes,—intermeddled with by no stranger. Visiting his people, speaking kindly, yet faithfully to the sick, ministering in the house of death, encouraging the timid, cautioning the unwary, reproving the erring, leading back the wanderer, pointing penitents to the cross, feeding and guiding the church, expounding the law of duty, exposing the deceptions of false teachers, pointing the world to God by a pure life and a faithful teaching,—these are tasks, always striking and impressive, yet often failing to arrest attention and excite interest. Men get used to the hoary-headed Alps, and to the majesty of Niagara, until they cease to attract attention; though the first view of them may have overpowered the soul. Regularity is often a garment, hiding the form of grandeur, and stripped off only by the hand of novelty. There is nothing greater in a miracle than in a thousand constant occurrences; but the miracle draws attention to the greatness, while the law hides it.

Mr. Cheney had a character and a method; and so, striking as they might have been, having once become familiar, they ceased to startle and impress as they had done in the beginning. They who heard him once, when he spoke as he was wont to do in his pulpit, found much that was striking and impressive,—much worthy of remembrance; but hearing him repeatedly, though he grew not less interesting, the impressiveness arising from the novelty was wanting. He labored on, month after month, and year after year, in the same field, among the same people, and in the same earnest ways,—doing most, perhaps, when arresting least attention.

In the early history of the Rhode-Island Quarterly Meeting, he was prominent and influential. He was prompt in his attendance on its sessions, and always doing what he could to render them interesting and profitable. From a meeting of the church at Olneyville, he seldom allowed himself to be absent, save as necessity detained him. His heart was strongly and constantly set on his work; and he was always seeking and embracing opportunities to carry it forward. The church frequently received accessions, and revivals of greater or less extent marked the history of his labors at Olneyville. The war which he was carrying on with public evils, seemed never to blind him to the wants of his own immediate sphere. Though his public labors were abundant, and he was often summoned abroad, he never forgot that he was the Olneyville pastor. For his own congregation did he feel that he must first provide. They had his deepest sympathies, and his highest efforts. Frequently away in answer to the multiplied calls which he received, still he bore his people on his heart; and was always happy if he could learn something of fresh interest to carry them on his return. And so, though his pastoral life may have been, for years, somewhat uniform, still it was the uniformity of perpetual conflict, of earnest study, of abundant labors, and of high success.

He was often solicited to preach at the organization of churches, at the dedication of houses of worship, at the ordination of ministers, and to act prominently in the conventions assembled to promote the great moral causes in which his heart was so deeply enlisted; and, generally, he was ready to do whatever he was able in all these varied spheres of labor. His natural activity had not at all abated by means of his religious consecration; and it now found abundant room for display in the sphere to which he was wedded.

The Freewill Baptist Denomination became enlisted in the work of Foreign Missions, at about the time when his labors were attracting public attention, and while he was busy in studying the gospel in its practical applications. He took hold of this new work with his usual zeal and strength. Rev. Amos Sutton, of the General Baptist Denomination in England, who had been sent as missionary to Hindostan, visited this country in the year 1833, and attended the Freewill Baptist General Conference, with a view of inducing the denomination to send out missionaries to that foreign field. His appeals were powerful and not in vain. He travelled among the churches, and every where was received with confidence, and pleaded with power. The result was, that two missionaries with their wives were sent out, a Foreign Missionary Society was organized, and the churches set about the work of raising funds to prosecute the enterprise. At a public missionary meeting, held soon after Mr. Sutton's departure, Mr. Cheney was invited to be present and speak on the subject. So far as is known, this was his first public effort of this kind. The following copy of the Resolution and remarks, is found among his papers.

SPEECH ON MISSIONS.

"*Resolved*, That we highly appreciate the Christian benevolence of the English General Baptist Foreign Missionary Society, in sending and sustaining among us their faithful missionary, the Rev. Amos Sutton; to set before our churches the perishing condition of the millions of heathen among whom he has been recently laboring."

Mr. President :—In offering the resolution which has just been read, we do not intend to ascribe to human instrumentality the honor which belongs to God alone, to give flattering titles to men, or to make invidious distinctions ; but simply to give honor to whom honor is due.

We must advert to the numbers and circumstances of our English brethren, in order to appreciate, fully, the amount of their sacrifices, and the extent of their liberality. They number only about one third as many as the Free Will Baptists in this country. They not only support regular pastors in almost all their churches, but, for about thirteen years, have sustained a Foreign Mission in the very heart of idolatrous India. And this is done, it should be remembered, while they are burdened by a system of taxation much severer than ours—being compelled by law to support the established church. Surely, we can scarcely appreciate too highly such self-denying, wide-spreading, far-reaching, heaven-resembling benevolence as this. It bears the stamp and signature of heaven, the broad seal of the Father of Mercies.

And, sir, we can scarcely help imbibing a portion of the same spirit, while we contemplate the results of this heaven-born charity. Not to advert particularly to India, where converts have been made in sight of the bloody car of Juggernath, to see a religious body, a whole connection starting into life, and girding on the missionary harness, and shouting as it were for the battle,—this is soul-cheering.

Why, sir, we see a Freewill Baptist Foreign Mission Society formed; auxiliaries multiplying, and missionaries already in the field; a Home Mission springing into existence as by enchantment; a missionary spirit spreading, &c. &c. Surely, we have not estimated too highly that benevolence which, disregarding distance, locality, nation, and all other minor considerations, reached even to us and warmed us into a missionary life.

There is but one topic more to which I will advert before I sit down; and that is the character and spirit of their agent who has been among us, and has but recently gone from us. I think I see the character of our English brethren in their agent. A cold, heartless, formal, covetous people, would send no such agent as this. No, sir, I read the character of the society in their man; and how does it read, sir? Untiring activity, unconquerable perseverance, entire consecration to God; faith, hope, charity, but, in him, the greatest of these is charity. We would send our words across the deep, and say, we ought not, must not, cannot, forget the faithful labors of their devoted missionary, dear to them, dear to us, and dear to all the friends of Zion. No; his appeals still ring in our ears; his labors will not be in vain. We would say to them;—We thank the great Head of the church for directing your attention to us, and you for your liberality in bestowing on us the labors of your missionary.

Sir; I hope we as a Society may partake largely of that spirit of missions which pervades the hearts of our English brethren; that we may be co-workers with them in cultivating the great field of gospel labor, and with them share in reaping the harvests of immortality.

In reading these public discourses and addresses of Mr. Cheney, it must be remembered that he was very little accustomed to writing, that his preparatory sketches contained but an outline of what he usually said, and that the spirit and manner of his public speaking were such as to fill even common thoughts with freshness and force. And then his mind was so open to suggestions from the circumstances surrounding him, so accustomed to make the first use of his uppermost thoughts, that there would sometimes appear to be but a remote relationship between the prominent characteristics of his discourse and the previously prepared outline.

In the year 1840, Rev. O. R. Bacheler, who had received an appointment as missionary to India, was publicly set apart to that work by appropriate religious services. Mr. Cheney was solicited to preach the sermon on that occasion, and accepted the service. Those who heard the discourse as it was delivered, will probably recognize, in the annexed sketch, but the meagre skeleton of the living, glowing effort to which they listened. The outline will be valuable, however, for its thought and its suggestive force; and so it is presented here.

MISSIONARY DISCOURSE.

"Go ye, therefore and teach all nations; baptising them in the name of the Father, and of the Son, and of the Holy Ghost; Teaching them to observe all things whatsoever I have commanded you: and lo I am with you alway, even unto the end of the world. Amen."—*Matt.* XXVIII: 19, 20.

These words fell from the lips of Him who spake as never man spake; of Him who bore in his hand the sceptre, and on his head the crown of triumph over principalities and powers, as through a baptism of blood, he came forward and made a show of them openly; of Him who having gone down to the grave, came up with the keys of death and hell in his hand; of Him who as wonderful, counsellor, and mighty upholder, exclaims;—"All power is given unto me in heaven and in earth." Hear him. Every word is emphatic. '*Go*,' not remain quiet;—'*ye*,' that is apostles, chosen, partially qualified, and in a few days shall be fully so; '*teach*,' that is, make disciples of '*all nations.*' Mark has it,—"Preach the gospel to every creature."

From these words, thus uttered, we deduce the following sentiment, viz.: *The cause of Missions is the cause of God.* To sustain this position the following considerations are presented.

1. *The nature of the Commission.*

Christ says by another Evangelist, "As my Father hath sent me, so send I you." In connection with this, note the Baptismal qualification on Pentecost; the sheet let down from heaven to urge a doubting one to open the door to the Gentiles; the calling of Saul of Tarsus, and his work; the separation of Paul and Barnabas by the Holy Ghost. In this great commission and its attendant circumstances, we have the broad seal of heaven's approbation on the missionary enterprise. It may be objected that this work was confined to the age of the apostles; which leads us to remark,

2. *That the promise confirms what the commission requires.*

That promise is,—Lo, I am with you alway, even unto the end of the world. This promise was confirmed to the apostles, and has also been to the modern missionary. Add to this the facts,—That they were to commit the same trust to faithful men; That the world still lieth in wickedness and needs now the glorious gospel of the blessed God preached unto it as it did then; That God has given some apostles, some prophets, &c. for the perfecting of the saints. And finally under this head, we note the predictions or promises touching the spread of the gospel, and the mode by which it shall prevail. All this shows the mission cause to be of God, as it is the appointed means of fulfilling these predictions.

3. *It is in full accordance with the Second Commandment;* "*Thou shalt love thy neighbor as thyself.*"

The missionary enterprise bears on its brow the clearest, brighest, noblest, evidence of obedience to this law. The world was like the man among the thieves; and this cause approaches it like the good Samaritan.

4. *The example of Christ and his Apostles shows it.*

See in Christ the first, the prince of missionaries. See him divest himself of his robes of glory, and clothe himself in the robes of a servant. What a picture is that! It becomes the missionary to study it well, to look at it till changed into the same image. See Paul, Peter, Silas, Barnabas, Philip, and a host of others, hazarding their lives,—not counting them dear, cheerfully laying them down. And why? There is but one answer,—the cause was God's. It was this which led Christ and the Apostles to the labors and sufferings of the missionary life.

5. *It is seen in its results.*

See Paganism in all its strength,—fortified by age, customs, appetites,—shaking, trembling, falling, before the missionary of the cross throughout the Roman empire. To whom is England indebted for freedom from savage barbarism; to whom are we indebted for the spirit of missions and the labor of missionaries? The exposure of children for sale in the market at Rome, led missionaries to Britain. See the results. Should we wonder if similar scenes should lead to missions in our own land? See the results in the British West Indies, in the isles of the sea, in Burmah among the Karens, and even in our own field in Orissa. Whole nations have, at least nominally, adopted Christianity;— in Greenland, Labrador, and in more than thirty islands of the South Seas, and many villages in the very heart of heathenism. A few years ago it was doubtful whether Judson and Newell could be supported by the American Church; but now they are counted by hundreds.

And the results reaped by those who have given to sustain these missions have been striking. Who has not observed that those individuals and churches prosper most, who have most of the missionary spirit? They scatter yet increase; they sow bountifully and reap bountifully.

6. Finally, it is seen in that *it bears the image, and is in accordance with the dispensations, of the great and blessed God.*

Of him it is said that he is Love, and his tender mercies are over all his works. He is good to all in Creation, in Providence, in Redemption. In goodness he reigns. God so loved the world that he spared not his own Son, but delivered him up freely for the unthankful and the evil. He gave his word, Spirit, and the ministry of the gospel. And why all this? What is the design? obviously to bless and save men. Well this is the object of missions, *to bless and save;* to lift up man from his ruin; to restamp him with the image of God; to lift him up to equality with angels, to fellowship with Christ and the Father; to place the crown of beauty and glory on his brow.

Now the missionary enterprise is only the flowing of the stream of benevolence from the heart of the God of love. This cause, in its object, in its sacrifices, in its measures, and its results, bears the image and the superscription of him who made all of one blood; who loved all so well as to give his Son; who in the dispensation of his Spirit invites all to take the water of life freely. It is full of moral grandeur and sublimity. Does God love and pity? Do his bowels move? Did Christ hasten to man's rescue? So is it with the missionary of the cross.

REMARKS.

1. If the cause of missions be the cause of God, then all objections must fall to the ground.

What are some of these objections? First, That the heathen being ignorant are not accountable, but will be made so by teaching them. But is ignorance bliss? If so, then our knowledge is calculated to make us unhappy; we ought not to educate our children;—and Christ need not have died.—Second; It is in vain to teach them. Third; It is not our duty, there is so much to do at home. Fourth; It is a money getting scheme.

To all this it would be sufficient to reply, if we had no other answer, that God has commanded it, Christ has set the example, and every objection is in direct opposition to the Second Commandment.

2. We may see also what is the duty and what is the condition of the church. It is her duty, First; To pray for the Evangelist, that the word may have free course and be glorified; that the Lord of the harvest

would send forth laborers ; that the kingdoms of this world may soon become the kingdoms of Christ. Second ; To give her gold and silver, her sons and daughters to this cause. Third ; To clear herself from guilt, to be pure, that others may see her good works.

O may we not ask if this is the condition of the Church ! See Mammon enthroned in her temples ; and rather than lose her gains, she will even tolerate, yea apologise for and sanction the horrid sins of Intemperance, Licentiousness and Slavery. We may well ask how such churches can have the missionary spirit.

3. We may learn what should be the character of those who engage in this work.

First. They must be men of God. It is God's work ; and the men must be men of deep piety, holy men, pure-minded, single-eyed men, full of the Holy Ghost, if much people is to be added to the Lord. Second ; Men of discretion, prudence, knowledge ; of zeal, courage and patience. Third ; Above all, they must have the spirit of faith and hope,—stagger not at the promise of God through unbelief ; though they see him not, yet they must believe. And finally, he needs a heart as large as the world of sinners, overflowing with unquenchable love.

4. If the sentiment of this discourse be true, then should the heart of the missionary of the cross be cheered and strengthened. When trembling with solicitude about engaging in this work, let him remember, *It is God's cause.* Let this thought cheer him, when he asks,—" Can I, can I say farewell." When languor, disease, and desponding come, when the hour of death

arrives, still should he remember, the cause is God's,— it is well.

5. Finally, suffer the word of exhortation. Let a deep conviction that this cause is God's, fasten on your minds, O ye professed Christians! Weigh the matter well; and if conviction is produced, then act as though it was God's cause; give it a large place in the warm feelings of your heart.

Sinner, if this cause be God's, what is the value and price of your soul. What goes our brother for? It is to preach that gospel to others which you have despised and rejected. Seeing you judge yourselves unworthy of eternal life, lo! he turns to the distant gentiles.

Dear brother, bind this truth to your heart. When I look at the toils, sufferings, sacrifices you go to encounter; when I survey the field of darkness and peril within which you are to dwell, I feel that you will need it. When the heart is faint and the hope is wasting, cling still to the promise of your Master, "LO I AM WITH YOU ALWAYS."

The subject of Licentiousness attracted Mr. Cheney's attention at an early period in the effort for its removal; and, as usual, he was one of the first to identify himself with the enterprise, when the cry of imprudence and indelicacy rang out from the public lips. The cause was supported by truth, and its advocacy was required by duty; and this was sufficient to settle his own course. The following is a sketch of an address delivered before the Moral Reform Association of Providence. It is but a mere outline; but it is an outline such as he would be likely to fill up with earnest and burning words.

ADDRESS ON MORAL REFORM.

I. Definition.

LADIES; There is an evil in the land; an evil deep, wide spread, fearful, in the land of bibles and of Christianity, among all ranks in society. It blasts, scorches, withers, the fair and beautiful. Its name is Licentiousness; and its nature is terrible.

What is this sin? Ans. 1. The unlawful, unscriptural intercourse of the sexes. 2. It is a violation of the seventh commandment, as expounded by the Savior. 3. It is a practical abrogation of the marriage institution. 4. It is giving one class of the propensities the control over reason and judgment and God's law.

II. Object.

Now the object of this association is to free the land from licentiousness; to lift up the marriage institution to its high and honorable station in the minds of of all people; to guard our domestic circle with purity as with a wall of fire; to turn the currents of public thought and feeling into a pure channel; to purify the church, so that she may appear clear as the sun; to purify the great fountains of thought and feeling, that all that is filthy and offensive to a God of purity may be done away; to open blind eyes and unstop deaf ears; to refuse the seducer as well as the seduced our confidence until the wrong is repented of; to discountenance whatever leads legitimately to this evil.

III. MEASURES.

1. Show where the seat of this sin is.
2. Its alarming prevalence.
3. Its direful results.
4. The Press and Pulpit must be enlisted.
5. The Seventh Commandment must find its place.
6. Females must be enlisted.
7. Marriage Contracts must be formed in the light.

Who shall employ these means?

Ans. All the wise and good. But especially Parents—pre-eminently Mothers. Females, also, by refusing to associate with the licentious. Ministers have a work to do also, by precept and example.

> "The pulpit, in the sober use
> Of its legitimate peculiar powers,
> Must stand acknowledged while the world shall stand,
> The most important and effectual guard,
> Support, and ornament of Virtue's cause."

IV. OBJECTIONS.

1. It is too delicate for public discussion.

This is urged earnestly, and so even ministers leave it untouched. But, 1st, God did not think so when, from the blazing top of Sinai, he said, "Thou shalt not commit adultery." 2d. So did not Christ when he expounded this law in his sermon on the mount. 3d. So did not the prophets when they made such frequent and striking use of adultery as a figure; and so did not the apostles. 4th. If the objection be allowed, it seems that there are some prominent portions of Scripture which it is not profitable to preach! 5th. This objection seems to be an impeachment of divine wisdom in giving prominence to this evil. 6th. How, then, are men, and especially the youth, to be warned of her whose steps take hold on hell?

V. Motives.

1. The magnitude of the evil. This is seen from various considerations.

1st. It discourages marriage. This institution keeps the moral world in being. Once gone, social virtue would expire, education cease, government be destroyed, and religion there could not be.

2d. In a multitude of cases it supposes seduction. Treachery, lying, perjury, are the preparatory steps.

3d. It brings untold wo, that treads out the holiest feelings of the heart. Look at this picture, from Pollok, of female wretchedness in its desertion.

> " Upon a hoary cliff that watched the sea,
> Her babe was found—dead. On its little cheek,
> The tear that nature bade it weep, had turned
> An ice-drop, sparkling in the morning's beam;
> And to the turf its helpless hands were frozen.
> For she, the woeful mother, had gone mad,
> And laid it down, regardless of its fate
> And of her own. Yet she had many days
> Of sorrow in the world, but never wept.
> She lived on alms, and carried in her hand
> Some withered stalks she gathered in the spring.
> When any asked the cause, she smiled and said
> They were her sisters, and would come and watch

Her grave when she was dead. She never spoke
Of her deceiver, father, mother, home,
Or child, or heaven, or hell, or God, but still
In lonely places walked, and ever gazed upon
The withered stalks and talked to them;
Till, wasted to the shadow of her youth,
With woe too wide to see beyond, *she died.*"

"Can a mother forget her child, that she should not have compassion on the fruit of her womb?" Yes, with woe like this she can and does.

4th. It hardens the heart, and speedily destroys all moral principle. Look into the tenements of prostitution. Whoso enters there seldom returns. Around these places, impiety, blasphemy, treachery, drunkenness, perjury and murder flourish. It fits speedily for perdition.

5th. It ruins the peace and hope of families, and covers with shame innocent children.

2. God has repeatedly expressed his abhorrence of it. The view he takes of it may be learned from God's voice heard at Sinai; from the flames that curled around Sodom; from the plagues that brought thousands upon thousands of Israelites to a terrible grave; from the awful loathsome disease attending the profligate; from the groans of the dying, decaying, conscience-smitten criminal.

3. Love to our neighbor, to the church, and to our country. Their safety requires our effort.

4. Our own interests, safety, and welfare. God has linked our duty and interest together. O that we might see it! We may deem ourselves safe, and so did those who are now victims. The paths of temptation are

every where open, and the work of destruction is carried on with strange boldness. Who, unless forced to do so, would believe that sin is bartered in the market ; that damnation is held up as a commodity for bargain and sale ; that the destruction of the human soul should be publicly announced, authorised and guarantied as a privilege ; and that patents should be made out, signed and sealed, for populating more rapidly and extensively the world of woe. In such a life, let him that thinketh he standeth take heed lest he fall.

CHAPTER VIII.

"REMEMBER THEM THAT ARE IN BONDS, AS BOUND WITH THEM."

The position taken by Mr. Cheney on the subject of Slavery, has already been noticed. Nor was it enough for him to define and maintain a position. His warfare against it was by no means confined to defence. When released by his local triumphs from immediate attack, he was busy in carrying the war into the camp of the enemy. The hold which that subject had taken upon him was deep and strong; and in proportion as he saw, or thought he saw, desertion and cowardice among those who ought to be the defenders of Freedom, did he multiply and intensify his own efforts. From the time he entered the lists in the Olneyville pulpit, his heart was always set on fire by the view of despotism; and whenever he spoke on that subject his fervor was almost sure to kindle, and his speech would go forth in a series of condensed and fiery expressions. His whole being seemed to become a battery, luminous with the discharge of red hot epigrams. He could not reason coolly over the abstract question of the moral wrong of Slavery. To him, its wrongs were all real, concrete things. While others were constructing a syllogism or critically examining a text in the Pentateuch, he was gazing on the sale of souls from the auction-block, and listening to the wail of African despair.

He never seemed to covet, in his dealing with American Slavery, a calm, cool, prudent, passionless wisdom; he rather strove to approach the offenders in the spirit of a rebuking prophet. He swept down at once upon the hosts of oppression, never condescending to a parley, scorning all flags of truce, and scarcely regarding the plea for clemency; and those who did not join in the crusade he could hardly acquit of treachery. The Anti-Slavery conclusions to which other men arrived by patient reasoning and hesitating steps, he seemed to grasp by intuition; and wondered, sometimes with manifest impatience, that while he saw every thing clearly, others saw only men as trees walking. Whether this was the best course, is not now the question; we are not asking what was wisdom, but what was the fact; not what he should have been and done, but what he was and did.

The following outline of a speech delivered not long subsequent to his avowal of abolition sentiments, at a public convention in Providence, will illustrate what has been above stated. The exact date is unknown; but the allusions, as well as other circumstances, place it near the period referred to.

SPEECH.

"*Resolved*, That it is the duty of the American Church thoroughly to examine American Slavery; and if found to be sinful, to use that peculiar influence which God has given her, for its immediate and entire removal."

Mr. Chairman;—I think myself happy in being permitted to speak for myself. Yes, thank God, Slavery has failed to shut every meeting house and padlock every lip. I am happy to speak on such a topic, too—the duty of the Church—and its duty too in relation to such a subject;—a subject which is shaking the nation. Incompetent as I am, I feel it to be a privilege to offer my thoughts on this topic. The spirit of Slavery has sought to injure my reputation, to drive me from my pulpit, to sow discord among my brethren, simply because I sought to expose some of its enormities in the light of God's word. But it overreached itself and failed.

Moreover, the church among which I labor have come to the conclusion that Slave-holding, and Slave-trading are sins, and that Slave-holders and Slave-traders are sinners, such sinners, too, that they will not admit them to membership and fellowship; and they have dared to publish these conclusions in their official organ. For this they have been condemned by one of the papers in this city—a paper making pretentions to fairness and neutrality. From such fairness and neutrality we may well say, in the language of the Episcopal Liturgy, "Good Lord, deliver us."

A few queries this political examiner of churches, has put forth.

1. Why did not Christ say Slavery was a moral evil?
2. Why was he silent respecting the whole subject?
3. Why, among the Christians of Judea, Greece, and Rome, were none dismissed for holding Slaves?
3. Why, among the specifications of immoral acts in the New Testament, is this nowhere to be found?

It is no part of my business now to reply to these questions; but the very fact that such inquiries are seriously made, shows the ignorance which prevails, and the importance of having this subject discussed by the church. In support of this resolution I wish to present the following thoughts.

1. We must examine Slavery in order to know what it is.

Some say it is a divine institution; others say it is of the Devil. One part of the church affirms; the other denies. There is the same division on this subject too in the ranks of the ministry; one part fellowship and another disfellowship the Slave-holder.

Now the manifest duty of the church in this case is, to examine thoroughly in order to learn what and who is right. Whether it be divine or otherwise, a political or a moral question, can only be learned by examination.

2. It must be examined in order to learn what relation it sustains to the church.

It may or may not be so located as to be out of the sphere of the church. The church may or may not have a duty in regard to it; may or may not be affected by it; may or may not affect it. But how is this to be known without examination? How *can* it be known while the whole subject is tabooed?—forbidden to the press, the pulpit, the conference and prayer meeting?

3. It must be examined in order to learn the measures necessary to its removal.

Be they Abolition or Colonization measures, they must be examined before we can judge of their adaptation or efficiency.

4. Discipline is a duty of the church. Now the question is, do we or do we not fellowship the unfruitful

works of darkness? Slavery must be examined in its character and relations before we can determine.

5. The precepts of Christ and his Apostles enjoin this duty. "Search the Scriptures," "Prove all things," "Come out from among them and be ye separate."

6. The highest interests of the church demand this examination. 1st, Her Peace. How long before the church will learn that the peace of God is not to be obtained by smothering discussion! How many rents must be made before she will learn wisdom! How can she escape the dark suspicion that she loves darkness rather than light, so long as she shuts her doors in the face of honest inquiry! 2d, Her Purity. How can she keep herself pure if she shuts her eyes to the character and work of her members; if she refuse to look at her own spirit and test its features by God's word? Impossible! She may become the home of every pollution and yet know it not, if she refuse examination. 3d, Her Strength. This cannot remain unimpaired; for truth and purity constitute her strength. Necessity is laid upon the church. *She must act;* she cannot avoid it, for Slavery is in her midst, and she must either approve or disapprove. The simple question is,—will she act in the dark?

The church is charged with inconsistency in sending the gospel to the heathen, and neglecting the heathen at home; in exercising and requiring examination on other topics, and in neglecting and refusing it on this. Do not our Baptist brethren say on the subjects and mode of baptism,—come let us reason together? Do not our Unitarian and Universalist friends say,—come let us examine? How is it then that Orthodox and Heterodox here unite, and, strange to tell! unite to stop discussion! Strange that, in this age of sifting, weighing, guaging, the age whose motto is "onward," the descendants of the Pilgrims should be found opposed to free discussion. Why, it is asked, do churches and ministers speak against the idolatries, caste, and pollutions of heathenism—against the violations of the Sabbath—against duelling—against all national sins except man-stealing and the man-traffic?

We must examine. Our character as a church is suffering among the churches abroad; and all the eloquence you may send abroad will not redeem her from becoming a by-word, unless she set seriously about this work. A part of God's people have been directed by the Angel of Truth to look into the chambers of imagery possessed by this dark system, and they have started back in amazement. In the language of an eloquent female, "The Angel of Truth has descended and rolled away the stone from the door of this dark den, and, as he sits upon it, directs the world's eye to explore it." There it is; and the church must be amazingly guilty which will not examine. They who have been to the portal and examined have found no soundness in it,— have found a system of highhanded robbery,—robbery of body, soul, wife, children, wages,—*all.* They have examined, not by torture; they have looked only upon what was obvious; but they have found a system that rivals the Inquisition in its cruelties. It reeks with licentiousness; it revels in abominations.

Our resolution says—"and if found to be sinful." What an *if* is here! If it be sinful to do what? Why to buy and sell human beings as property!—to turn a man into a thing!—to annul marriage!—to legalize fornication and adultery! It is to separate parent and child, husband and wife; to withhold from the laborer his hire, and deny him God's word; to violate the First Commandment by obliging the Slave to obey *man* rather than God; to violate the Seventh, by selling husband from wife and giving them another, and by promoting promiscuous intercourse; to violate the Tenth, by coveting the poor man's wife, and children, and wages, and even himself; to violate the Eighth, by stealing men and receiving and holding them when stolen. If this be *not* sin, then it is difficult to tell what could be sin.

But why is the church bound to use her peculiar influence for its removal?

1. Because Slavery is *what* it is—*Sin.* The Southern church admits this.* This is what Southern politicians are afraid will be proved to the conviction of the Southern conscience. Now if it be a sin, and a sin of such magnitude, it is the real mission of the church to labor for its removal. The church is appointed to be the *Stone*, the *Mountain*, the *Light*. Slavery tram-

---

* This was generally true at the time this was delivered. It is not till recently, that attempts have been made to justify Slavery on moral and Scriptural grounds. It was generally conceded to be sinful until the practical and disagreeable duty of repentance was insisted on. And then commenced a defence of what it was determined not to abandon.—G. T. D.

ples on God's law, on God's word, on God's image, on Jesus Christ in the persons of his members, and has the church no duty?

2. Because Slavery is *where* it it is. It is in a Christian land; aye, in the church. Yes, the wolf in sheep's clothing has leaped into the fold, claiming to have come from heaven. Now if Slavery be sinful, then the church is bound to put it away, or come out from those who will not do so. She is set by her great Head, to reprove and rebuke, and required to have no fellowship with the unfruitful works of darkness. She has armor,—she is bound to put it on; a sword, and she is bound to wield it.

[The sketch closes here, though it appears unfinished. The conclusion was, probably, on another sheet, which has not been discovered.—G. T. D.]

At a date somewhat later, Mr. Cheney was invited to deliver the Annual Address before the Providence Female Anti-Slavery Society,—a body embracing, at that time, a large measure of talent and moral worth. As in most other cases, a sketch only remains of what was a strong and impressive effort. The manner of his speaking it would be impossible to convey; and the luminous flashes of thought and the impetuous bursts of feeling which gave a large measure of the force possessed by his efforts, he could never anticipate, and

Perhaps never took the pains to recall. These sketches however, meagre as they are, do not a little to exhibit the mental features of that life as it flowed on over the channel of years. Save the personal recollections of those who knew him, these are all that remain as mementoes of those past years, and they will be prized somewhat, at least for their intrinsic value, and much for their associations.

ADDRESS.

Respected Friends; By your invitation, I stand here to address you, though deeply sensible of my inability to do justice either to my own wishes, your expectations, or the great cause of bleeding humanity which has brought us together. But I may—I ought to—expect your candid attention, for the sake of the cause I am to plead.

This question of Slavery has become the *Great Question* of the nation and the world. There has been much to make it so. Little did I think, when I commenced the ministry of mercy, that I should ever be forbidden to ask mercy for the suffering and the dumb; that I should see the house of God shut by the spirit of slavery; females mobbed by gentlemen; men scourged and lynched for speaking the truth; pure minded men outlawed; the press broken, or basely bowing at the feet of despotism; the temples of liberty in flames; God's ministers brutally murdered; man's decree set above God's law; and, worse than all, these vile abominatians winked at, tolerated, apologised for,—by the Priest and Levite, while they march by in stately dignity on the other side.

Let me advert for a moment to the objects of this association. Why are the mothers, wives and daughters of our land gathering together by thousands? Is it to rebel against him who has been styled the *Lord of creation;* to dispute his title to supremacy? No. Let not the rulers tremble. Is it to insist upon the right to form marriage connections with the African race—to amalgamate, as has been charged upon them? If they did wish this, it would be hardly needful to make any great expenditure of time or effort to secure it; for it is now progressing at a fearful rate. Is it to discuss the ever varying fashions—the next party or ball. Oh no If this were all, their lordly traducers would hardly deem them out of their proper sphere. Nor is it to present the banner of blood; not to greet the warrior as he returns from the fields of carnage; nor yet to sing and dance and be toasted. What then? Why, a wail is on the breeze of the South—the wail of woman in her agony. The sound of the lash, and the clanking of the chain is heard; and that lash and that chain is on the back and limbs of woman. The voice of the mother is heard pleading for her child; and then comes the voice of the virgin daughters pleading for their honor and their virtue, but pleading in vain. The miseries and woes of woman—these have roused the matrons and maids, the mothers and daughters of the North.

But what is it proposed to do?

1. To sympathize, pity and pray for the slave, and

the so called colored free man, as he lies trodden down and degraded.

2. To bear their united testimony against the sin of slavery. To exhort, reprove, and rebuke the upholders of this iniquitous system.

3. To aid in turning public attention to this deadly evil; to fix the gaze of the nation—the church—the world upon it; to urge mothers to stamp hatred to oppression upon the tender heart of every child that nestles in her bosom; to encourage the hearts and strengthen the hands of their fathers, brothers, husbands, and sons, in the great battle of freedom. It is so to concentrate the rays of light and of truth upon the foul den of slavery, that,—scorched, blasted, withered,—it shall flee to the pit whence it came and be seen no more.

Their object will not be gained till no slave's foot shall tread the soil of freedom; till the sound of the lash and the clank of the chain shall be heard no more; till the pulpit, the press, and the hall of legislation shall be unshackled and free; till the key of knowledge shall be put into every hand; till liberty shall be proclaimed to all the inhabitants thereof; till the whole land shall be what it has been declared,

"The land of the Free and the home of the brave."

But what can woman do,—what measures can she adopt?

1. She can *pray*—to man, to Congress, to God.
2. She can plead,—with relatives, Christians, opposers, with a persuasive eloquence almost irresistible.
3. She can circulate information. What can she do? Let what she has done, tell. She has proved herself

able to lay the naked truth on the naked heart of the church, the nation, the world. Who wrote the "APPEAL," that thrilled thousands? A woman. Who wielded the pen in the cause of liberty so powerfully that Napoleon felt his despotic throne in danger? A woman. Who plead the cause of freedom before the Massachusetts Legislature? A woman. Upon whose lips have thousands hung with delight among the cities and villages of New-England? A woman's. And even in the pathway of blood, where man's heart has faltered, she has stood up and stayed the hand of violence. The very effort to drive her from the field, shows that she wields a power whose results are feared. But I will glance at a few OBJECTIONS.

1. Associations are dangerous.

Granted. And so is intellect, and will, and health, and property, and society. This objection, however seriously urged, and by however eminent men, seems to me to impeach the wisdom of God, who has given man a social constitution, and has associated his people together to bless the world. Shall good men cease to act in an associated form because pirates, &c. may do the same? What is our *Glorious Union*, so called, but an association.

2. But it is not the appropriate place and work for woman.—First; Woman in extraordinary cases has tilled the ground;—at the South not a few of them are thus occupied still. Is this perfectly appropriate?

2d; They associate for many other purposes not less publicly than for this, and no reproof meets them.

3d; It was customary for women to associate for good

in the days of the Savior, and of the Apostles; as when they ministered unto him, and when they brought spices to anoint him.

3. But the North has nothing to do with Slavery.

Ah, if the North *had* nothing to do with it, it would have died long ago. It is the North that consented to its being, and it is the North that has kept it in being, and it is the strong arm of the North that keeps it in being now. Look at the votes in Congress; read Jay's view; observe the influence of the D. D.'s; behold the Northern pulpits dumb on the subject, or eloquent with apologies.

4. It is interfering with that with which we have no concern.

Yes; just as we interfere with the heathen; with the rumseller, with every other class of sinners.

5. It will lead to amalgamation.

How! O the hypocrisy of this charge! Are the thousands of mulattoes at the South, the fruit of emancipation or slavery?

6. The slaves will cut the throats of their masters.

Will the objector please tell us how many throats have been cut by emancipated slaves.

7. But the two races cannot live together.

Well, then let them live apart; only take the yoke off their necks and see.

8. But they cannot take care of themselves.—It is quite too late for this objection to have force. Try them and see. England claimed that the colonies could not take care of themselves, and that she held them as dependencies for their good.

Well, then the object is grand, your measures peaceful and powerful, the objections groundless. Then think of the MOTIVES which urge you on.

1. What has been done.

England has given freedom to the West Indies. France is preparing; Denmark is on her way; thousands of noble spirits male and female are roused, pledged, and sworn before high heaven to faithfulness in this cause.

2. What is doing now.

A plan for a world's convention is proposed. Abolitionists are multiplying in all circles, and gathering strength even from their apparent defeat.

3. The solemn requisitions of duty.

Its plea is urged by the voice of millions perishing; the voice of humanity; the voice of mercy; the voice of Jesus; the voice of God.

4. The Church is in danger.—The leprosy is on her; onward to the rescue!

5. The necessities of the country. Either the nation or slavery must die. Let the blows of your patriotism fall thick and fast.

6. The world's hope is bound up in this question. Never while slavery lasts can the world's jubilee come.

Are you indifferent? Listen to the wail of agony till your hearts are stirred. Are you contending for trifles? Think of the woes and wrongs of the slave, until his redemption shall command your power.

Whoever else faltered in the dark days of the anti-slavery enterprise, Mr. Cheney stood firm. The friends of the slave looked to him with confidence, and their confidence was not misplaced. How much he did to give reputation to the cause of freedom, and to bring supporters over to it, cannot be known. His ministerial brethren of the same communion were encouraged in their efforts to bring the churches into the attitude of hostility to the whole system of slavery. He made it prominent in all his associations with them. He aided them in the solution of the problems presented by the enemies of emancipation. He reasoned, whenever he deemed argument necessary, and pleaded, where inactivity needed to be overcome. He was confident that the abolitionists occupied the only tenable ground, and this confidence made him ready for conflict every where, and nurtured an enthusiasm which roused almost every spirit that came under his anti-slavery influence.

Among anti-abolitionists he was a marked man. They knew his character and dreaded his power. They seldom encountered him in open or private debate. His character and the character of his efforts made it a hard matter to sneer at him; in the use of satire and invective they knew him to be rather dangerously expert; and he had proved his heart to be as impervious to flattery and bribes and threats, as the skin of a Rhinoceros to musket balls. Aristocrats checked their conversation and looked after him significantly as he passed them in the streets; and demagogues and cowards stepped aside with averted faces when they encountered his keen piercing eye. In one form or another, would his hostility to slavery appear in a large proportion of his public efforts. He could show slavery either as a cause, or effect, or companion of almost every other evil; from the magazine of its terrible facts, he could bring forth an illustration of almost every principle; and, in the form of a conclusion, he could draw out a weapon from almost every subject with which to wound it afresh. Few knew him without knowing that slavery was an excrescence in his eye, and a stench in his nostrils. And wherever there was an effort made to discriminate between the man and his anti-slavery, to do honor to the first and dishonor to the second, it must either be so secret as to elude his vision, or recoil on the head of the courteous critic. An incident, occurring in the Spring of 1840, will illustrate this. He was invited to preach and baptize in a manufacturing village a few miles from his residence, on a Sabbath, and consented to do so. He baptized at noon, and was on his way to the ample school house—(where the Baptist meetings were usually held,) crowded with people who had assembled to hear him preach. Before reaching the place of worship a note was put into his hands. He opened it and found it to be from the Agent, —and a large owner—of the village, stating that he was heartily welcome to the use of the Company's school house, but specially requesting him to say nothing on the subject of slavery. He read it; stopped, hesitated a moment, and turned about, saying, as he folded the epistle,—" I shall not go into that house with any such restrictions." He remarked that he did know that he should have deemed it necessary to say any thing on that subject; had made no arrangement to do so; but that his lips were to be sealed on no such subject by human dictation. He preached another discourse that afternoon in a private dwelling, and he did not forget either slavery or its Northern defenders.

CHAPTER IX.

CHANGES IN SENTIMENT.—INVIOLABILITY OF LIFE.

From what has already been learned of Mr. Cheney's history and character, it must appear no extraordinary thing if his opinions on many subjects underwent more or less striking changes. Serious, earnest thought he had been very little accustomed to exercise until his serious life began. He had been educated in the religious tenets of the Puritans;—that was the only system of theology which he had ever really studied. He had, to be sure, obtained a mere smattering of Universalist philosophy, but this operated rather to quiet all thought on religious topics than to induce study; and besides, he was too busy in his round of dissipation to leave time or inclination for sober reflection.

In his religious study he may be said to have begun with extreme faith. That is, he accepted as unquestionably true the religious opinions held by the great mass of the christians with whom he had been acquainted. Over the points of Calvinism he had many a weary struggle when his mind came to be aroused, and he had come to confide in his logical deductions. He found himself unable to reconcile the doctrine of election, as then held, with his notions of divine justice and impartiality. He looked in vain for harmony between the doctrine of total depravity, as then explained, and the obligations of men to love and serve God. He could not divine how man could retain any responsible freedom, after God had foreordained whatsoever should come to pass. The impossibility of falling from grace, found no support in the testimony of his consciousness or in his observations upon human character. And above all, the reading of his own English bible seemed to build still higher the barriers between his faith and the generally accredited sentiments for whose sake he was carrying on his investigations. It was suggested to him by hoary men, whose reputation for piety and wisdom was high, that the rebellion of his heart against Calvinism indicated its want of submission to God; that when his soul was acquiescent in the sovereignty of Jehovah it would glory most of all in his wise purposes to save and destroy. Mr. Cheney was troubled. He had great confidence in his accusers; he supposed them speaking from an experience which the gospel had begotten, and for the want of which he feared he was guilty. But yet he could not believe. His nature plead stoutly for freedom in all its moral life, and his bible would impress him yet more and more with the impartial goodness of God. For much that was done, he felt that men were responsibly guilty; and his bible revealed to him the protests of God against all the works of transgression. Wretched hours did he spend on his knees before God, asking for grace to subdue him if he was yet unsubdued,—pleading for the true light if as yet it had not gladdened his eyes. Quietness came at last, though not precisely as he had looked for it to approach. He happily remembered that inspiration had left this testimony; that the offerings of human love to God are "accepted according to that a man hath, and not according to that he hath not." He was conscious of a deep love of the truth, of a sincere desire to know the truth, and of a settled purpose to obey the truth so far as it was revealed to him. Satisfied that God asked only what he rejoiced to yield, he dismissed his fears and prosecuted his study.

The result was, he became firmly settled in the belief of those sentiments known as Arminian. He rejected what is usually called Calvinism in all its phases, and opposed it with all his force. To him it ever appeared as scripturally false, as philosophically absurd, and as practically evil. He fought it with texts, with logic, with ridicule, with the charge of immoral consequences; and seldom contemplated it in any other aspect than that of a fearful barrier to the progress of religious truth. He traced its parentage to the FATE of ancient Paganism, and found it latest born in the philosophical ATHEISM of his own time.

He had never, so far as is known, sympathised with the church where he first united in respect to Restricted Communion; but his convictions in favor of the opposite practice gathered strength with his thought. In reply to an inquiry from a brother respecting his method of disposing of certain objections to Free Communion, he wrote quite a lengthy epistle, which was subsequently published in the "Freewill Baptist Magazine" in 1839, and then issued in pamphlet form for the sake of a wider distribution. The argument was close and lucid, and was read with much satisfaction. No reply was ever presented to it.

Mr. Cheney's views in respect to Civil Government, and its authority and prerogatives, were, in the earlier part of his ministry, those generally entertained about him. The discourse on the Sixth Commandment,—a sketch of which is presented in chapter sixth,—shows plainly that he not only believed in the right of Government to take life for murder and defend itself by war, but that he had reasons ready to be given for the faith that was in him. In the sketches of an argument, in favor of legislation for suppressing the Rum Traffic, found among his papers, he is discovered insisting most strenuously upon the obligation of Government to suppress that business by the forcible measures which it is authorized to employ. But these views he did not always retain. Sometime about the year 1840, he began to waver in his support of Government as it was, and as he had been doing it. He had become acquainted with the friends of peace; had heard their reasonings, had read their declaration of principles, and become deeply aroused by the miseries of war. With a noble candor he set himself to examine the subject; more anxious to secure the truth than to preserve a reputation for consistency. He applied himself to this work of examination faithfully, and soon reached certain conclusions. The war-spirit was opposed to the spirit of Christ; no war could be carried on without the war-spirit; all wars then were wrong—offensive and defensive, domestic and foreign. All preparations for war were wrong; and so armies and navies were outlawed by Christianity. All endorsements of the war-spirit and war-principle were wrong; to support Governments based on the war-principle was, therefore, wrong. For the same reasons that Government was forbidden to wage a war against the lives of the many, it was forbidden to destroy the few ; and, for the same reasons it might not take the life of the individual. Human life was inviolable, and the love and mercy inculcated in the sermon on the mount, and exhibited in the life and death of Christ, were alone to be employed with the sanction of the gospel, to discipline offenders, and guard the interests of men. Whether this was the precise reasoning which led him on is doubtful; but in some such order as this did he advance from one conclusion to another, till he occupied the ultra peace position ; a position which he defended with skill and ability, for more than ten of the last years of his life.

These views were adopted after careful deliberation and at some sacrifice. Mr. Cheney says, " They brought me into collision not only with my former self—of whom I entertained a very good opinion—but also with my best, my dearest friends, who had stood by me in the darkest hours of former trials." But truth was to him more sacred than friendship—duty was to be consulted before consistency. What the views were, in detail, and what the reasons assigned for them were, will be more fully exhibited hereafter.

This change of sentiment wrought out some practical results. Soon afterward occurred that civil contest in R. I., between the Government and a large portion of the people of the State who had sought to supplant the existing Government by another, on the basis of a new Constitution guaranteeing the right of suffrage to the masses of the citizens. The feeling ran high. The Auto-biography thus speaks; "It set father against son, and son against father; mother-in-law against her daughter-in-law, and a man's foes were those of his own household. I was misunderstood and misrepresented. When I counselled the Suffrage party to peaceful measures, I was accused of being unfriendly to their rights; and when I told the Government party, who had set themselves in battle array against their brethren, that their weapons were carnal and their measures anti-christian, then I was called a dangerous man —a no-government man. There were advocates of both parties in the church and congregation. I was opposed to both parties, so far as their use of force was concerned. I could not countenance the force-gatherings on Federal Hill, nor at Chepachet; nor could I approve the processions and force-movements of the Government. I regarded both anti-christian, and so I frankly and openly declared. Both parties sought to array all possible power under their banners. My influence was sought, humble as it was; but I could not give it to the measures of either party; the object aimed at by the suffrage party I regarded right, as did probably a large majority of the people. And I conceived that the Government party was mainly responsible for the fearful condition into which the State was thrown; for at almost any time during the contest, they could have allayed all the difficulty by an extension of the right of suffrage, and without the compromise of any principle. I uttered these thoughts, and they who had been friends were friends no longer. I was represented as a dangerous man ; and I was informed by a friend that my name was on the list of those marked to be sent to prison. Many supposed me actually incarcerated. I am sure I am ignorant of the reason why I should or should not go to prison. But I felt but very little fear or uneasiness about the matter. I have since wondered why I felt so calm. But so, thank God, it was."

That was a fearful time in many respects. The State was declared under martial law. Nearly every bridge was guarded ; men were arrested on slight pretences, and peaceable citizens were in danger of meeting violence. Both parties seemed bent on triumph, and appeared ready to fight for success ; but the contest ended without much loss of blood. Yet Mr. Cheney was left unmolested. He had occasion to go out of the State to attend public meetings, and, without solicitation, was furnished by the Governor with a pass to go where and when he pleased. But he had no use for it. He was so well known that his face was his passport, and his character his recommendation. Many of the meetings in the State were for a time given up, and Brown University sent home its students. But the Church at Olneyville held on its way—though having in it strong advocates of both party-positions—never lowering a jot its pulpit testimony. Thus passed the memorable spring and summer of 1842.

After quiet had been restored, a day of Thanksgiving was appointed by the authorities. Of this Mr. Cheney thus speaks :—" I preached in the morning of that day in the Olneyville meeting-house. There were but few present, and those mostly of the Government party.

The other party had no thanks to offer for what seemed to them a forcible trampling upon their rights. The Governor of the State was present. My text was; 'The wrath of man shall praise him, and the remainder thereof he will restrain.' I endeavored to show how the wrath of man had been exhibited on both sides; how God had made and would make such wrath to praise him;—that is show forth his glory, wisdom, power, and love, and how he would restrain such wrath. It was indeed a trial to me to condemn most decidedly the course of the Government party, while the Governor and other friends of that party, were present, and especially as they were my personal friends; but my convictions of truth and duty required me to do it. The Governor omitted attending meeting after this discourse; and, with a friend, I called upon him to learn the cause. He said he did feel unpleasant when I so pointedly condemned the Government of which he was the executive; but when I told him that I intended no personal reflections on himself he seemed much pleased, and afterward continued his attendance on that meeting so long as he resided in the place."

In the afternoon of the same day, Mr. Cheney attended a Peace meeting in the Fountain Street Church, Providence. Mr. Adin Ballou was expected to be present and speak, but from some cause failed to arrive, and Mr. Cheney was called on to address the meeting, which he did. Mr. Amos C. Barstow—at the present time, (1852) the Mayor of Providence—was present and took notes. He afterward had a public meeting announced at the same place, for the purpose of replying to Mr. C., and sent word to that effect in a note addressed to his opponent, and politely inviting him to attend. Mr. Cheney now took notes, and announced, at the close of the meeting, that he should reply to Mr. Barstow on the same evening of the following week. Thus went on the discussion for several weeks before crowded audiences. At the last meeting Mr. B. was not present, and so the discussion closed as informally as it had begun. All agree in representing the discussion as courteous, able, close, comprehensive, and earnest. It went over the whole field of argument covered by the questions of Peace, and the rightful authority of Civil Government.

It is somewhat difficult to present, within any reasonable compass, Mr. Cheney's views on this subject, and the reasons urged in their defence. He said and wrote much, and the papers left are in a state of confusion. His strongest reasonings on some one point will, perhaps, be found in the heart of a sermon, or sketched out as an intended reply to some specious objection. The substance, however, of what he wrote and said is probably very well exhibited in the following condensed propositions and reasonings. They lack very much the spirit and force with which he was wont to speak on the subject, and something of the force belonging to passages on the same subject scattered over his writings. But, as a whole, they seem to be the best compendium to which access can be secured.

HUMAN AUTHORITY OVER LIFE.

Can one person rightfully take the life of another, under the Christian Law?

I reply in the negative, and urge the following reasons.

1. Because the Sixth Commandment in the decalogue is still in force, viz. "Thou shalt not kill."
I do not argue that it is unrepealable or unchangeable, but that its authority is recognised by the Savior.

2. The ceremonial and judicial laws of the Jews, which gave the right to take life, have been repealed by the Savior. See Exodus, xxi. 23; and Matt. v. 38, 39. And moreover those laws were never in force among other nations. The mere absence, therefore, of divine legislation under the new dispensation really abrogates.

3. There is no precept under the Patriarchal dispensation sanctioned by the gospel, which authorizes life-taking. The passage in Gen. 9: 6, "Whoso sheddeth man's blood," &c., wears the aspect of a prediction, and has been so regarded by many able commentators, who have nevertheless upheld capital punishment. It seems of the same nature as the prediction of Christ, "They that take the sword shall perish by the sword." A statute of that kind should be explicit. Christ repealed the Jewish law which required life for life, and is it probable that he would lend his sanction to another of the same character? And are we to infer that he does thus lend his sanction, in the absence of any intimation to that effect? And if it was a law of divine

justice, of perpetual obligation, that the life of the murderer should be taken, why did he so faithfully guard the life of Cain—setting a mark upon him, lest any finding him, should slay him?

4. The instinctive love of life and the strong desire to preserve it, give no authority to take life; for our instincts are not to control but to be controlled by the christian law.

This law of instinct or necessity, which is urged so frequently, deserves examination. We ask,

1st. Where shall we find this law? Is it in the Decalogue, or in the Sermon on the mount? It may be said that it is found in man's nature. Is this so? Is there a law impelling him to take life? May he not, *can* he not avoid it? Is he not taught to give up his own rather?

2d. Who is the author of this law? above all laws as it would seem to be. " There is one Lawgiver;" where among all his statutes is this all-controlling enactment? I hear his mighty tread on Sinai; let us examine his *Ten Words*. Is it there? Let us listen to Him in whom dwelt all the fulness of the Godhead; the expounder of that law written in the heart.

3d. Who is to be judge when this law obtains? a law that abrogates all other laws. This is a fearful question. Has the great Lawgiver told us when all his laws are null and void, and when might makes right? Or is it left to man's weak *judgment;* or to man's *fears*, or to man's *propensities?*

In truth the gospel knows no such law; it is derogatory to the great Lawgiver to imagine it. True, we have instincts and propensities given to aid in preserving life. But how they shall operate, the gospel alone prescribes. The pirate, duellist, thief, robber, assassin, all plead this law; and if men are themselves to be judges, who shall dispute their claim?

But is there no such law? No! When necessity rules there is no accountability, and of course no law. When man's moral nature is controlled by his physical nature absolutely, then what is he? Why, simply an animal.

5. Man's organization shows that God did not originally design him to kill. He has no teeth, no claws, adapted to such a purpose. And as to his inventive powers, who will dare assert that they were given for any such end? And when he was to use his powers for such an unnatural purpose, God prescribed the mode by a special message.

6. Man has no discretionary power given him over human life. This discretionary power over life, if it exist, is restricted to beast, bird and fish, &c. God has not given to man dominion over his fellow.

7. The teachings of Jesus forbid it. See his exposition of the Sixth Commandment, Matt. v.: 21, 22; of the Judicial Law, Matt. v.: 38, 39; his rebuke of James and John, Luke ix.: 55; his rebuke of Peter, Matt. xxvi.: 52; his explanation of his quietness to Pilate, John xviii.: 36. Hear him say, "Love your enemies;" "Pray for them that despitefully use you and persecute you;" "Whatsoever ye would that others should do unto you, do ye even so to them;" "Forgive men their trespasses." The spirit and practice here taught seem to me to forbid life-taking.

8. The example of Jesus. See him reviled, persecuted, apprehended, smitten, buffeted, mocked, put to death. What did he say? what did he do? Now hear him say, "Learn of me;" "Follow me;" "It is enough for the disciple that he be as his Master." And a voice from the lips of the Eternal cries,—"This is my beloved Son; hear ye him."

9. The design of Christ's mission into the world. Luke ix.: 55, 56. "The son of man is not come to destroy men's lives, but to save them."

10. Apostolic precept and example. Rom. xii.: 19, 20; "Dearly beloved, avenge not yourselves," &c. 1 Pet. ii.: 20, 24. So says Paul; "Love worketh no ill," &c. For the weapons of our warfare are not carnal," &c.

11. The historical fact that the early Christians refused to fight; and gave only the simple reason that they *were* Christians. This charge is brought against them by Celsus, and admitted by Origen.—See Peace Manual.

12. Life-taking in self-defence leads inevitably to war, civil and national, with all its horrors. And war in its origin, spirit, and measures, is anti-christian, is of the devil, and its awful results show it. Says Robert Hall,—" War is a temporary repeal of all the principles of morality." It leads to a violation of most, if not all the commandments of the Decalogue. See its destruction of life, estimated by Dr. Dick at fourteen thousand millions. See the famine and pestilence which follow in its train; its cruelty; its licentiousness; it sets brother against brother with a sort of conscientiousness, and

sends hundreds of thousands of souls to destruction. It is the place where all Christian virtue is put under ban. Bonaparte boasted that he could convert his whole army to Mohammedanism by a single order of the day. He also said; "The worse the man the better the soldier; and if they were not corrupt they must be made so." Wellington said:—"No man who has any conscientious scruples about religion, has any business in the army."

13. It stands in the way of the work of missions. It opposes the spread of the gospel. See China, India, the Seminole Indians. The emperor of China once said; "Wherever Christians go they whiten the soil with human bones." The Turk at Jerusalem said to Wolfe, the converted Jew,—"Why do you come to us?" The reply was,—"To bring you peace." "Peace!" retorted the Mussulman,—"upon the very spot where your Lord poured out his blood, Mohammedans are obliged to interfere to prevent Christians from shedding each other's blood."

14. It exposes Christianity to the scorn of infidels. An infidel paper thus comments on a suggestion touching the spiritual improvement of the army;—"This means, we suppose, that if the army and navy become pious, a sort of holy sanctification will be thrown around the business of killing, which will secure the eternal salvation of those engaged in it."

15. We cannot tell when and whom to kill. It must be all guess work unless God tell us,—and that he has not done.

16. There is no moment in which we may cease to love our neighbor, so as not to regard his highest good. Can we kill him for the sake of his highest good?

17. It is doing evil that good may come; not a transient, physical, temporal evil merely; but a fatal, final, eternal evil. Now will property, family, government, liberty, or even life, or the whole world, compensate for the loss of a soul? Can the whole creation utter a groan too deep or shriek too piercing over such a loss? This principle erected the Inquisition, instituted the order of the Jesuits, banished the Baptists, hung the Quakers;—it is the devil's masterpiece!

18. It shows a want of confidence in God. See Raymond's travels among the smugglers of the Pyrenees; William Penn; the Quakers in Scotland; Adam Clarke when beset by a mob. They confided, and so found deliverance.

19. The Christian advocates of life-taking shudder at their own progeny. Now if fighting be needful, you should prepare. But you shrink,—and the more holy the more you shrink. Satan can go to work with courage, and in such a contest he will be the victor.

20. Objections brought against this view can be answered, or are not strong enough to set aside the previous reasons. Some of the principal objections will be noticed.

1st. It denies the right of self-defence, and this is sacred. Property, liberty, life we may,—ought to—defend.—But Christ says, give up cloak, coat, life.

2d. The precept given to Noah.—This has been noticed.

3d. The Mosaic code.—This has also been noticed.

4th. We are to obey magistrates—to be subject to the higher powers—to submit to every ordinance of man for the Lord's sake, &c.—But what is the extent of the obedience and submission here demanded? Ans. We are to submit and obey when the requirements do not conflict with God's word. When they do conflict, Peter and John have settled the question by saying, "We ought to obey God rather than man." The question then resolves itself into this, Does the Christian law authorise Government to take life, or does it authorise a Christian to take life when the Government commands him to do so? Now to attempt to answer this by saying that the Christian law requires obedience and submission, is to give no answer at all; for *the* question is, What is the *extent* of the obedience due? Now we ask for a "Thus saith the Lord," telling us that obedience is due even to the taking of life.

Where does Government get its just powers. Our declaration of principles affirms that they originate in the consent of the governed; and that man has certain *inalienable* rights, among which is life. Then it follows—First; That no man has a *right* to take his own life. Second; That *he* cannot confer the right to take it upon another. Third; Then the *people* cannot impart any such right to Government. Unless it can be proved that *one* man has the right to take the life of another, then *no numbers* have that right; or, else God has given to a number of men called the Government that right. And if so, has he given to all governments or to certain ones that right? and if only to certain ones, where and what are those privileged ones? Blackstone says; "The State has exactly the same power, and no more, over all its members, that each individual had naturally over himself and others."

5th. *It is said that we can take life in love.*—Well, admit this to be true, would it not be a dreadful necessity? Lord Hill, when told of the success of the English arms in the East, exclaimed, almost with his last breath, "*Horrible!*" And will not every Christian, before he imbrues his hands in his brother's blood, wish as plain a command to kill, as he finds in the Decalogue against it? What Christian, filled with God's love, would not rather lose his life than to save it at the expense of staining his hands with the blood of his brother.

6th. *God is unchangeable. He has taken life, therefore we may. He has once authorised it, therefore it is right now.*—God *has* commanded to kill. He gave life, and so has a right to take it away; and a right to take it by what means he pleases—earthquakes, fire, pestilence or sword. He often uses the wicked as his rod or sword, and accomplishes his purposes by them though they think and mean it not. So with Sennecharib and Cyrus; so Abraham armed his servants and punished the plundering kings.

Now it will be admitted by all that to take life is very difficult to be reconciled with loving our neighbor as ourselves; and still more with the commandment,—"Love your enemies,"—"Overcome evil with good." Now may not all God's approbation of life-taking by human beings be simply *the approval of toleration or permission*, as was the case with Polygamy, Divorce and Servitude? "He suffered all nations to walk in their own ways." "The times of this ignorance God winked at."

7th. *Consequences are held up.* Anarchy, Piracy,

Robbery, the Destruction of Religion are predicted.— Ans. 1st; Recollect we are not discussing the question, whether a wicked world would be better or worse without a life-taking Government; but whether Christians are authorised to have or sustain such a Government, and especially in the hands of the wicked.—Ans. 2d; How did Christ and his apostles get along without the aid of such a Government; aye, even *against* the Government, for *it* was often their fiercest persecutor.— Ans. 3d; Many of these consequences are imaginary. See the Friends in the Irish Rebellion. Look at all the records of Christian faith and submission.

But what have been the consequences of the union between Christians and life-taking Governments? Look at the Mother of Harlots,—what is that on which she rides? A bloody Government! Rev. xvii. 1—6. Who has waited to do her bidding, and kindled her fires of persecution? Who drives Indians from their council fires? Who tramples on three millions of human beings? It is Government; and by virtue of the support which God's people have lent, it baptizes itself with the name of Christian.

8th. Much stress is laid on the alleged fact that the centurion, who was commended for his faith, was not condemned for his business; and that John Baptist did not condemn the soldiers who came to him.— There is no proof that they did not. The record is simply silent; and so it is silent on many other things— Idolatry, Slavery, Games. Shall we infer that they were approved?

9th. Christ paid taxes.—Certainly; and in perfect

accordance with his teachings; "Resist not evil,"—
"Be subject," &c.

10th. He directed his disciples to buy swords.—
Certainly; but for what purpose? Not to fight, for he forbade such a use. But evidently to fulfil the Scriptures, and to rebuke Peter.

11th. Paul appealed to Cesar, and was escorted by an armed force, and said "if he had done any thing worthy of death;" implying that there were things worthy of death.—Paul evidently meant worthy according to the law by which he was being tried, without at all adverting to the question whether the law was good or evil.

12th. The principle forbids the correction of children, and the restraining of any being from the commission of a crime by force.—Not at all. Children, before they become moral agents, should, must be dealt with by physical means. So with maniacs. So a murderer may be restrained by physical force, if done for his good; *perhaps* his life might be taken if it could be *proved* that it was for his good. But our knowledge is not the measure of our action here. Our brother's life must be held sacred till God authorises us to take it.

13th. But suppose a villain was about to take the life of your wife.—Well, if it would be my duty or privilege to kill him, should I not have the same duty and privilege in respect to her if she were about to kill somebody else? No! no! There is no safe guide here but the Cnristian law. Following that, we shall be led in the paths of righteousness and safety.

These views Mr. Cheney made particularly prominent during the latter part of his life. Their importance seemed to be ever present to his eye. In their prevalence he seemed to see the prophecy of the world's social, civil, and moral regeneration. He inculcated them frequently from the pulpit, urged them upon the young, and refused to take any position or endorse any practice which seemed to sacrifice them. He would courteously refuse any civil distinction which friendship or confidence or respect sought to lay upon him. He would not support any measures to accomplish a most praiseworthy object, if, in doing so, his testimony against life-taking was to lose any of its strength. He mourned over the miseries of Intemperance, and toiled as did few men for their removal ; but he gave his unqualified approbation to no legal measure to remove them, however little prospect there was that life-taking was actually to follow. He longed to see the governmental agencies of the country dedicated to the cause of freedom, and rejoiced when the strong men of the land lifted up their voices in the hall of legislation in the cause of the oppressed ; but he would not seek even the slave's disenthrallment through the political action which he regarded as an endorsment of the authority over life, which the Government had assumed to exercise as its fundamental right. His convictions restricted him to the use of moral power in his dealing with men ; and did something to give him his large efficiency in that great department of action. He charitably allowed others to lean on the civil law, but his support was the truth and authority of God.

CHAPTER X.

THE FREEDOM OF THE TRUTH.

Mr. Cheney had seen so much of oppression in life, and been so much saddened at its fruits, that he became jealous of every institution and every influence which seemed tending to fetter either body or soul. He claimed freedom for himself, and for others. He quarrelled with all sorts of despotism as with a deadly foe. The tyranny of custom, talent, influence, and public sentiment,—all alike he opposed with his earnest remonstrances, and his own fearless and defiant rebellion. Freedom in thought and in its expression, he demanded for himself and sought earnestly for others. He desired to see the largest possible equality, consistent with obligation, prevail in every department of life. Voluntary organizations for moral ends he felt to be necessary; and yet he ever seemed to fear in them a tendency to the accumulation of power in a few hands. He did not suppose that the masses always acted wisely, perhaps sometimes less wisely than would the few, but he did not therefore feel inclined to justify the absorption of all authority by a handful of men. In freedom he knew there was peril, but he knew also that there was death beneath the reign of despotism; and so he chose life—running a fearful gauntlet,—developing its energy as it struggled on—rather than the torpidity which came over the soul from the touch of its chains.

Religious freedom, especially, did he set himself to guard. He would have no Bastile dungeons for heresy, no gags to stop the mouth of honest inquiry, however irreverent might seem its questions. He believed that theoretical error might take up its abode with high sincerity; and that harsh condemning words uttered over such souls, were neither wise nor just. He loved, in himself, activity of intellect in matters of religious faith. He did not believe that wisdom had died with any college of cardinals or assembly of divines, who had ever undertaken to fashion a creed for the world. With John Robinson, he held that higher light was yet to break forth from the divine word, under the study of years and the developments of Providence. He insisted that no one should swallow unquestioningly the theology of any man's preparation, whether administered in Botanic or Homeopathic doses. He would have all men feel that they were responsible for the principles adopted and the applications given to them. The religious sentiments adopted, and the modes of worship chosen, he insisted should be left to every individual, acting under the guidance of his own understanding and the eye of God.

As a result, he was most strongly attached to the Independent form of Church Government. He disliked Episcopacy, and could not sympathise with Presbyterianism. He did not doubt but these last forms of Government would serve to consolidate, systematize, and save the churches from excesses. But he liked no consolidation which was brought about by external pressure; a system which swallowed the individual, which lessened his strength and restrained his christian freedom, he could not approbate; and he would suffer an occasional excess sooner than assume tyrannical powers to check it. He believed an individual church the highest—indeed the *only*—ecclesiastical tribunal recognised in the New Testament; and the only one with whose existence the safety and welfare of the church consisted. Voluntary association by the churches, for counsel, encouragement, edification, and moral strength, he heartily approved; but even these he watched, not without jealousy, lest the association should gradually exercise and the churches gradually concede a kind of authoritative supervision. When he carried a request from the church at Olneyville to be admitted into the Quarterly Meeting, before presenting that request, he obtained an assurance that the church would be permitted to withdraw from that body, whenever the church should deem it best to do so. In matters of discipline, he regarded the action of the church as final on earth. He protested against the idea that any other body had rightful power to annul its decisions, or that any aggrieved member or members had the right to appeal for adjudication to any other human ecclesiastical body. He did not claim that the church would always act wisely or right; but that God had vested disciplinary power in no other body. He regarded this principle a vital one. Between this Independence and the Romish Hierarchy, he saw no stopping-place, save such as was indicated by a local and doubtful expediency.

This independence he saw, with sorrow, was gradually being sacrificed by the Freewill Baptist denomination. In the year 1844, the Boston Quarterly Meeting and the Boston church were involved in some unpleasant difficulties. The Quarterly Meeting regarded the church as unfaithful to its obligations; and the church regarded the Quarterly Meeting as unjust in its requirements and oppressive in its policy. An appeal was carried to the Yearly Meeting, and a Committee chosen by that body to meet a Committee of the Quarterly Meeting and the church. Of this Committee Mr. Cheney was chairman—a post generally assigned him in such cases. A meeting was appointed at Boston, where a hearing of the case on both sides, more or less full, was had. The Report of the Yearly Meeting Committee, besides a statement of the facts, contained a series of Resolutions; the first of which asserted the right of a church in good standing in a Quarterly Meeting, to withdraw from such Quarterly Meeting whenever it might deem it proper. Against this sentiment the Committee of the Boston Quarterly Meeting earnestly protested in a lengthy and elaborate reply, which was published in the Morning Star, the principal periodical of the Denomination. The door of discussion was now fairly open; the gauntlet had been flung down and boldly and fairly taken up. On both sides appeared ability, earnestness, sincerity, and inflexibility. The controversy went on through the press, conducted on the one side, to a great extent, by Mr. Cheney. It was carried to the next session of the Yearly Meeting held at Waterford, Mass., Sept., 1845; where the champions measured their swords and tested their forces. It was an occasion adapted to call out Mr. Cheney's strength, earnestness, fire and skill. The Yearly Meeting sustained the Committee by a small majority. An appeal was then taken to the General Conference, held at Sutton, Vt., in Oct., 1847. Here the subject was discussed strongly and earnestly, and after two or three votes, now supporting the principle and now disapproving it, the whole subject was referred to the next Conference, which was held in Providence and Olneyville, in October, 1850, the scene of Mr. Cheney's labors in the gospel. To that Conference and its action on that question he looked forward with almost a nervous anxiety. His interest in the matter had rather gathered than lost strength, and what disposition would be made of it he could not predict. As the time of assembling approached, he spoke of it often; and though his words were calm, it was easy to see that his soul could not be wholly quiet. He had, in past years, not felt all the sympathy with the Denomination that was desirable. He had feared that its spirit was growing conservative, and its policy was leaning towards ecclesiastical despotism. But time had drawn him to it again. The separation of himself from it, which he had previously deemed a probable event, was now a thing not seriously thought of. He desired that this mooted topic might be so disposed of as to promote charity and sympathy ; but he felt that he could not sacrifice a jot or tittle of his principles, even for the sake of peace. With deep and earnest feeling would he speak of it to his brethren in the ministry, and meekly ask advice.

The Conference assembled. In talent, and the spirit of consecration which seemed to pervade it, it gratified and surprised even the most hopeful. Mr. Cheney was chosen Moderator. After the disposition of preliminary matters, and attending to some of the less important items of its business, the question of Church Independence came up. Mr. Cheney was out at the time; having been called away to render some pastoral service. No sooner had he entered the Conference and learned the topic of discussion, than his eye might have been seen flashing, and every tone of his voice indicated the activity of an anxiety which he was struggling to hide. He gazed upon every new speaker, whose position on the subject he did not know, as though he would penetrate his spirit and read the fact which he hardly had patience to wait for the lip to utter. He listened an hour, and then calling one of his assistants to the chair, announced his wish to say a few words. But he was too deeply anxious, to command his power as he desired, or as was necessary to do justice to himself. His feelings, long kept under restraint, once finding an outlet, rushed up impetuously through his lips, like jets from a volcanic crater. His speech was largely made up of a succession of abrupt questions, announcements, and retorts, intensified by his vehement manner and his piercing glances. The very interest he felt to commend that subject strongly to the understanding and heart of the Denomination as represented there, was so deep as to defeat his object. Of this no one was more conscious than himself, and he hardly knew afterward whether to laugh at or regret it. It is only needful to add, that the Conference decided that question, so far as it had authority to decide it, in favor of the Independent principle, and in a spirit of conciliation and Christian fraternity.

While this subject was pending, Mr. Cheney was constantly interesting himself in the work of impressing his convictions upon others. To a young man about to leave the scene of his studies, he wrote ;—"I am happy that young men who are so soon to take the posts of responsibility in the state and the church, have so ample an opportunity to fit themselves for their work. I am only anxious that, while they avail themselves of the labors and aids of others, they may still learn to depend upon themselves. I want the young brethren when they come out from —— to be free, free as the wind." .... " I want you to examine seriously this question of Church Independence, and be prepared to take and defend a position upon it. Study it well. It is one of the great questions of the age." And at home in private conversation, in ministers' meetings, in Conferences, and in his own pulpit, he gave ample proof that his heart was set on what was, to him, a great and important object.

There was a time when he was deeply occupied with the question; What tests of church membership is it proper to introduce? The guilt of the churches arising from their fellowship of slaveholding, he felt to be very great, and desired to free himself and the church at Olneyville from all participation in the offence. To him, slaveholders seemed almost the chief of sinners, and an apologist for slaveholding seemed to him a willing partaker of the guilt. Was it proper for the church to welcome sin? If not, was it proper for her to welcome obvious palpable sinners? If not, was it proper for her to welcome those who joined hand in hand with the sinner, and endorsed his character as every way worthy of a seat in the circle of Christian confidence? Accustomed to trace out a principle to its logical consequences, he found it difficult to reach a stopping place in this multiplication of tests; and at last rested on the principle that *Christian character* was all that should be required as a condition of church membership. This discussion was being carried on in connexion with that of the Independence of the churches; and was earlier disposed of. His conclusion still left a difficult question unsettled, viz. What is essential to Christian character? But he left that question to be answered by others; deeming it practical and simple. A difference of opinion on almost any point of doctrine, usually regarded as fundamental, constituted, in itself, no serious barrier to his Christian sympathy. "To live and let live," the maxim of social charity, he appended, "Think and let think," which he regarded the maxim of *Christian* charity. He had passed through marked changes of sentiment himself, and been highly honest and earnestly sincere through them all; and he believed others could be thus affected as well as he. Such changes, indeed, he thought men would be almost certain to experience, if their understandings were kept awake and their candor tarried with them. He thought character might be very corrupt even with the endorsment of a good creed, as most others believe; and he was equally settled in the conviction, that a most miserable creed might be earnestly held to, and yet the heart remain the very sanctuary of high Christian goodness; a sentiment which finds fewer supporters. And so in dealing with others in his Christian intercourse, he was usually more anxious to learn what they *were* in fact, than what they *professed* in theory.

Another point of belief there was,—which, perhaps, would have been quite as appropriately developed under the head of changes in sentiment—claiming some notice. To outward ordinances and observances he attached less importance than did many of his brethren, especially in the latter portion of his life. Forms, he was disposed to leave to the choice of those who were to adopt them. The two ordinances, Baptism, and the Lord's Supper, he always accepted as enjoined by the gospel; but beyond these he had no guide but expediency. His reverence for every thing outward in religion grew less and less; while his veneration for that which was inward was perpetually increasing. Tithe, mint, anise and cummin, were insignificant things in his eye; judgment, mercy, and faith, were all vital. Traditional rites, sustained by testimony gathered up from the fathers, he could smile at with indifference or incredulity; but a principle developed by Christ, was to him what the voice from the burning bush was to the prostrate Moses. To him, Paul's declaration was full of meaning; "The letter killeth, but the spirit giveth life."

These views found an application to the question touching the authority of the Sabbath. In the early part of his ministry he held to the sanctity of that day as strenuously as any occupant of the pulpit, and urged its claims as strongly as he was able. In the lectures on the Ten Commandments he gave prominence, especially, to the Fourth. Several discourses were delivered on that, and the law of the Sabbath he interpreted and applied with no ordinary strictness. The prevalent laxity in respect to its observance he rebuked sharply.

Not a few among his auditors felt that he was as objectionably plain and severe on this subject, as on Rumselling and Slavery. He then held the Fourth Commandment as he held the rest of them; prescribing a moral duty with the force of a positive enactment; and so he faithfully taught. In subsequent years his views, on this subject, underwent a change. He began to ask whether the observance of the Sabbath could ever be suggested to the human mind as a duty in the absence of positive instruction and requirement. And if it was a positive institution, he began to ask whether it had ever more than a local and temporary existence, like the Passover and Circumcision. The Jewish Institutions were in force after Christ, only so far as he had brought them forward and incorporated them into that dispensation which he introduced. Had Christ thus brought forward the Sabbath? and, if so, when and where and how? And when and where and how did he make the change from the seventh to the first day of the week? He studied over these questions, discussed them more or less, and finally concluded that there was no such evidence in support of the Sabbath as a divine institution now, as to justify dogmatism in respect to it.

The writer is not aware that he ever gave a formal

and full development to his views on this subject, in any consecutive statement; and so any attempt to exhibit them might do him injustice. He appears to have meditated this, and once set himself about it; but there is only found enough to indicate the field of discussion which he intended to explore, and the manner in which he proposed to effect it. The following is a copy of what is found among his papers.

THE SABBATH.

QUESTION. IS THERE ANY CHRISTIAN SABBATH?

I. Will what is said in Genesis establish it?

II. Is a *Christian* Sabbath found in the Fourth Commandment?

III. Has such a Sabbath been predicted by the Prophets?

IV. Has such a Sabbath been appointed by Christ?

V. Had the Apostles authority to appoint; and, if so, *did* they appoint such a Sabbath?

VI. Is the example of the Apostles binding on us? and, if so, did they observe a Christian Sabbath?

VII. Does man's nature, or the physiological law demand such a Sabbath?

VIII. Does Christianity, or do Christian Institutions, require the arm of the civil law for their preservation or propagation?

1. Is the Christian Sabbath found in Genesis.—Here note the theory of creation. If Geology be true, then neither Christian nor Jewish Sabbath is here. But, on

the common opinion, how can a Christian Sabbath be found here? indeed how can *any* Sabbath be found here. *God rested and hallowed;* and here the record ends. True, Moses records, in the Fourth Commandment, that God assigns as a reason for it his resting and hallowing. Here mark that, if there was a Sabbath in the beginning, there is,

1. No record of any such direct appointment. A belief that there was such is based on inference or assumption.

2. No directions what to do, or what not to do on that day.

3. No evidence that such a day was observed by any till the Jewish Sabbath was appointed. The division of time into weeks has been urged. But this is assumption, conjecture; the division might have existed for the sake of sacrifices or other reasons. If it was like the Jewish ordinance, or like the so called Christian ordinance even, should we not have had at least a hint of it in the history of Abel, Noah, Abraham, Isaac, Jacob, Lot, down to Moses? God rested, therefore I must rest. Well, God created, therefore I must create. Must I do as God did, simply *because* God did it? What God does is not authoritative unless he commands it.

But again. God never rests. What then is the meaning of his resting? &c. It is simply ceasing to do what he has been doing. But it is said that it is only a seventh portion of time that is consecrated. Well then has God designated that portion or not? If not, then we may choose as we please.

[Here the discussion closes.—G. T. D.]

To these views Mr. Cheney attached importance; but he never obtruded them uncourteously upon the attention of others. He held them in prudence, seeming to remember that they might be practically abused; and, as a matter of fact, he exhibited as little laxity in his Sabbath life as most of those who held firmly to the views he had abandoned. He did not, by any means, attach a low importance to the Sabbath, as a day of respite from physical toil, as a period for religious thought and social worship; but he found reasons for prizing the day without regard to the question of its positive force. He did not often state these views in the pulpit, for reasons best known to himself. It *might* be that he saw that the Sabbath was sufficiently disregarded, and feared that others would fail to grasp the moral argument as he had, and that to remove, in their minds, the positive obligation to sanctify the day, would be to make them entirely reckless in respect to its observance. What he would have liked to see, was a more faithful and general devotion of its hours to moral and religious improvement, *because it was so adapted to human nature and wants;* and not because of any such reverence for it as made it to be regarded the exaction of positive law. But he may have seen reasons for believing that, just so far as it was taken out from the sphere of divine legislation, it would cease to command the respect of the very persons who most needed its influence. By this it is not meant that he wanted confidence in the truth, or that he feared to utter it. From such causes he never suffered, but he probably thought that there was no special cause for his speaking often on this topic. The *practice* of his congregation, so far as it supported the observance of the Lord's Day, was what he desired it to be; and to be earnest about matters that were simply or chiefly theoretical, was something foreign to his nature. Yet he never withheld his views on this subject when they were solicited; and seldom failed to express his decided dissent when he heard the opposite sentiment insisted on.

Few of his congregation, comparatively, and few of his brethren in the ministry, probably, ever came to sympathise with him in these views. As he had done formerly, so they did still regard the Sabbath as, in some sort, the ordination of God, claiming the service and reverence of christians as well as of Jews. They regarded him as deeply sincere in the opinions he entertained on this topic, and in no danger of scandalizing even the most scrupulous of intelligent christians by any practical laxity. Even if he had come to feel in regard to the Sabbath as Paul felt about the meat which had been offered unto idols, they were satisfied he would never indulge himself in what was lawful yet not expedient,—in that which, though seeming to him innocent, in itself, would yet cause his brother to stumble. The liberties which he might conscientiously take with the hours of the Sabbath, they felt sure he would not take if it were likely to weaken the restraints of morality upon others. And so, though they might have regretted his position because they deemed it an erroneous one, it gave him a fresh opportunity of exhibiting his scrupulous tenderness for weak consciences—his readiness to sacrifice for the sake of another's feelings.

In the Ministers' meetings, he would open his heart and lips on these topics with freedom. As the teachers of others, he wished them to hold the truth strongly, and exhibit it carefully. He supposed they were not children, able to digest nothing save the diluted milk of theology; or if they were thus weak, he evidently thought it time to put them upon a more manly regimen. What he regarded their errors he combatted with argument; and what seemed to him their superstitions he would sometimes seek to riddle with sarcasm, and shatter with the blows of what seemed to the antagonist, his irreverent radicalism. And though, for a time, hearts would seem sorely wounded by his attacks, he seldom left any other impression than that he meant it all for their good.

Those Ministers' Conferences, if their history could be written, or their features Daguerreotyped, would constitute some of the best delineations of Mr. Cheney's soul. There he was himself, in all the varied aspects of his greatness and of his defects. All that was characteristic in the man, found there free expression. Sometimes his soul was before us in the vexed storminess of its vehement feeling; and then there broke out the touching, pathetic, beautiful tenderness, which fell on all hearts to melt them. There glanced, light and feathery, the arrows of his piercing wit, and there his deep and genial humor broke forth in its freeness. There he welded the links of his strongest logic, and there his sudden bursts of eloquence came forth to startle and astonish like the unexpected discharge of an electrical battery. If there was any power of thought in the natures about him, he would wake it into life ; and some of his abrupt sentences, thrown out at random apparently, in the course of a close argument or in the midst of a heated declamation, would furnish a text for weeks of deliberate thought. Few, who have enjoyed them for any length of time, will forget them ; and few will go to them for a long time to come, who were members in past years, without feeling the greatness of the vacancy occasioned by the absence of him whose attendance was so punctual, whose labors were so abundant, whose counsels were so valuable, and whose influence was felt like the storm or the sunshine by all the hearts about him. There his memory will long be precious, and lips will tremble with tenderness in the utterance of his name.

16

CHAPTER XI.

COMEOUTISM.

The preceding chapter has exhibited Mr. Cheney's charity in respect to all mere outward things, and his tendencies toward a purely spiritual unity of all who sympathised in the attachment to great and just principles. But in these tendencies he always kept himself within the bounds of practical moderation; and followed faithfully what seemed to him the clear, steady light of scripture. In breaking loose from the trammels of mere human prescription, he ever paused in reverence before what were to him the appointments of God.

He trusted his bible; its clear voice was what settled many a question for his understanding and his heart. He approached the law and the testimony, feeling that it was always safe to confide in the teaching of that great oracle. He could not be drawn to abandon it by the cords of personal friendship, nor by the strong attachments of the cause he loved, when it turned its back upon the wisdom revealed from heaven. On these points he was tested thoroughly; tested by temptations presented to the most vulnerable part of his nature, and presented under circumstances best adapted to give them power. How far he would go, and where he found the "Hitherto," which held him perpetually in check, this chapter will more or less fully reveal.

Enough has been presented to satisfy the most skeptical of the reality and strength of Mr. Cheney's attachment to the Anti-Slavery enterprise. And, as a result, he was most warmly attached to the firm friends of that enterprise during its stormy and perilous days. They who braved the popular odium which Abolitionists were then meeting, were heroes in his eye ; he believed them worthy descendants of Huss and John Rogers. They had proved their sincerity. He regarded them as the chief shrines of freedom in an age when a shameless despotism, under the shallowest and meanest of all pretences, was hunting liberty from the land. And when they stood firm, and calm, and uncompromising, amid the surges of mobocratic violence ; when they cheerfully perilled all for the sake of the poor slave who had no eye to see, and no tongue to thank them for their sufferings in his behalf, he gave them his full heart's confidence, his ready defence, and his cheerful co-operation. He felt for them more than the ordinary attachment of a personal friendship ; and at the same time, he felt that their accusers, revilers, and persecutors, were both insincere and cowardly.

The leaders in this Anti-Slavery work were, to a great extent, identified with the measures that have usually come to be designated by the term "Garrisonian," —Mr. William Lloyd Garrison of Boston being, in some sense, their head and leader. There were men of high talent and moral worth connected with this school of Reformers. Mr. C. frequently attended their meetings, listened eagerly, and sometimes spoke from their platform. The startling facts, the strong reasoning, the brilliant and impassioned oratory, the fierce, withering invective, and the radical measures which successively passed in review before him there, produced a deep impression on his mind. There was very much there that found correspondencies in his own nature. He was firm, earnest, vehement, radical, impulsive, and benevolent, by virtue both of his constitution and his habits; and these characteristics all appeared before him in the development of these champion abolitionists. And so they were his chosen co-laborers; and many of them became personal acquaintances and friends. Whoever villified them, was almost certain to meet his rebuke. Whoever suspected them, he regarded as either ignorant or bigoted or pro-slavery; and none of these were, in his eye, venial sins.

A State Society was formed in R. I. under their auspices; and of this Society Mr. C. early became both a member and an officer, and continued to hold that station for years; lending his influence and labors to give it character and efficiency. These leading advocates, grew, gradually, less and less guarded in their language and policy. Their condemnations grew more sweeping, and their crusades more fierce. From condemning the ministers as unfaithful men, they began to condemn the ministry as an order; from contending against the positions and character of churches, they came to contend against all church organizations; from opposing false interpretations of the bible, they came to oppose the bible itself as a barrier to truth and freedom. Not all known as Garrisonians went to this extent, nor did any of them in all places; but this began to be the attidude of the body. Mr. Cheney still retained a large measure of his faith. He insisted, against the assertions of his friends, that they were misunderstood and misrepresented. Where a prominent element of Christianity had been so strikingly exhibited, it was hard for him to believe that the very foundations of Christianity were wanting.

On the 16th and 17th of November 1842, the R. I. Anti-Slavery Convention was held in Providence. Scarcely was the meeting opened, when its radical character began to appear. The ground taken by several of the speakers was, that the Sabbath, the ministry, and the Church, were the great obstacles in the path of the Anti-Slavery enterprise, and that their abolition was imperatively demanded. This sentiment furnished the principal staple of nearly all the speeches made on the first day of the session; and the speeches were interspersed with the harshest epithets, and the most severe and indiscriminate charges levelled at the head of ministers and churches. Ridicule took the place of facts, and sneers were used to do the work belonging only to sober argument. Moderation seemed to be designedly abandoned, and courtesy was unceremoniously kicked out of doors. Of that Convention thus speaks an Anti-Slavery man who attended it:—

"Of all nests of vipers, from the days of the Pharisees who laughed Jesus Christ to scorn, to the time of holding that meeting in Providence, I never read or heard of any body which exceeded that Convention in uncourteousness, scorn, contempt, or contumely, toward every minister that arose to speak, without stopping to hear what he had to say. It was enough to know that he was a minister, and from every part of the house came forth hisses and cries, 'O, he is a minister! nobody can be a minister and a man, or a friend to the Slave;' and *slang*, that bespoke it the foam of an irritated but caged serpent of the most venomous or red dragon sort, was poured forth in torrents.'"

One man there was, nominally, at least, of their number, who opposed this position; but his polished eloquence and platform power—scarcely equalled in this country—did not suffice to turn the current of this Convention.

Near the close of the first day's session, a young minister of the same denomination with Mr. C., whose Anti-Slavery labors have always been abundant, arose to make a brief defence, and indicate what appeared to him the real obstacles to the progress of the Anti-Slavery enterprise. Some one asked for the name of the speaker; whereupon one of the leading men of the Convention responded in a sneering, contemptuous tone; "*No matter who he is; he's a Clergyman, I'll warrant you.*" The speaker was announced, and, amid hisses and sneers, concluded his speech.

This was too much for Mr. Cheney's endurance. Up to this time he had been silent, under the influence of such feelings of disappointment, wonder, and regret, as may be conceived only in part. If he spoke at all, he must utter his convictions and express his feelings; and it was hard to bring himself into a conflict with these heroic ideals of his former days. But this attempt to gag a true man and brother;—this attempt to silence by sneers and clamor an honest earnest spirit, simply because of his profession; this exercise of a petty tyranny never exceeded in injustice and meanness by any pro-slavery mobocrats;—this was a torch flung into the magazine of his explosive nature. There was sorrow enough mingled with his indignation to make him calm; and virtue and worth enough in his cause to rouse his great courage, that never knew fear, up to its highest point of activity and development. The mask had fallen off from his antagonists, and pity did not plead with him to spare them. The scene which followed can only be understood by those who knew the parties and understood the issue. Verbal description it is not worth the while to attempt. Suffice it to say that the rest of that Convention was a close hand to hand moral battle; and in the front ranks, meeting the enemy at every turn, and wielding his weapons with a skill and an energy that made every blow tell powerfully on some vulnerable part, stood Mr. Cheney, firm as a rock and dauntless as a lion.

Says that young minister alluded to; "The defence which Brother Cheney made of my rights, the lashing which he gave to those who treated me with such contempt merely because I was a 'Priest,' as they frequently termed it, was searching and annihilating. Never, I think, did Brother Cheney win a more triumphant victory, or wear the laurels achieved more deservedly."

As a result of this discussion, a new Anti-Slavery Society was formed in the State the same year, and to this Society Mr. Cheney gave his sympathy and support till the last. He held himself aloof from the official positions in the old Society which he had before occupied, and was careful not to become identified with its policy, or the unqualified defender of its principles or measures. Yet even here the tendencies of his mind discovered themselves. He did not sweepingly denounce the body, nor take advantage of his ability to thwart them in all their efforts. There were individual members of that School of Reformers who would not endorse this crusade against religious institutions, and his sense of justice forbade him to treat them otherwise than as their personal characters and public efforts warranted. He could still and did still honor their courage and sacrifices, though condemning their policy and rejecting some of their principles. He regarded them as earnest and efficient defenders of freedom, even while he repudiated some of their chief modes of warfare. Their practical reprobation of the doctrine of expediency, which seemed to him the great curse of the American people and churches, still commanded his respect; though he protested against the injustice of their indiscriminate invective. As fearless defenders of the rights of the weak he wished them success; though, as violators of the law of Christian propriety, he regarded them as perpetrating both a wrong and a blunder. He rejoiced that their exposures were arousing the public conscience; though he regretted that their excesses should shock and arm it against themselves. He saw, in the general indifference to human rights, some sort of an apology for the extreme methods of defence which they were adopting; though they were methods opposed to his idea of duty or wisdom.

Besides, the attacks they received from the political and religous censors of the land, he regarded as unjust. If they sinned, he felt sure that they were " sinned against" quite as fearfully and frequently. To him, *their infidelity* was hardly more to be dreaded, than the sanctimonious connivance of popular ministers and churches at the sins of Slavery. The popular clamor of indolence and conservatism for their crucifixion, he would not and could not aid in swelling. And so his position became an independent one. All parties alternately looked upon him as an ally and an opponent. When he condemned the infidelity of the Radicals, the Conservatists gave him their hand; and when he pointed his artillery at the inconsistencies of the Conservatists, the Radicals regarded him as passing through the process of conversion to their faith. Partly from an ever growing liberality in his opinions, and partly, perhaps, from his belief that there were fewer excesses connected with the Garrisonian School ; and partly, perhaps, because the encroachments of the Slave Power seemed to demand more rigorous and radical measures, he had probably more sympathy with that body of men in the last years of his life, than for some time subsequent to the Providence controversy. He attended their Conventions more or less, sometimes spoke from their platforms, and remained an interested subscriber to their paper—" The Liberator"—up to the time of his death. Some of the leading men of that body he always looked upon as high examples of ability and worth. He believed them deeply conscientious, truly benevolent, really full of courage, ready to sacrifice for the Slave's sake, and, in spite of their errors and excesses, doing a high service to the cause of human freedom. And believing all this, he was at no pains to conceal it, either from the friends or foes of the men in question.

This detail has been entered into, because it seemed necessary to make his position understood; especially since it has been misapprehended. Some, judging chiefly from the strong ground taken at the time of the Convention, have supposed that he always afterward kept himself entirely aloof from all positions which implied sympathy with, or confidence in the Garrisonians. Others, having seen him on their platforms and heard him denounce the position of the Church as he was sometimes wont to do, set him down as a disorganizer and conducter. Both alike seem to have misunderstood him. He was unqualifiedly attached to no party; was the servile follower of no leader. He would sympathize with every party so far as his conscience and judgment endorsed its principles and policy; and when they could not do this, he was willing to stand alone. But he ever clung to the bible and the Church as God's richest gifts to the world; counting it his chief joy to enforce the teachings of the one, and labor for the efficiency of the other.

The following discourse, preached at the dedication of a house of worship, will, perhaps, be the best exposition of his views touching some of the points involved in the preceding statements. Grateful to his *Christian* friends will it be to know that these were the sentiments which were carried even to his grave.

DISCOURSE.

THE IMPORTANCE OF CHRISTIAN ASSOCIATIONS.

"Not forsaking the assembling of ourselves together, as the manner of some is."—*Heb.* x. 25.

The text suggests for our consideration the importance of Christian Association. By Christian Association we mean the *assembling together* of Christians for mutual benefit and mutual co-operation, to promote the glory of God in the highest, Peace on earth, Good will to men. Their importance may be seen in the fact,

I. That associations of the good have existed from the time when the morning stars sang together,—from the time when "men began to call on the name of the Lord." In olden time, as indicated by the author of the book of Job, the sons of God came to present themselves before the Lord. The Commonwealth of Israel was an association; and in ancient days they had places where prayer was wont to be made. Prophets and holy men of old spoke often one to another, and the Lord hearkened and heard; and, what is more, a book of remembrance was kept. It may be seen that God approved of these associations of the good, to receive and impart benefit.

II. From the fact that Jesus instituted such an Association. First, when he said, "On this rock will I build my church;" and, Second, when he said,—" Tell it to the church." In the first of these remarks he recognizes that great association including all believers in heaven and earth; in the second, he recognizes a local association whose members could be reached.

III. From the fact that Jesus did so much to reveal the character of the association. He taught, 1st. The foundation of such an Association; viz. Jesus Christ. 2d. Who are members of such an Association; viz. believers, lovers, doers. 3d. Who was its head or Ruler; viz. Christ. 4th. Gave their rule of faith and book of discipline. Taught how to labor, in what spirit to labor; whom and how to exclude, and how to regard such as were excluded. 5th. Taught the equality of the members.—"One is your Master, even Christ, and all ye are brethren."

IV. Association meets a primary want of human nature. 1st. Man is a social being. His physical, intellectual, and moral natures all show that he was formed for society. Man's organization utters the same truth as God's word; "It is not good for man to be alone." Now Christian Association harmonizes with this nature, and meets a part of this want. But, 2d. Man is a religious being; he has the religious sentiment. Deeply has God planted this in the human breast. Now with a social and religious nature, man needs Christian Association. Nothing short of this meets his necessities. Man will worship, *must* worship. Moreover he will worship with his fellows. It is of vast importance, therefore, that he exercise himself in *Christian* worship. And, 3d. He is a dependant being—dependant on God and man; and so needs the prayers, sympathies and aid of others as they are furnished by Christian Associations.

V. They meet the wants of a world lying in wickedness. Christian Associations are the concentrated salt of the earth—concentrated for diffusion,—the concentrated light of the world to illumine it; cities on its hills; Christian Light-houses to direct the myriads of tempest-tossed sinful souls how to avoid the whirlpools of despair, the rocks of peril, and the gulf of perdition;—to guide them to the haven of peace.

From these associations are to go forth those principles and practices which are to purify and regenerate the world. Here the war-loving and war-practising world is to behold—taught and lived—a peace that changes swords into ploughshares and spears into pruning-hooks. Here is to be seen embodied a love that seeketh not her own—stronger than death. Here is to be displayed, to all revengeful, worldly, beholders, the forgiving spirit of Jesus;—" Father, forgive them, for they know not what they do." Here is to be taught and practiced that world-embracing and world-harmonizing rule, "Do unto others as ye would that others should do unto you." Here is revealed, in teaching and life, the Fatherhood of God and the brotherhood of man.

Now we urge that the world needs such *salt*, such *light*, such a practical gospel, such a living embodiment of Peace on earth and good will to men; and that Christian Associations seem alone able to supply that need. These world-saving truths needed an embodiment, and they had it in Jesus of Nazareth; they need it still, and they have it in Christian Associations.

VI. Christian Associations are the only avenue through which a Christian can meet the claims of God, of his brother man, and of the world, upon him. If a brother is perishing in yonder river, or by fire, or wreck, and *one* is unable to rescue him, two or three or more others are obligated to aid; united effort is needed, nay, demanded. And this includes both the spirit and form of Christian Association in its simplest character. So if one voice will not appropriately swell God's anthems of praise, then a multitude which no man can number should be heard; no one would be justified in such a case in singing on his own hook; his voice is needed in the band. If one hand, one arm, one heart cannot perform a required service, there must be a union of minds, hands, hearts, or the work will not be done.

VII. Such associations harmonize with our views of the heavenly state. There heart meets heart, soul meets soul, voice meets voice. It should be so on earth; for this we are taught to pray; and we should make earth as much like heaven as possible. A *home*, a *mansion*, a *city*, a *multitude*, *music*,—all these speak of Christian Association. There are strong reasons for their perpetuity; they are in accordance, 1. With the uniform practice of the good; 2. With the teachings of Jesus; 3. With the soul's nature; 4. With the world's wants; 5. With the claims of God; 6. With the heavenly state; and we may add with every tendency of a Christian heart. So that if there was no day for their enjoyment indicated, he would make one; if no particular time specified, he would set one.

REMARKS.

1. We may see what is *true* and what is *false* Come-outism. There is a scriptural come-outism. "Come out," says Paul; "Come out," says the Revelator. But come out from what? The answer is,—

Come out from an apostate church; come out from man-made, and man-imposed ceremonies; come out from shadows and antiquated customs that have been abolished; come out from an anti-christian church, the mother of harlots; but never come out from the Bride, the Lamb's wife, never come out from a true church, for that is needful for the soul.

2. We learn how to test the character of all associations of men, from the system of Fourier upward or downward. So far as they leave out the religious element they must fail. Man's deepest necessities are the religious; and associations making no provision for these are destined to be dashed in pieces like a potter's vessel. They may be literary, civil, ecclesiastical, or philanthropic; leave out Christianity in its essence and they must die, for the spirit of life is not in them. Every association, whatever its character or profession, is to be tested by this standard.

3. We see the wisdom and goodness of God in establishing such associations. Christian churches are these, and no more. Jesus said, "Go preach," &c.; that is, in effect, kindle up these beacon lights; where two or three gather in my name, there is a light. These circles were to be formed in every land, that thus unto principalities and powers might be known, by the church, the manifold wisdom of God.

4. We see that if such associations be of God, then a great hierarchy with a human head, claiming infallibility, whether called Roman, Greek, or English, is a mighty mistake. And more than that, all jurisdiction, claimed by one of these bodies over the rest, is assumption. In other words, Bible Associations—New Testament As-

sociations—are independent bodies; having One Lord, One Faith, One Baptism, One Foundation, One Head, and that not human but divine. Hence Presbyterian jurisdiction, or Episcopal jurisdiction, or Quarterly Meeting or Yearly Meeting, or Conference jurisdiction, are equally to be repudiated with Romish claims. They are of human origin, and have no divine authority. "Tell it to the church," is the teaching of Jesus; and the only appeal from that jurisdiction is to the court of heaven.

5. We see that our individual responsibilities embrace our social obligations.—We must be judged as individuals, but can never fulfil our duties as isolated beings. Monasteries and Nunneries are not of God, nor the celibacy of the clergy. "Am I my brother's keeper?" will be answered by "The voice of thy brother's blood crieth unto me from the ground." If we neglect the claims of the poor, the crushed, those among thieves, we shall meet the censure of him who said, "Inasmuch as ye did it not unto the least of these, ye did it not to me."

6. We see the duty of Christians, in villages, towns, cities, and country. To associate, meet, assemble, unite, for their own and the world's benefit. The word of God is to be read, the sense given and applied; children are to be trained in Christian principles and Christian practice; and where can it be so effectually done as in Christian associations. They are to exhort one another; pray one for another; aid each other in bringing Christian principles and practice to every family and individual within their reach. What a work

is this! to cast the leaven of the gospel into every department of society.

7. We see the need of a place to meet. A poet has said, "The groves were God's first temples," but the groves will not always suffice. And so we have here this beautiful house. We attach no peculiar sanctity to place; yet there is a sweetness and preciousness in association, and it will sometimes give to a place something of its own interest.

8. We see the need of a *time* in which to associate. And hence the fitness of the Lord's Day. And although we attach no holiness to time more than to place, yet we can say with Watts, "Welcome sweet day of rest." Welcome the time for its fitness—its uses. We do not confine meetings to one day in seven. Man's social nature and spiritual wants, and the world's needs seem to demand more frequent association; and what man needs, let him have.

9. The Christian Association or Church here, will see the work they have to do. Not to keep lamp light, or moon light, or sun light, but *Christian* light before this people. Each should be luminous alone, but when united they should blaze and burn with spiritual radiance and heat; their influence should be seen and felt in all this region. They have the Sunday School to organize and sustain—the children to care for. They have the word of truth to preach; and assemblings for prayer and conference and exhortation to maintain. Not a child should be left untaught, not a family unvisited, not a sinner unwarned, nor a needy, sick or dying one uncomforted or unaided.

*17

10. We see of what these associations should be composed; viz. of new creatures, lively stones, Christians.

11. We see where these associations should exist. Where there are two or three disciples there should be regular associations.

12. The glory and beauty of these associations are seen, 1st. In their foundation. 2d. Their Head. 3d. Their stability. 4th. In their gifts and ministry and power. 5th. In their peaceful character, their simple but efficient discipline. 6th. In their benevolent spirit. 7th. In the benefits they confer. 8th. In the bow of hope and promise around and above them—exceeding great and precious.

Brethren, will you associate and work? Will you all work? Will you be in charity with each and all? Will you prove by your spirit and fruits the worth of Christian association?

CHAPTER IX.

SERMONS.

It seems proper to make a selection from the discourses of Mr. Cheney, with a view to present the methods of sermonizing which he adopted, and lay up in a permanent form some of the more striking exhibitions of truth with which his ministry was marked. His preparations for the pulpit usually consisted simply of an arrangement of his thoughts, the choice of what he intended should be his chief illustrations, and the very briefest designations, in a few particulars, of the language he was expecting to employ. And in the heat of his earnest speaking, new thoughts would occur to him, fresh illustrations crowd around him, and the phraseology he had regarded as fixed, would be set aside for that which gushed up spontoneously as an envelope of his ideas. The result was that his best sketches were not always followed by the best delivered sermons; and a prosy, meagre outline, may have been the herald of a discourse that startled the audience by its rare force, and lived in the memory for years, as among the happiest things connected with the ministry of the Olneyville Pastor.

The following discourses have been selected chiefly on the ground of their variety, and characteristic qualities. They show the author in the various phases of his character, and the specific features of his teaching. And yet even these are exhibited to a great disadvantage; for, to get a just view of Mr. Cheney or his sermon, one needed to hear him preach it. They are selected from among the usual sermons preached to his own people; and few of them probably produced any very unusual impression in the delivery. No particular regard will be paid to the order in which they were preached; because there seems no necessity for observing it, and because it is a very difficult thing to ascertain.

SERMON.

CONSECRATION TO GOD.

Glorify God in your body and in your spirit which are God's."— I *Cor.* vi.: 20.

The requirement of this text may be simply stated as Consecration to God; and, in considering it, I shall note;

I. Some things implied in consecration to God.

II. What is that Consecration?

III. Give some reasons why such consecration should be made.

IV. Make an Application of the subject.

I. What is implied in Consecration to God?

1. The existence of a God to whom this consecration is to be made. If there were no being who could rightfully claim such service, there would be no propriety in such a precept.

2. It implies the existence of beings who are rational,

and free; capable of making such consecration. No being destitute of moral perceptions, could do such a work.

3. It implies a rule, law, or standard, by which such consecration is defined and enforced. Or in short, a Being to whom it is to be made; beings *by* whom it is to be made, and a method *in* which it is to be made.

II. What is that Consecration?

To consecrate is to set apart, dedicate, or devote to the service and worship of God. So to consecrate ourselves, is to devote the powers of body and spirit to the service of God. Or, in other words, we glorify God when we use our bodies and spirits as God would have us use them. In other words still, consecration is obedience of heart and life to the commands of God. It implies especially, 1. The control of the appetites; and 2. The government of the passions.

First. We glorify God in body when we eat and drink and sleep and exercise so as to give the body the highest degree of physical strength and health; so that it may be the fitting residence of the mind or spirit,— that bright image of the Deity. Health and strength, and life even, may be sacrificed to the claims of the higher law, when the law of love demands it. The Samaritan risked his own life in an act of humanity. And, in obedience to the higher law, the dungeon, rack, or stake may be met. A mother may yield the body, and the law which calls for its highest health and strength, to the higher claims of a sick and dying child.

Second. We glorify God in body when we make the appetites and passions of the body submit to the commands of God, as they are seen and felt by the reason and judgment. By so doing the spirit will become clearer and stronger.

We glorify God in spirit,

First. When our affections are placed on the supreme, infinite Spirit; the pure, holy, and lovely One.

Second. When we aim, strive to know God, and Jesus Christ, and the will of Heaven.

Third. When we yield to that will as fully as we can learn it, that is, follow our highest convictions of right.

Fourth. When we copy the example of Jesus, in humility, in tenderness, in love, infaith, in diligence, in boldness, in patience, in endurance.

III. Why should such consecration be made?

1. The Supreme Ruler of the universe demands it. "Thou shalt love the Lord thy God with all thy heart," is the high, the universal, the unalterable command.

2. God's creating, upholding, and redeeming gifts are reasons why we should consecrate ourselves to him who gave such gifts. "God so loved the world;" "He made us a little lower than the angels;" "He bought us with a price." The privilege to be and the power to enjoy flow from him. Our bodies and spirits are his; yet they are ours to use, and hence we should use them right.

3. Not to do so is rebellion against the just Ruler of the universe. It is to side in with Satan. It is to say; "We will not have this man to reign over us." It is to cry,—"crucify him!" It is to say "His blood be on us and on our children." This is awfully dangerous.

4. Not to do it is to cut ourselves off from the aid which we might receive in times of need. The hour of weakness will come, the hour of destitution; the hour when no human aid will avail. Then shall we need to be in harmony with God, that his power, wisdom and goodness may flow into the soul. O the misery of that being who consecrates himself to any being or thing short of God! See the whole world groaning in its agony, because consecrated to the lust of the flesh, the lust of the eye, and the pride of life.

5. Such consecration secures pure enjoyment, unalloyed happiness, permanent peace. It meets the highest claims of the reason and of the conscience; it meets the command of God, and the teachings of Jesus. It meets the wants of all the faculties of both body and spirit, it gives exercise to them all, and keeps them all in harmony; and hence, peace like a river, joy unspeakable, and hope so bright and sure.

6. It is the condition of our highest usefulness. It is only when thus devoted, that we begin to do ourselves good. Before this, we do ourselves constant harm. Now we begin to be light to the world. Now, in the family, in the social circle, in the church, our influence is felt. Now, with a heart full of love and a countenance radiant with joy, we go forth like angels of mercy to bless and save the lost. And when such a consecration is made, the moral vibration is felt in all worlds. The moral electric chord is struck, and an influence is sent from the farthest reach of moral being up to the throne of God—the great moral centre of the universe. "There

is joy in the presence of the angels of God over one sinner that repenteth."

APPLICATION.

1. We see our duty for to-day ;—to consecrate body, soul, spirit, all. Reasons high as heaven, deep as hell, broad as moral obligation urge to this.

2. What a spectacle of beauty and sublimity is presented when blooming youth consecrate themselves to God! Not to enter the nunnery, or the monastery, not to bow at the shrine of fashion, not to present standards to the worshippers of Mars, but to enter a world of misery, want, and woe, to bless and save it; to enter a world of temptation and trial, to suffer and endure, to overcome and triumph.

SERMON.

FREEDOM AND ITS RESULTS.

" Am I not free ?"—I. *Cor.* ix. : 1. " As free and not using your liberty for a cloak of maliciousness, but as the servants of God."—I. *Pet.* ii. : 16. " For, brethren, ye have been called unto liberty."—*Gal.* v. : 13.

I. The term freedom is applied, sometimes, to things which have no internal self-moving power ; but act or move as they are acted or moved upon. We say, in common speech, " free as air ;" " free as the birds." Now air moves as it is acted on, and birds act from instinct. Neither, therefore, has that freedom which is the basis of a rational mind ; neither has a self-determining power. They move and act as influences around them compel ; and want all controlling power over those influences. Some make all intelligences subject to the same or similar agencies; not only with Pope, "bind nature fast in fate," but, beyond Pope, bind the human will also—yea, even the will divine.

But we think, 1st. That God is free; bound only by his perfectly balanced character or disposition; and 2d. That all rational beings are free;—and are very sure that *man*, made in the image of God, is free. We think so;

1. Because he is in God's image.
2. Because God treats him as free. He does this, 1st. By placing him under law. 2d. By threatened penalties and offered rewards. 3d. By invitations and persuasions. 4th. By lamentations over his rejection of truth. 5th. By judging him at the last day.
3. Because man perceives right and wrong; feels condemned when he does wrong, and approved when he does right.
4. Because he is *conscious* that he is free.
5. Because he is constantly condemning and approving others as if they were free.

The terms free and freedom, then, are mostly applied to human beings.

1. They are applied to all human beings who have come to years of understanding, except the insane or idiots; to all who are moral agents. They have power to choose or reject, to obey or disobey, that is, so far as the will is concerned.
2. They are applied to those who have political liberty. New-Englanders are therefore called free, in opposition to such a people as the Russians.

3. They are applied to those who have personal liberty; as the people of Rhode-Island in opposition to the slaves of the South.

4. They are applied to those who have been freed from sin and brought into the glorious liberty of the children of God. So, figuratively, we speak of the freedom of the press, of speech, of the pulpit, of worship.

But freedom to think, act and speak; that is, power, liberty, or privilege to do this, is man's birth-right,—heaven-descended, God-given.

II. If this be so, then there are certain RESULTS or consequences.

1. Such a being—i. e., a free being—is placed under law. He inquires what is right, and it is law that tells him. Of course such a being is responsible for his obedience or disobedience to the law. Then he can sin. Then he may continue to sin. Then he may die in sin. Then he may be punished for his sin. Then he may continue forever to sin. Then endless punishment may be received. Admit the freedom, therefore, and you admit endless punishment as a possible result.

2. The doctrine of absolute predestination and unconditional election cannot be true. If man is free, he is certainly not bound. But God cannot decree who shall or who shall not repent, and leave the subjects of such decree to repent or not.

3. Man determines his own moral character. If there was no freedom, the character of all sentient beings would be fixed by their Maker, as certain as the hills. But freedom implies that the character is determined by the possessor.

4. We see how sin entered into the world. Freedom alone could make a pathway for sin. If there were no free beings there would be no sin. But if beings are free, then there is necessarily a possibility of sinning. Hence God is not the author of sin, but of freedom. Man is the author of sin, in the abuse of his freedom.

5. Through freedom God receives the highest honor and the sweetest praise. The laws by which the material world acts, moves—the mineral, vegetable, animal,—indicate wondrous power, skill, goodness; but who perceives, and appreciates that power, skill, and goodness, but free beings? But *could* we perceive and feel all this, and yet know that it was all choiceless, what would that be compared to the joy arising from a choosing, loving heart.—We see, then, that without freedom, God must have remained an "*Unknown God.*" Joy might have been felt, but its great source, origin, cause, must have remained unappreciated and unseen. Hence man was made, and man was made *free.*

APPLICATION.

If such be the origin, nature, and results of freedom, then we may see,

1. That freedom is a God-given right to man.

2. An abuse of this high gift must bring on man the direst curse. It takes a fallen seraph to make a Devil.

3. How aggravated must be the guilt of those who would deprive man of this right in any of its forms! Hence the guilt of despotism in Church and State,—of slavery and caste.

4. We see why there are such conflicts among the Go-

vernments of Europe. Freedom, like the burning lava, will find its way to the surface, upheaving, overturning. Despotism struggles to choke freedom; and the contest convulses the world.

5. True freedom and true happiness are identical. Where one is there is the other. The sons of God are like God,—free and happy.

6. No people can be virtuous, happy, or useful, without freedom;—freedom of speech, of the press, of worship.

7. Our privilege and duty are before us;—to be free and prize it, to defend freedom and spread it.

8. Sinners are voluntary slaves. Satan binds them with their consent and aid; until they are sometimes forced to cry with Paul, "O wretched man that I am, who shall deliver me from the body of this death!"

> "Ye slaves of sin and hell,
> Your *liberty* receive;
> And safe in Jesus dwell,
> And blest in Jesus live:
> The year of Jubilee is come,
> Return, ye ransomed sinners, home."

SERMON.

GOD'S LAW AND ITS WONDERS.

"Open thou mine eyes that I may behold wondrous things out of thy law."—*Ps.* cxix.: 18.

I. God's law. This implies;—

1. The being of a God. If there were no God, there could be no law; all would be fate or chance.

2. That God has a rule of action, or is himself governed by law. By being thus governed we mean, that he acts in accordance with his own conceptions of right, which are always perfect.

II. What is meant by God's law?

1. God's will or purpose by which he himself acts.
2. God's rule or method of governing worlds of matter.
3. God's rule or method of governing worlds of mind.
4. God's rule or method of governing worlds of moral beings.
5. God's will made known to men.—In his works,—the operation of those works in Providence ; or as made known to prophets, apostles, and by his Son.

God's law physical is wonderful. God's law mental is wonderful. God's law moral is wonderful.

III. What are its wonders?

1. It is wonderful in in its extent. Take Mitchell's farthest star, whose distance is such that it will take twenty millions of years for light to reach here, though travelling at the rate of about eleven millions of miles per minute. But God's law reaches that star and regulates the transmission of those rays. Take the millions of animated creatures that populate a single drop of water, and God's law is there. Take the divisibility of matter until you are lost ; and yet God's law is present in the least particle. It reaches all the thoughts of all intelligencies, and all the pulsations of all moral beings.

2. It is wonderful in its simplicity and its adaptations. These features are seen in the law of gravitation, which wheels the planets and lifts the vapors ; which

draws the mighty waters to the ocean, and regulates the weights of commerce.

3. It is wonderful in its inflexibility. Violate it, and its penalties are certain, whether it be physical, mental, or moral.

4. In its clearness and comprehensiveness. Look at the law as it is expounded by Jesus—Love to God, and love to man. And then that its just applications may be known, he directs us to the inner chamber of the soul, where God has Daguerreotyped the law which tells us what we are to do to our neighbor.

5. It is wonderful in its spirituality. It does not simply take cognizance of action, but reaches down to the purposes, desires, motives, and thoughts.

APPLICATION.

1. What a glorious being God must be—the author of this law!

2. What a glorious being Christ must be—the end, the fulfiller of this law!

3. What guilty beings men must be, who knowingly violate such a law!

4. The gospel is only a later edition of this law, developing it in new forms—the glorious law of liberty.

SERMON.

THE NATURE AND DEVELOPMENTS OF GOD'S LOVE.

"Behold what manner of love the Father hath bestowed upon us, that we should be called the sons of God."—I. *John*, iii.: 1.

I. The nature of a person or thing is,

1. That which it is in itself, organically, constitutionally.

2. That which it is by custom, practice, habit. By nature men are said to be children of wrath; and without natural affection. So there is the nature of the bird, of the beast, of the fish, and of the insect, and a vast variety of subordinate natures among all these. So we have human nature, angelic nature, and divine nature. So by habit there is found the nature of demons.

Now we cannot speak of God's nature as organic or constitutional; for, being self-existent and eternal, he was not organized; but we may and do speak of his nature as manifested, developed. And, indeed, when we speak of an emotion, a passion, *as love*, we speak not of a creation, but of an exercise; not of organism, but of action; not of passive being, but of voluntary power. The nature of God's love then, is, negatively,

1. That it is not *instinctive*. The tribes of irrational animals have this love, some of them in a high degree. The love of most animals for their young, and of some for the old and infirm teaches this.

2. It is not simply *emotional*. I do not affirm or deny here that God is the subject of emotions; but

simply state that such emotional action does not include all that is meant by God's love.

3. It is not *associational;*—that which is produced by associating with each other.

4. It is not sovereign or mysterious, as has sometimes been asserted. It is the love of a sovereign, but not sovereign love.

5. It is not the love of *gratitude;* for who can bestow favors upon God?

But, affirmatively, the nature of God's love is,

1. Like its author, eternal.

2. It is *impartial;* that is, loving things and persons according to their real value.

3. It is *unchangeable;* not fickle, variable, uncertain; but the same yesterday, to-day, and forever.

4. It is *free;* not bought or paid for, so much for so much.

5. It is *extensive;* heaven-high, and world-wide. It reaches the smallest animalcule, and embraces the mightiest angel. In a word, God's love is associated with pure truth and justice, and all-embracing wisdom.

II. Let us look at its developments.

1. In Creation. Observe the tendency in all creation to produce happiness, when not abused. What scenes of grandeur and beauty for the eye! what melody for the ear! what variety for the taste! and what capabilities in the eye and ear to receive delight!

What sources of pleasure in the social relation; father, mother, son, daughter, husband, wife! God's love created all these capabilities. Behold what manner of love is here! So in the acquisition of knowledge. There is delight here, purer and rarer than that which comes through eye or ear.

And then the highest, purest of all joy, in doing good to others. This it is largely that makes the joy of God.

2. In Redemption. Here we have God's love developing itself in another set of circumstances. A world has revolted. Man, made in God's image, has fallen, is lost. The crown has tumbled from his head. Now let us look at infinite wisdom and see its plan to save. See power unlimited executing that plan; and while you steadily gaze, you will perceive that all this proceeds from God's great heart, whose pulsations of benevolence are sending to all the news of mercy, and you will exclaim, " Behold what manner of love the Father hath bestowed upon us." 1st. In the plan of mercy. 2d. In the promise of a Deliverer. 3d. In the gift of his Son. 4th. In the mission of Jesus. 5th. In his unfolding and developing his Father's heart. Mark Jesus tempted, Jesus weeping, Jesus sweating, Jesus bleeding, Jesus groaning, Jesus dying. What intensity of affection! what manner of love! See his love in the Spirit's influence; and also in the great commission, " Go ye into all the world," &c.

3. In his patience and long-suffering, his unwillingness that any should perish. He sends rain and sunshine on rebels. Deeper than the compassion of a mother for her child, is the tender, patient affection of God. Here is the love of pity, tenderness, compassion, dropping tears, uttering groans, sweating blood, and crying, amid mockery and scorn, " Father forgive them."

4. In the arrangements made for a higher state of

bliss for his children. 1st. A mansion, a home, sweet home. 2d. A resurection. 3d. An incorruptible body. 4th. All that the tree of life and river of life typify; all that Eden's bowers and John's beautiful city indicated. All this comes from the same heart that clothed the earth with beauty, that filled it with fragrance and music. Behold what manner of love is here.

APPLICATION.

1. We may see the character of the Ruler of the universe. "Our Father," is his appropriate name. Not a being whose love is fickle, but ever in accordance with justice, reason, truth.

2. We learn our indebtedness to Christ. It is in him and through him that we learn of the Father. God in Christ is the lovely One.

3. We see what man ought to be, and what he may be. He should be like God; and he may rise up as a son and heir, to inherit all the fulness of his love.

4. We see the folly and guilt of those who reject God and his wondrous love, Christ and his glorious manifestations.

SERMON.

JESUS THE WONDERFUL.

"And his name shall be called Wonderful."—*Is.* ix.; 6.

The high propriety of this appellation, as applied to Jesus, may be seen,

1. In the vastness of his views. He appeared as a

Jew, but how wonderfully had he emancipated himself from Jewish bigotry! He came to bless nothing short of a world. He grew up in a carpenter's shop at Nazareth; and yet his knowledge abashed the sages of his time. He lived among the most peculiar of people and in a most peculiar age; and yet the interest attaching to his character is neither local nor temporary.

2. In the calm confidence which he always cherished in the accomplishment of his vast objects. He proposed to change the religious sentiment and life of the world. And yet he knew his own stay was brief; that not even his own disciples understood his intentions; that he should meet an ignominious and violent death; and that civil power, learning, and religion should combine to crush, into contempt and forgetfulness, his principles and his name; but he never despaired. His heart seemed always full of hope, and his language, bespoke his calm, settled, quiet confidence in his success, even when all outward circumstances predicted nothing but defeat.

3. He was wonderful in the authority which he claimed. He wore the robes of a peasant, but he claimed prerogatives that would have seemed presumptuous in a Roman Emperor. The Mosaic system and sacred temple and Sabbath, he handled as though he was their Lord.

4. He was wonderful in his patience.—Pure and spotless and wise himself, corruption and ignorance and superstition must have tried him in others. But the mistakes, the prejudices, and the bad spirit of his friends;

5. *He was wonderful in his benevolence.*—He did not share at all in the narrowness of feeling prevailing about him. Others sought only the glory of Judea; he sought the good of the world. His benevolence was world-wide in its expansiveness. It reached the whole human race. He loved man as man. See this in the parable of the Good Samaritan. As he approached, the prophet cried, "Ho every one that thirsteth, come ye to the waters." And he closed his ministry on the earth, that had given him a life of suffering and a death of ignominy, by the command; "Go ye into all the world and preach the gospel to every creature." None of his enemies saw the least indication of revenge; and every needy outcast felt confident of his sympathy. His suavity of manners attracted all to him, and his love was ready with a blessing.

6. *He was wonderful in combining the highest dignity of character with the deepest condescension.* He associated with publicans and sinners, yet there was nothing which encouraged the low and vulgar; side by side did he stand with earth's loftiest dignitaries, yet he discovered no pride or ostentation. With a majestic calmness he says to Pilate, "I am a king;" and then with the sweetest humility he washes his disciples' feet.

APPLICATION.

1. *We have here a beautiful example.*—In dignity of character, simplicity of manners, sweetness of spirit, purity of intention, and in a whole-hearted self-sacrifice,

Jesus stands before us as a pattern. Wonderfully pure, lucid and bright is the example of Jesus, worthy of all acceptation.

2. Here is a Guide of wonderful skill. No tempter ever misled him. Follow him, and ye shall not walk in darkness.

3. Here is One wonderful in power, all exercised for the protection and good of such as love and trust him. Earth, sea, and air, diseases and death, obey his bidding. Devils tremble, angels minister, the heaven opens, and the earth quakes at the sound of his voice. See the loaves, the fish, the lepers, the blind, the dead, all at his control. Wonderful power! and all waiting on the wants of mortals.

4. And all this you reject, O ye thoughtless sinners. This is he whom you crucify afresh, O ye backsliders. Will you do it still?

5. This wonderful One we are about to remember at his table. Will you go away, O ye who profess to love him?

SERMON.

JESUS THE BEAUTIFUL.

"He is altogether lovely—*Songs* v.; 16.

The topic suggested by these words, as usually understood, is the beauty of the character of Jesus. We shall inquire,

I. What constitutes beauty or loveliness?

II. What renders the character of Jesus beautiful?
I. What constitutes beauty or loveliness?

To this we reply, in general terms, that the chief elements of beauty seem to be, 1st, Harmony; 2d, Usefulness.

1. For any thing or person to be beautiful, it, or he, or she, must be in harmony with itself, or himself, or herself. In face, in form, in gait, in manners, if there be want of harmony, there is want of beauty. It is harmony of each part with the whole, and of all parts with each other, that constitutes the beauty of architecture, of painting, of music, of sculpture, and,

2. It must be in harmony with all around it, or with the Universe. The architecture, the music, the painting, must be in the right place, and at the right time, or beauty is sacrificed. Merry music at a funeral, or a dirge at a wedding, would not be in harmony with circumstances, and so would not be beautiful. Each of two men wrought a figure to stand on an eminence. When seen on the ground, the one received the praise; when elevated to the intended height, it was given to the other. The beauty was in the adaptation to place. So actions which are beautiful in a child, would be any thing but lovely in old age. So in oratory and preaching, adaptation is beauty. So in style. "It is true, by the Gods," is beautifully earnest. But to see "a passion torn to tatters" over a trifle,—

"Ocean into tempest tossed
To waft a feather or to drown a fly,"

how absurd, how offensive to good taste, how destitute of beauty! So the beauty of the body is having all the members harmonise—having the head, the feet, &c. just where they should be and just as they should be. So the beauty of the mind is in its rightful balance; the judgment, the passions, and all other powers in their rightful place, and wielding their rightful degree of power. So the beauty of society, from the family upward, consists in its harmony—each member being in its place.

So then harmony, proportion, fitness, is an element of beauty, in things, persons, actions. So God's worlds are beautiful; they move in harmony, showing the happy balancing of forces.

2. The second element of beauty is usefulness. When God created this world, he pronounced it good, *very good.* The bud and the blossom are beautiful, as they give promise of fruit. We are terrified at power without wisdom to direct it; we shrink from skill without goodness,—for we feel that we are in danger.

There is then no beauty of character without goodness; and the beauty of moral character is holiness. Hence there is nothing really and truly beautiful that is not good, or that does not tend to good.

II. What renders the character of Jesus Christ beautiful?

1. Much has been said of the beauty of his person; but of this there is no solid evidence. The beauty of Jesus is the beauty of character; and he will be found beautiful in proportion as he is found in harmony with his relations, in harmony with his declarations, and in harmony with his mission.

Let us look at the relations he sustained.

He was God's only begotten, appearing in the form and authority of God. Did he sustain the dignity of that relation? Did he do so on the banks of Jordan? Did he do it in the wilderness in his conflict with the tempter? Did he in the temple? Did he when confronting the Lawyers, Pharisees, Sadducees, Herodians? Did he when teaching on the mountain? Did he in the garden? Did he before the bar of Pilate? Did he on the cross? Did he on the third day as he arose from the dead? Did he when a cloud received him up out of sight into heaven? Was there a word or act in all his life that was inconsistent with his lofty origin? Not one.

Look at him in his relation to the law of God, ceremonial and moral. Perfect harmony is here likewise. The law was in his heart. He magnified and made it honorable. Look at him in his relations to men. How did he act towards his parents? See his obedience to them, and his care of his mother. His brothers and sisters, did he disown them? How did he act toward the suffering? His eyes filled with tears at their woe, and virtue went out all around from him, to heal and bless. How toward the guilty penitent? Go and sin no more. How toward his enemies? Rebukes them sharply; weeps over them; prays for them; dies for them.

2. Was he in harmony with his declarations? Who ever entangled him in his talk into an inconsistency? Who ever caught him in an untruth? The beauty of truth shone clear in him; for he was the truth.

3. Was he in harmony with his mission? He came to seek and to save; and when and where did he turn aside from this great work? Did Satan seduce or frighten him in the wilderness? Did the Herodians at Jerusalem entice him to seek a crown? Did toil weary him of his work? Did he faint utterly in the garden, or quail at the mob? Did he show any weakness before Pilate? Did he falter when the hour and powers of darkness were all around him; when friends forsook and a disciple denied? Did he repent of his undertaking when crowds reviled him, wagging their heads? Did his conduct in these trying scenes harmonize with his teachings and mission? Did he, like thousands, disavow his declarations and compromise his principles? No. No. He scorns to save himself by treachery. "Thou sayest that I am a King;" "To this end was I born," are the frank confessions to Pilate.

Behold in all these scenes the beauty of unbending integrity, uncompromising fidelity, unshrinking firmness, unwearied patience, and unconquerable love.

> "Here his whole name appears complete;
> Nor wit can guess, nor reason prove,
> Which of the letters best is writ,
> The Power, the Wisdom, or the Love."

Here is seen in its full proportions his character, and it is truth and goodness incarnate, it is indeed beautiful, very beautiful,—"altogether lovely."

SERMON.

IMPORTANCE OF ADHERING TO OUR CONVICTIONS OF DUTY.

"Thy God whom thou servest continually, he will deliver thee."
Daniel vi: 16.

Note Daniel's character, condition, and conduct. Its immediate effect; upon the King; upon his enemies.

1. Such adherence as this is the only ground of inward peace. We are so constituted that a violation of a law is followed with pain. If a physical law, the effect is physical pain; if a moral law, it is moral pain. This moral pain involves the loss of self respect; it implies the condemnation of the conscience, for it cannot be destroyed, and there are times when its voice will be heard. And this agrees with the assurance,—"There is no peace to the wicked."

2. It exerts a most happy influence upon the character. It makes its virtues grow strong, its courage enlarge, its moral power multiply. Its absence, on the other hand, leaves one with no fixed principles. He has no settled standard, and hence no fixedness of purpose. He becomes all things to all men, in a most vicious sense. His object being his own pleasure or profit, he can never be trusted. Trying to please all, he pleases none. God made him a man, and he has made himself a slave.

3. It is the only method of obtaining more light respecting truth and duty. "Then shall ye know if ye

follow on to know the Lord." "He that followeth me shall not walk in darkness." These assurances, as well as our own observation, show the dependence of light upon fidelity.

4. It attracts attention to the truth and to its advocates. The virtue of fidelity is seldom left unnoticed. Heaven, earth and hell gaze on the faithful soul. See Job. He was the observed of God, of Satan, of his human enemies and friends. It has been so with all such characters in and out of scripture. Examples.

5. It advances the cause of truth. Truth, in a fair contest, is always the victor. The great difficulty is to present it fairly, and let it be seen as it is. Falsehood resorts to mobs, and fines, and faggots, and the inquisition; and what is this but the confession of her moral weakness?

6. It restrains the wicked. Herod heard John gladly, and feared him when dead. So vice is always troubled in the presence of such high virtue.

7. It lays the foundation for great good in the future—a good whose magnitude justifies any cost to which fidelity may be subjected. The virtue may, perhaps, be sneered at, at the time, but it is reverenced afterward, and inspires multitudes to practice it. See Job's patience, Moses' meekness, Abraham's faith, Christ's life, teachings and death.

8. By contrast, it shows the evils of the opposite course. See the mother of harlots, once the Bride of Christ! How came she thus? See the great ecclesiastical organizations, becoming the bulwark of Slavery. Whence is this? See the United States' Constitution

guaranteeing support to despotism. How came it there?
Why has ***** a sword in his hand, and a Colonel's
commission in the Massachusetts Volunteers, who once
contended for the inviolability of human life? Why
does ***** present that sword to a military chieftain,
after having written a Prize Essay on Peace? Why
does ***** justify fighting in Rhode-Island, after having once, before the public, solemnly committed himself to the cause of peace? We will not judge the
heart, but fear that fidelity here may have been wanting.

This rule violated, makes sinners, and fills perdition.
This rule kept, makes angels. This rule adopted by a
sinner, is conversion.

APPLICATION.

1. We see the seal of reprobation set on the doctrine of expediency; viz: That we may do evil that good may come.

2. We see the power of truth. Truth uttered faithfully, lived faithfully, is eternal and mighty.

3. We see the method in which reforms progress. The leaders are sacrificed; but in after years their ashes are gathered with reverence.

4. We need the strength of God in the day of trouble.

SERMON.

THE BETTER COUNTRY.

"But now they desire a better country, that is, a heavenly."— *Hebrews* xi.: 16.

I. What is meant by country?
II. What by the better country?
III. Why is it a better country?
IV. Who will enjoy that better country?
V. Reflections.

I. What is meant by country?
1. Country is the place of one's birth.
2. Our place of residence, or our adopted place of residence.
3. Thinly settled; not abounding in cities.
4. Earth,—in distinction from heaven.

II. What by the better country?
1. The land of promise, or Canaan, which Israel sought through the forty years' journey in the wilderness.
2. The rest that remains for the people of God,— which Canaan typified.

III. Why is it a better country?
1. It is free from physical evils,—Poverty, dishonor, shame, persecution, sickness, painful separations, death.

1st. There is no War with its fields of blood, sacked cities, and its unutterable horrors. 2d. No Slavery with its untold abominations; its whips, its gags, its coffles and prisons, its blood-hounds and infantry to hunt down flying bondmen. No Slave Ships from whose holds human beings are taken to feed sharks—more merciful than man. No 'land of steady habits' to refuse the colored man his rights. No United States' Constitution, or Court, or Officer, to return the fugitive slave. 3d. No drunkards or drunkard-makers, to go through the land followed by a train of woes.

2. It is free from intellectual disease. No insanity; no such defects in the reasoning powers as makes the soul the victim of dangerous and destructive errors.

3. The body and intellect are free from weariness. They shall not tire in their action, shall not lose their force in the toil to which they shall be dedicated.

4. It is free from moral evils. There are no God-haters; no Jesus Christ-haters; no man-haters; no malice and rage; no covetous, no seducers.

> "Those holy gates forever bar
> Pollution, sin and shame;
> And none will gain admittance there,
> But followers of the Lamb."

O, it is better, *far better*, than this country we now inhabit.

But again it is better, because,

1st. There is greater knowledge. 2d. There is greater, more intense, love. 3d. The society is of the highest, purest kind. 4th. It far exceeds in beauty all that we have ever seen below. 5th. It excels in music. Justice and mercy, righteousness and peace, harmonize, and their blended utterance is full of melody. 6th. It is more extensive. Its fields of glory we can never explore; its sources of wisdom we can never exhaust. 7th. It is permanent. It will be home, sweet home, always forever home; our and our Father's home.

    IV. Who will enjoy it?
1. The pure in heart.
2. The poor in spirit.
3. Those persecuted for righteousness' sake.
4. The penitent.
5. The believing.
6. The obedient.

REMARKS.

1. We are all citizens of one great country, and that country is the world; and our countrymen are all mankind. We have all one blood, one Father, one Savior, one Judge.

2. There is a better country, and we may enjoy it; a heavenly, a prepared country; and into that shall be gathered the citizens of every earthly land, whose hearts are fitted for the heavenly inheritance.

3. That which is often called patriotism, is treason against God, a trampling upon the second commandment, a crusade against the government of heaven.

4. The prejudices we have against men of other lands and colors is anti-bible, anti-christian, anti-heaven.

SERMON.

MAKING KNOWN GOD.

"Whom therefore ye ignorantly worship, Him declare I unto you."—*Acts* xvii.: 23.

In these words we note,
I. That there is a great fact stated.
II. There is a great duty involved.

The fact is that men ignorantly worship an unknown God. The duty is that of making known to all men the character of the true God.

The fact implies,

1. That there is a great Supreme Being. All races of men are impressed with this idea; Idol worship in all its forms implies this. Why are all men disposed to worship, if it be not so that there is a great Being who made the heart conformable to this service? In the religious rites which are adopted, savage and civilized nations give their testimony to this great first truth. They find it written out on the face of the heavens and earth. It is imaged in man's organic structure, and daguerreotyped on his heart.

2. It implies also that man has a capacity for perceiving and feeling that there is a God. The fool hath said, and may still say, there is no God; yet a voice shall be heard within, troubling the thoughts as did the hand-writing on the wall. He has windows to his soul, and he has hard work to keep them shut. Phrenology, consciousness, and observation, prove this.

3. It is implied that this Being can be known. That is, his existence and character and will may be known; not his essence. By searching, we cannot find out God in this last sense. Nothing but an infinite mind could grasp an infinite mind. But it is possible that very much should be learned of him.

If there be a God, he is certainly able to make beings capable of apprehending him. He will also be disposed to be known; for we can hardly conceive of an intelligent being who does not cherish this desire. And the fact that beings exist, endowed with a nature ever turning itself to the idea of a God, proves God's disposition to be known.

But how is this to be done?

1st. By the things that he has made. These things declare him. So says David. "The heavens declare the glory of God, and the firmament showeth his handy work." So says Paul. "The invisible things of him from the creation of the world are clearly seen, being understood by the things that are made." Old Ocean, with its hoary locks, and its wild bass in the anthem of nature, speaks of him. So do the mountains of granite, the vast prairie, the volcano, the tempest, the earthquake, the mighty heavings of material forces; the vast, the grand, the sublime; the voice of Niagara. The beautiful things of earth and sky, scenes, colors, sounds. The useful materials for food and raiment; man, and his capabilities; the senses and their uses; the intellect and its powers; the moral sense with its clear dictations of right; "the human face divine," that mirror of the soul, showing its features to others; *all these* declare HIM, who is the great Master-soul, the Maker of all.

2d. By the teachings of his Spirit. Holy men of old spake as they were moved by the Holy Ghost. This is proved by the testimony of those who have had this revelation; by miracles, signs, and wonders, which God did by them, and by predictions which were fulfilled.

3d. By the teachings of his Son. "God—hath in these last days spoken unto us by his Son." And he is the great, the reliable Teacher, above all others. "No man knoweth the Father but the Son, and he to whom the Son shall reveal him."

4th. It is implied that men may and do mistake the character and will of God, and so ignorantly worship. This is clear from the text, and from facts. Pagans, Jews, Mohammedans, Christians, cannot all be correct in their views of God; much less can all the various sects among these. The God of Calvin, and of Arminius, in his character and will, must be somewhat different. It is so of Arius and Augustine, or of Trinitarian and Unitarian.

5th. It implies that there is a cause or reason why men ignorantly worship. 1st. This fault is not in God; for he has revealed himself most clearly. 2d. The fault is in man, when there is fault, for there may be ignorance in a greater or less degree, even where there is very high honesty of heart. Yet even this shall have proceeded originally from some violation of the divine law. 3d. But the great primary cause is, men have "not liked to retain God in their knowledge;" they have "loved darkness rather than light;" they have been "blinded by the God of this world."

II. The duty involved, is,

1. To obtain correct views of God; so that the Being whom we worship shall not be some great *Unknown*, some vast abstraction, but a reality.

2. To make known Him who is true to all our race. O, what a work is here, for the pulpit, the Sabbath School, for every sphere where we may gain access to the minds of mortals!

APPLICATION.

1. Is not this a glorious Being we have declared unto you? It is the God of nature, of the bible, of man, of the universe; the pure and living God. It is no partial, sleeping Deity; but powerful, wise, and good.

2. Multitudes worship an unknown God. The Greeks had an altar erected, and thus inscribed. But all who worship any other than the true God, worship Gods unknown. Jupiter, Mars, Venus, Bacchus, were worshipped of old, but they were all imaginary, as are many of the divinities of the present time. They do so who worship a God without mercy, justice; who is partial or terrible as a grim idol, or as passionate and weak as themselves.

3. Will not those ignorant worshippers rise up in judgment against us, if we, in our higher knowledge, do not worship at all?

4. We may see the wretchedness of those who worship false or imaginary deities. The soul is constantly crying out for a divinity, but finds it not.

5. We may see the tendency there is in us to make God like ourselves. Men seek the sanctions of religion for whatever they resolve not to abandon; and so we have a War God, a Man-Eating, or a Man-Stealing God.

SERMON.

THE VISIT TO THE MOUNT.

"It is good for us to be here."—*Matt.* xvii. : 4.

Two questions present themselves.
I. Was this declaration true?
II. If so, why?
I. It was true.

1. Not because the Apostles were always correct in their opinions or actions. See Peter and Paul at Antioch, and Paul and Barnabas when they parted. But it was true,

1. Because they were led or directed there by their Master. "Jesus taketh Peter and James and John his brother, and bringeth them up into a high mountain apart." It is always good to be where the Master tells us to be. In heaven all are where he tells them to be, and doing what he tells them to do.

2. Because they saw the glory of their Master. He was transfigured before them. He stood revealed in

the brightness of his Father's glory. It was good to see this.

3. Because they heard the Almighty Father's voice, ratifying and sealing the mission of his Son. "This is my beloved Son, in whom I am well pleased: hear ye him." It was good to hear this. It was adapted to strengthen their faith; to send them down more confident in their Master and their work.

4. Because they saw and heard Moses and Elias; thus having the highest assurance of a spiritual world.

5. Because they heard Moses and Elias and Jesus converse respecting the death of Jesus. Surely it was good to hear about that which was so important, and which they would afterward understand more fully. In short, it is good to be where, 1st. The highest authority utters its voice; where the highest truths are announced; 2d. The great Exemplar is pointed out; 3d. The glory of the opening future is seen.

> "The opening heavens around us shine,
> With beams of sacred bliss."

APPLICATION.

1. We see the value of a preached Gospel. The highest authority is there; the great Exemplar is there; the glory that eye hath not seen is there.

2. The value of the Scripture record. The highest truths are there.

3. The value of the Conference Meeting. It is good to be there, to talk over the great truths revealed on the mount.

*20

4. The value of meditating upon, and understanding the death of Christ.

5. It is good to be where God would have us be; to hear what God would have us hear; to do what God would have us do.

6. It is sometimes good to be where it is not good to stay. Peter did not see this, and so said, "Let us make here three tabernacles." It is good to be at meeting, but not good to stay always. It is good to labor, but it is also good to rest.

7. It is often good to be where we would have thought it *not* good to be; to suffer what we think is not good to suffer.

The following Sermon is founded on the same incident as the former; and among other things it will serve to show the various uses he made of the same passage. It has been often said by himself and others, that it was almost impossible for him to repeat a sermon, even when having before him the same outline. The same general thoughts he could, of course, present a second time, but the specific impressions left on his audience would vary widely. Only a few of the ideas in the former discourse will be found repeated here.

SERMON.

THE GREAT CONFERENCE.—TEXT, *Luke*, ix.; 28—35.

The Conference described here was not great in its numbers; for it consisted of only six members—half the number that afterward assembled in the upper room. In this respect it did not compare at all with the gathering on the day of Pentecost, when more than three thousand listened to the sermon of Peter. A little handful surely, yet we think it was *great*.

1. It was great in the character of those who composed it. MOSES was very great in his possession of the learning and wisdom of the Egyptians; he was great in his position; in his nearness to God, as he approached him face to face in the mount; and especially was he great in his choice to suffer affliction with the people of God rather than to enjoy the pleasures of sin. Look at him as he stands before the bush that he may be prepared to stand before Pharaoh. Look at him as he stands with the mysterious rod, stretched out,—the emblem of coming wrath or of coming mercy. See the magicians quail before him. Look at him as he stretches out his hand towards heaven to implore mercy on his foes. Look at him as he descends from the Mount of God, his face all radiant with the glory caught in that sacred communion with Jehovah. See him, at the age of 120 years, his eye not dim and his natural strength not abated, ascending the mount to see the goodly land,

and then laid to rest by his Maker. He is one of this great conference.

Another is Elijah or Elias. It was he who confronted alone four hundred and fifty of the priests of Baal, and proved them liars. See him boldly taunt them with their folly. Look at him as he builds the altars and has the water poured upon them. Look at him in his prayerful might, as rain is withheld and rain given at his request, and as fire comes down at his call. See him as with his mantle he smites Jordan, and piles the waters in a heap. See him in a splendid chariot of fire as he rises to heaven, while Elisha cries out,—" My Father, the chariot of Israel and the horsemen thereof!" He too is on the Mount, as one of this great conference. The great heads of the legal and prophetical dispensations are there.

But the representatives of the new dispensation are there also. There is bold Peter, who first answered " Thou art the Christ the Son of the living God,"— that declaration which was the rock for the foundation of the church. The zealous James and loving John, sons of Zebedee were also there.

And then the son of Mary, the Nazarene, the great prophet of Nazareth was there. He of whom bards had sung with rapture, was there. He of whom Moses in the law and prophets did write, was there. The Shiloah of Jacob was there. The wonderful, the counsellor, was there. The stem and rod of Jesse was there. David's Lord and son was there. He of whom the angels had sung in Bethlehem was there. The opener of eyes and ears was there. There he stood, all clothed in light, the Son of God, the chief corner stone uniting the two dispensations; in himself the head over all things to the church.

And, finally, the Father was there, and his voice was heard out of the beautiful cloud, saying; "This is my beloved Son." Great in the character of its members was this conference.

2. It was great in its subject of converse. The glory of God in the salvation of the world; peace on earth and good will to men; the fulfilment of the law and the prophets; the wonderful decease of Christ; his great work and mission; the plan by which God could be just and yet the justifier of him that believeth in Jesus;— these were the various features of that great subject which called together that great conference.

3. It was great in its object. We may suppose this to be to make known to his disciples more clearly his character and mission. 1st. He showed them that he was greater than Moses or the prophets. In this conference this was clearly seen; his transcendant brightness and the voice from heaven clearly decided this. And this was important, as may be seen in Peter's strong attachment to Jewish rites. 2d. To show them that the law and the prophets were closing their mission, and parting with their authority; that a new dispensation was about commencing. 3d. To open before them a glimpse of heaven, or of the glorified state. See his raiment, his countenance; it was somewhat like Paul's journey to the third heavens. 4th. In short to prepare the three, who were to witness his death, to stand firm and trustful, not staggering through unbelief

at the promise of God, but to testify in faith, "This is the Son of God." And so in after years, Peter says, "We have not followed cunningly devised fables—but were eye witnesses of his majesty."

4. It was great in its results. It did impress them deeply and favorably. Peter exclaimed, "It is good for us to be here." It did strengthen their faith. "We heard him in the holy mount," was the decisive proof, which was given to skepticism, of Jesus being the Messiah.

APPLICATION.

1. We do well to ascend the mount for prayer and meditation, apart, aside, alone, or with a few disciples. It will be good to be there, especially if we take Moses and the prophets with us, and Jesus to expound them. Moses and the prophets to tell us what was and was to be, and Jesus to tell us what is and is to be.

2. We are taught the transcendant character of the Son of God. Greater than Moses or Elijah, greater even than angels. Let us hear him reverently, according to the Father's direction.

3. We see how to have a profitable conference. Imitate Jesus in going up to commune with God; and imitate the disciples in gazing on his glory, and listening to the words of God.

4. We see what it was that specially, deeply interested them—the decease which he should accomplish at Jerusalem. This also is what should most deeply interest us.

SERMON.

THE LOOK OF LOVE.

"And the Lord turned and looked upon Peter."—*Luke* xxii.: 61.

This was a wonderful look. It had a wonderful effect. There was a mighty power in it. It reached Peter's head and heart; it touched his conscience and opened the flood-gates of the soul; remembrance was awakened and penitential tears began to flow.

It might perhaps be called a look of reproach, called forth by the deep ingratitude which the disciple had shown. Or it might be called a look of wonder, if Jesus who had foreseen and foretold this denial could feel wonder. Or it might be regarded as a look of pity over such weakness as had been disclosed.

It was a *revealing* look. It revealed the character of Jesus, the heart of God, and the weakness and guilt of man. It revealed the interesting fact that the divine and human can meet and do meet.

It was a look of love; and our topic will be, THE LOOK OF LOVE.

I. The eye that first beheld the earth rising from its formless state into order and life, the beauty of the beasts and birds and flowers, the first rising and setting sun, the moon in her brightness, the stars in their grandeur, must have witnessed a most lovely appearance. Morning stars sang together, and the Sons of God shouted for joy. Something looked on them and they looked on something, and *there* was *the look of love*.

Again. Adam slept. He awoke, and there stood before him one so like him and yet so unlike, bone of his bone and flesh of his flesh;

>———"grace in her steps, heaven in her eye,
> In every gesture dignity and love."

Adam looked on his heaven-formed bride, and it was *the look of love.* Eve looked on the God-given bridegroom, and it was *the look of love.* So when congenial spirits meet at the bridal-altar, there is *the look of love.*

Behold the young mother gazing on her first born, and there you shall see the look of love; and should that babe be in danger, that look of love shall rise almost to an agonizing intensity; still it is love's look.

Again. That was the look of love, when God gazed on the world with that deep interest for its welfare that gave his only begotten Son for its redemption. See that love embodied in Jesus weeping over Jerusalem, and at the grave of Lazarus.

> " O for this love let rocks and hills
> Their lasting silence break!"

And this love looked out in the drapery of mourning from the cross, when, in the form and words of compassion, it cried, "Father forgive them, for they know not what they do."

And so that look appears when the love of God is shed abroad in the heart; when the soul perceives the lovelines of truth, and the beauty of holiness, then by the soul's eye is the look of love discovered. And how shall it irradiate the countenances of the myriads that no man can number, when, on the mount of heavenly vision, they shall see Jesus as he is!

II. What is implied in this look?

1. There is a source, origin, or cause, from whence it springs. There is a heart in which it is generated, and out from which it flows, as a spring of living water. Thus when we see the material world, with lovely face beaming upon us, we know there is a source whence all this beauty springs. So when we see the moral being all radiant with moral beauty, we know there is a fountain from which it flows up to our view. So when the man face divine looks upon us in its sweetness, with its look of love, we know that down in the depths of the soul there is a flame of love that the waters cannot quench.

2. It implies that there is a medium by which this feeling is communicated. What a wonderful power has the human countenance to express the soul's emotions! Let malice and rage—those fires of hell—be in the soul, and how soon are they daguerreotyped on the countenance! When Cain was wroth his countenance fell. How the face will tell of the troubled sea that cannot rest! But when peace and joy and love fill the soul, it will be seen in the eye; the whole face shall glow with radiance. Let but the voice be heard, and it shall harmonize with the soul as it gives out its look of love.

It implies that this look has its uses; but these we shall see if we note,

III. Its power.

1. It has a revealing power. It tells of the source of love. It leads us back till we come to Him who is said to be Love. 1st. Creation is one of God's looks of love.

2d. Redemption is another of these looks of love. All along while this plan is being developed, God's face of love is seen looking out on us from the face of Jesus Christ. 3d. It tells of the joys which the Father has prepared for them that love him. 4th. It reveals our relationship to God, to angels, to the good and the pure. The look we see and the look we give tell who we are and to whom we belong. 5th. It reveals true happiness and how to obtain it.

2. It has a transforming power. "Beholding with open face as in a glass the glory of the Lord, we are changed into the same image, from glory to glory." Like begets like. Hence the proverb, " like priest, like people ;" that is, this is its tendency. A look of love has often produced a look of love where it had long been a stranger.

3. It has a convincing power. How that look, indicated in the text, convinced Peter! It gives often to the sword of the spirit its keenest edge.

4. It has a reclaiming and subduing power. It lays hold on every moral chord of the soul, it enters the holiest of all in the human heart, and there pleads with the eloquence of tears the cause of Jesus. It melts the soul into tenderness, and then says, "*return.*"

APPLICATION.

1. We learn the character of God. " God is love ;" and his looks through Creation and Redemption are the proofs.

2. Jesus is the lovely One. In his moral character we behold it. His love looks out in his life and death

with great power to subdue. O sinner, behold that face; scan that look. O backslider, look at that countenance and let it melt you.

3. We learn how to be happy. We must be loving, and we shall be beloved. An unloving being is wretched.

4. We learn how to be useful. Be filled with love. This love fills God's heart, and so he creates and redeems. This love fills the heart of Jesus, and so he works and dies. This love filled Paul's heart, and so he spends all cheerfully for the sake of Christ and of sinners. It fills Luther, and he becomes nerved for the battles of the truth. It fills Howard, and he spends fortune and life for the good of the outcast and imprisoned. Let it fill ours and our work shall be glorious.

5. We learn the way to teach children. The look and the tone of love, prompted by the heart of love, shall act on them with a magic force.

6. To give this look in all its power, love must fill the soul. The face is but the mirror, and the eye is but the window of the soul; and so the look will show its features and reflect its image.

SERMON.

A RECIPE FOR A HAPPY NEW YEAR.

"Happy is he that hath the God of Jacob for his help, whose hope is in the Lord his God."—*Ps.* cxlvi.: 5.

"Whoso trusteth in the Lord, happy is he."—*Prov.* xvi.: 20.

"Jesus answered and said unto him, What I do thou knowest not now, but thou shalt know hereafter."—*John* xiii.: 7.

Happiness has been said by a poet to be the aim and end of our being. Certain it is that all intelligent beings, from their very nature, desire and seek it. This implies that it is to some extent a lawful object of pursuit, and shows the importance attaching to the subject.

I. What is happiness? It is enjoyment, more or less full, complete, perfect. To have physical, mental, moral, and spiritual joy; to have all these departments of our nature ministers of pleasure. This is to be happy.

II. What are the conditions of human happiness?

1. We must be in harmony with ourselves. Every department and power of our natures must be filling its true sphere, exercising its just measure of authority, and doing its appropriate work. The physical must not be sacrificed to the mental, nor the mental to the physical, nor the moral to either.

2. We must be in harmony with our neighbor. As social beings we cannot be happy alone, nor independent of the aid of others. God has said, " It is not good for man to be alone;" and our nature and experience attest to its truth. And so he cannot be happy while hating his neighbor. He cannot spare his neighbor's sympathy and confidence. The absence of this harmony with his neighbor fills the world with evil. See the world as it has been; war, slavery, intemperance, oppression; would any of these evils exist if the second command had been kept?

3. We must be in harmony with God,—with God's character, will, law, word. God's law or will is in harmony with man's highest good; and so harmony with himself and harmony with God mutually imply each other. By self we do not mean his appetites, passions, but his nature; what he was designed to be,

and what he is capable of being. Now if man is in harmony with God's law, physical, mental, and moral, he is and must be happy. All beings are happy when they are fulfilling the end of their existence.

III. What are the chief elements of this harmony with self, neighbor and God?

1. Faith, trust, or confidence in God. If there be a God he is all wise, all powerful, all good ; and so he is to be believed, trusted, confided in. As social beings and dependent, it is impossible to be happy without confidence. The child, the parent, the wife, the husband, the friend, the christian, find happiness here. They wish some breast on which to lean, some heart in which to confide. Look at the holy men of old when tried, how they looked up in confidence to God and grew peaceful and happy. Without faith happiness has no foundation, life no comfort.

2. A right heart—a good conscience. Without a right heart no good conscience ; and without this last no happiness. A heart reproaching and condemning us, a guilty conscience goading us, must destroy happiness.

3. *Hope* in God. All evils are bearable while hope is among them; but without hope the heart breaks. So the Scriptures set a high value on hope. "Hope thou in God," cries the Psalmist addressing his soul, as if assured that this would dissipate his sorrow. "Which hope we have as an anchor of the soul." "For a helmet the hope of salvation." Hope is essential to happiness, for often its promise of something better in the future is all the legacy left us. A wild, waste, howling wilderness would this world be without it.

*21

4. *Love* to God and man ; love to truth, goodness, purity. Faith, hope, charity, or love, these three in the soul, and happiness is the sure result. When these three great principles are in full exercise in the soul, then there is, 1st, a right heart ; 2d, a good conscience ; 3d, a meek, humble spirit ; 4th, self-control ; 5th, self-denial ; 6th, an obedient spirit. Then in wishing all happy, and in aiming to make all happy, we are happy.

IV. What proof is there that this is the true recipe ?

1. Scripture testimony. The Old Testament says, " Happy is that people whose God is the Lord ;" and the New Testament says, " happy are ye if ye do them." " Who shall harm you if ye be followers of that which is good ?" " Great peace have they that love thy law, and nothing shall offend them." " Fear not little flock, for it is your Father's good pleasure to give you the Kingdom." " All things work together for good to them that love God."

2. Scripture examples. Enoch and Elijah, Daniel, Stephen, Simeon, John, Jesus. They tell of joy unspeakable and full of glory ; of peace like a river, passing all understanding. " Mark the perfect man and behold the upright, for the end of that man is peace."

3. Observation. Men of faith, hope, love, are the happy ones.

4. Experience. All who accept this recipe know that happiness is the sure result.

5. Man's nature, relations, and faculties, all show that, in order to be happy, we must believe, must be clear from guilt, must love God and keep his commandments. His nature can only thus be satisfied ; his re-

lations can only thus be honored; his duties can only thus be performed.

APPLICATION.

1. We see one of the great, the almost universal, errors of men, viz: That riches bring happiness. They *may aid* in increasing and diffusing happiness, but can never create it.

2. Another error seen here is, that fame will make one happy. A reputation resting on the popular opinion is but a bubble on the stream, a vapor in the morning. The fickle multitude may cry "Crucify him," before the echoes of their "Hosanna" have died away on the ear. In a word, we may see that happiness is not found in the outward.

3. We see our duty. If unhappy, we should seek to know the cause. Why? why? why? Is it thy poverty? Is it thy misfortune? Think. Is it not rather thy ambition? Does not thy soul long to be greatest. Is it not thy temper unsubdued, and unrestrained? Is it not thy stubborn will that refuses to bend to truth? Thy proud mind that will not part with its haughtiness? In a word, is not thy heart set on the earth? Do you not sow to the flesh and look for heavenly fruit? And then our duty is, 1st. To be happy ourselves. 2d. To teach our children how to be happy. 3d. To make all around us happy.

4. Who will take this recipe home with them and apply it? Let me tell you, proud young man, vain young woman, that your visions of happiness, founded on outward things, will vanish like a dream, and make

each year one of bitterer disappiontment, and deeper sorrow. But take this recipe, and the thousand wishes breaking, thoughtlessly and seriously, from the lips about you, will be realized in the enjoyment of a "Happy New Year."

SERMON.*

THE FUGITIVE SLAVE LAW.

"We ought to obey God rather than men."—*Acts*, v.: 29.

Let us seriously and thoughtfully ponder this answer of the Apostle. Seriously, we say; for, if we mistake not, we are called to decide the same question, at the hazard of fine, imprisonment, if not of death.

I. Note first, that the authority to which they refused to yield, was the highest ecclesiastical authority in Judea; and that they acted on the same principle when commanded to abjure christianity by the Roman powers, even to martyrdom.

II. What is implied in these words?

1. They do *not* imply that Family Government does not rightfully exist. "Children obey your parents," is a divine command; but even this obedience is required only *in the Lord*. We are not directly told, in the New Testament, what means may be employed

---

* The date of this discourse is very nearly fixed by its subject, object, and allusions.

to enforce this command. The Mosaic code admitted of life taking in Family Government.

2. They do not imply that there is no rightful Church government. Such government exists, and has its discipline marked out. "Obey them that have the rule over you," &c.

3. Nor do they imply the non-existence of Civil Government. "The powers that be are ordained of God." These are recognized by the Apostles, and obedience to them enjoined in all things not contrary to God's law; and submission to their penalties when refusing to obey, is likewise required.

But these words do imply,

1. That God is the supreme Ruler, Lawgiver, and Governor of individuals, families, churches, and nations. This is taught by Reason, by God's law, and by his Son.

2. That God's law is universally binding on all his rational creation; on men, angels, devils, churches, nations, courts, judges, juries, commissioners, congresses, presidents, kings, emperors, and constitutions. This higher law of the Most High God, is always and every where paramount.

3. That any law or statute which contravenes the law of God, is destitute of authority in the sight of God, and should be treated as null and void;—treated as Daniel treated the edict of Darius; treated as Shadrach treated the edict to bow down and worship the image; treated as the Apostles treated the requirements of the Sanhedrim; treated as the Son of God treated

the propositions of Satan. It should be said to such a law, "Get thee behind me."

4. That men are individually responsible to God for their conduct. We must give account of ourselves to God. And, of course, all are to judge for themselves how far they can rightfully obey Church or State.

5. That unqualified obedience to God's law is binding, under all circumstances, in view of all consequences, and in spite of all threatened penalties. *That law is never suspended.*

If these propositions be true, then may we not answer a question of deep interest that thrills the hearts of multitudes in the Free States; viz: What is our duty in reference to the Fugitive Slave Bill recently made a law by the United States' Congress? and what is the duty of the Fugitive Slave?

(Here give the Law, and indicate how it is usually understood.)

Its aim is to recover the fugitive, whose manhood prompts him to run the fearful risks of an attempted escape. It involves the wicked, heaven-defying claim of property in man; and it requires of all good citizens to recognize that claim and endorse it.

It demands that we aid the Slaveholder in robbing our brother of his inalienable rights.

It demands of us to crucify conscience, to stultify reason, and act as though the slave was a beast.

It requires us to put in peril the liberty of every citizen in the North.

It forbids us to obey the Golden Rule.

It forbids us to feed the hungry, clothe the naked,— to do what if we refuse to do we peril our souls.

And now is it asked, what is our duty?

1. To refuse obedience to the law.
2. To testify against the law.
3. To mark and rebuke those who support the law, and especially the masters in Israel.
4. To exert ourselves in all proper and moral forms to secure the repeal of the law.
5. To remember and pray for its poor proscribed victims.
6. To help the panting fugitive, and aid him in reaching a place of safety from the bloodhounds that are on his track, and from the liabilities of being taken back to his fearful prison-house.

Friends, here is the alternative. Which will you obey, God or man? Jesus Christ or Congress? May none of us sacrifice mercy, in the persons of God's poor, to this monstrosity in civil legislation; and, at last, meet the withering rebuke of Christ,—"Inasmuch as ye did it not to one of the least of these, ye did it not to me."

SERMON:

Addressed to Young Women.

THE ELEMENTS OF FEMALE EXCELLENCE.

"Many daughters have done virtuously, but thou excellest them all."—*Prov.* xxxi.: 29.

These words are a portion of a most interesting description of a virtuous woman. They are the words of King Lemuel, which his mother taught him. But who was Lemuel? This is unknown. "Certainly, not Solomon," says Dr. Clark. The description is written in the Acrostic form. The text is supposed to be the utterance of the husband of the woman, whose character had just been given.

The woman here described, certainly sustained the marriage relation;—yet she might be a *young* woman. Paul teaches that young women should be instructed to love their husbands. Be that as it may; since all young women ought to be prepared to sustain with honor and respect *that* and every other proper relation into which they may be called to enter, I propose to call the attention of the young women of this audience to some things which I deem needful to form the character of a virtuous woman,—to constitute one of those daughters which excel.

I. They should be intelligent.

1. Young women sustain many relations, from which arise many duties. If ignorant of these rela-

tions and duties, how can they honorably sustain the one or perform the other? And if they fail here, they fail, utterly fail, of securing the character indicated in the text.

Every young woman sustains the relation of daughter; usually that of sister, and prospectively that of wife, and mother. Ignorant of the duties connected with these relations, she can never be the excellent daughter, wife, or mother. For example; if she be ignorant of the laws of health, then may she ruin her own and that of those most dear to her. This may be done by badly ventilated rooms, ill adjusted dress, and badly prepared or improper food.

She should know what dress is fit for herself, and what is fit for her husband and children, if she have them; and she should not only know what is fit, but how to prepare and keep it in order. She needs to know the art of being neat—not simply of *seeming* to be so—and of keeping others so about her.

She should know how to prepare food that is healthful and savory. You may, perhaps, smile at these remarks, and be ready to curl your lip with scorn; but let me say to you young women, in all seriousness, that, unless you have a knowledge of household duties, the language of the text can never apply to you. Neglect these admonitions you may, but it will be at the hazard of one day weeping as did an accomplished lady, because she *could not make good bread.* Your face may be beautiful, your form elegant, your voice sweet, your reading extensive, your performances on the Piano inimitable; but *poor bread* from month to month will spoil it all. Fathers, mothers, husbands, children, need good bread.

2. Young women have minds, intellect, mental faculties, as well as physical. Hence the need of knowing what those faculties are, their use, the conditions of their improvement; and without such knowledge you can never excel.

3. Young women have social relations. God has said, "It is not good for man to be alone." True, this marriage relation is optional. But the finger of God points so clearly in one direction, that we have little doubt of his will.

How much knowledge is needed here; and yet how shrouded in darkness and ignorance is this subject. This relation, so full of importance, and so fruitful of wide and lasting consequences, is entered into with the strangest thoughtlessness; and wretchedness, misery, woe, and premature death—yea, even to the third and fourth generation—are the results. If in any earthly relation young women need knowledge, it is here.

But who shall utter a warning voice? Fathers and mothers, sons and daughters, seem to treat the marriage institution as a great speculation, deceiving and being deceived. He that hath ears to hear let him hear. Young women, enter not this relation till you know its duties, and can and mean to fulfil them.

In their social intercourse young women should know what is meant by good manners, good behaviour, the treatment of all with courtesy.

4. Young women have souls—have the moral sense; and so sustain moral relations. They have a

Creator, a Redeemer, and should understand their obligations to them. They have a soul relation to all the human family, and hence are bound to love their neighbors as themselves.

In short, they should know their physical wants and how to supply them; what their social needs are, and how to supply those needs; what their moral nature needs and how to supply those needs. They should know their relations and obligations to God; their relations and obligations to their neighbor; the value and importance of time and influence; what they should be and what they should do. All this their intelligence, if it be what it ought to be, will teach them; and all this ignorance will hide from them.

II. Female excellence requires the possession of a good moral and christian character. The elements of such a character you will find specified in Phil. iv. : 8. Whatsoever things are true, honest, just, pure, lovely, and of good report. These principles must be set like gems in your moral nature,—Daguerreotyped on the heart. Then will you be Kings' daughters indeed, all glorious within; and a beautiful moral character will be the result. When such a character as this is developed, there will be seen a virtuous woman, excelling even the Jewish matron. Such, of course, will be meek, mild, tender, pitiful, courteous, compassionate, making garments like Dorcas, weeping and breaking the costly box like Mary, last at the Cross, and earliest at the Sepulchre, doing what they can in Mercy's cause, like the Frys and the Dixes—'sisters of charity' indeed. Their motto will be that furnished by the singing angels,—

'Glory to God in the highest, on earth Peace, good will to men.'

III. The female character can never attain its proper development, unless the *temper* be properly cultivated and controlled. An uncontrolled temper destroys happiness, and mars character in all; but is peculiarly offensive in young women—daughters, sisters, mothers. It utterly unfits for the performance of any duty as it should be done. Sweetness of disposition will atone for many, very many, outward defects, but no excellence will atone for a bad temper. With a sweet disposition, a young woman becomes the desired one of every circle, bringing light, joy, and happiness, in her train. She brings a wealth above gold or rubies; a joy which no beauty could bestow.

Such an one lightens the infirmities of age, and stamps her beauteous spirit on childhood's tender heart. On her tongue truly is the law of kindness, and where she goes she scatters moral sunshine in her path.

> "Blessed temper, meek and mild,
> Docile as a little child."

Such sweetness of spirit would I have all the young women possess.

Need I present a picture of the opposite, ill-natured, violent, passionate, unreasonable, impatient, fretful, spirit? Alas, for those who possess, and those who are obliged to endure such a temper as this!

IV. Another thing needed to form a character for excellence like that in the text, is Industry. Such was the virtuous woman of King Lemuel. She was no idler, no gossip, no tale-bearer; but she put her hand to the work. She made 'footprints on the sands of time.' Her influence was felt. She was a busy body, not in others' matters, but in her own duties. No indolent, lazy young woman, can ever win the prize of excellence.

V. But to be what we ought to be, that must be *done* which *ought* to be done. Our duties must not only be known, but performed, and performed now—to-day.

Our duty to ourselves, body, mind, and soul, must be done.

Our duty to our children, husbands, fathers, neighbors, &c., must be done.

Our duty to our God and Savior must be done.

Our time must be improved, and our influence exerted.

In fitting ourselves for life's great work and heaven's great rewards, *work is to be done.*

Among those duties let me allude to a few.

1. Be decided. Let no consideration induce you to act contrary to your convictions. Follow not the multitude to do evil.

2. Be careful of your associations, your companions. Give no countenance to the immoral of either sex. Remember your character is too valuable to be trifled with. Give no countenance to a young man of licentious or dissipated habits, and be not deceived by professions. It is possible to smile and smile and be a villain.

3. Avoid corrupting books. All fiction is not injurious, but novels in general are trash, or worse.

4. Beware of corrupting amusements. The Circus, the Theatre, &c., are generally of this character. There *may* be some good there, perhaps, but, in order to get it, you run too much risk. Young people have their parties and plays; they may or may not be innocent. Let your amusements be rational; not childish or immoral.

5. Night associations, night company keeping, and late hours, are bad. They are evil, and tend to evil as do almost all works of darkness. A word to the wise is sufficient. In any association where you may be, if anything immoral is introduced, leave it instantly, if possible. Make no compromise with sin.

6. Is it needful for me to urge the misery and woe which the strange woman—the opposite of the virtuous woman—brings on herself and others? There is no deep more profound than that to which the vicious woman descends. No misery more keen than that which she feels. No influence more contaminating than hers. She is a moral malaria, breeding death wherever she goes. Let young women avoid every avenue which would lead to such a character and end as this. May the young women of this congregation be saved from any such fate.

7. Do you wish to be loved? I know you do; loved permanently, to be worthy of being loved, loved forever; loved by father, mother, brother, sister, husband, children, friends; loved by Jesus, by your Heavenly Father. Then be lovely, be virtuous. If you wish to be despised, scorned, hated, now and ever—

which I know you do not—then be idle and vicious, obstinate and ill-tempered.

In short, motives high, deep, wide, strong, urge you to be what you should be. "Educate the mothers," said the Indian Chief. "What shall be done for France?" asked Napoleon of Madame De Stael. "Give her mothers," was the reply. Let the young women make themselves what they may be and ought to be, and the mothers we shall have; and having them we shall have husbands and fathers and children. Many a moral desert would bud and blossom as the rose, and countless thousands rise up gratefully in the good time coming, and say; "Many daughters have done virtuously, but thou excellest them all."

CHAPTER XIII.

DISCOURSES.

It has already been stated that Mr. Cheney's public discourses were seldom written. In the last years of his life, he was induced to write more than formerly; and we have a few discourses from his pen which were fully written out by his own hand before their delivery. The two Essays which follow, were prepared for the Rhode-Island Ministers' Meeting, consisting principally of Freewill Baptist Ministers, who had united for the purpose of securing mutual improvement. The exercises consisted, chiefly, of reading and criticising Essays on the various moral and religious topics which were, from time to time, selected and assigned to the members. They are among the latest of his productions.

ESSAY.

THE ATONEMENT.

"Were the sufferings of Christ in the Atonement vicarious?"

On this question we remark,

1. "It is a faithful saying, and worthy of all acceptation, that Christ Jesus came into the world to save

sinners." Such is the record of the New Testament. His advent was announced by a Star before unseen, and heaven's minstrelsy over the plains of Judea. The wise men's mission, a troubled king and city, were harbingers of his approach. A stern voice was heard in the wilderness, crying;—"Prepare ye the way of the Lord, make his paths straight." On the banks of Jordan was seen the emblem of the spirit, and the voice of the Most High was heard, saying,—"This is my beloved Son, in whom I am well pleased." That heaven's power and goodness had come to earth, was attested by the opening of the eyes of the blind, the unstopping of the ears of the deaf, by the loosened tongues of the dumb, the leaping of the lame, and the raising of the dead. That wondrous wisdom had come to earth, might be known by the listening thousands who hung on the lips of Jesus, and wondered at the gracious words that proceeded out of his mouth. Truly the Light and Life were manifested;—the Son of God had come into the world.

II. We note that such a Being had been announced and anticipated. Jacob spoke of a Shiloh, Moses of a Prophet, and Isaiah of a God with us, of the Wonderful, and of the Lamb; and Malachi of the Messenger of the Covenant.

III. We note that the Prophets announced that he would be a sufferer. Isaiah speaks of his face being marred, of his being wounded, bruised, despised, rejected, and of the Lord's laying on him the iniquity of us all. He announced himself that he should, must, and ought to suffer; that he should be taken by wicked hands and slain; and speaks of laying down his life and of giving his life a ransom for all.

IV. We note that he did suffer. He was reviled, persecuted, slandered, betrayed and scourged. He was mocked and nailed to the cross. "He was obedient unto death."

V. The Apostles testify that he suffered. Paul says *died*—for our sins. Peter says he died the just for the unjust; he bore our sins in his own body on the tree. The Spirit is represented as testifying of the sufferings of Christ; and Paul speaks of filling up of the sufferings of Christ. And the writer of the Epistle to the Hebrews speaks of the Captain of our salvation being made perfect through sufferings. His agonies, his groans, his wounds, tell us that he did suffer. Heaven and earth attested to this.

VI. We note that the scripture record is that he suffered for *us*. It says wounded for *our* sins, bruised for *our* iniquities. By his stripes we are healed, says Peter, quoting Isaiah, who says, the Lord laid on him the iniquities of us all. Peter says, bore *our sins* in his own body on the tree. Paul says, whom God hath set forth to be a propitiation through faith in his blood, to declare his righteousness for the *remission of sins.* John says he is the propitiation for *our sins*, and not for ours only, but *for the sins of the whole world.* Paul speaks of redemption through his blood. Peter speaks of being redeemed by the precious blood of Christ. The blood of Christ cleanseth, says John. Shedding of blood, and giving life, and dying *for us*, show clearly that our salvation is closely connected with the sufferings of Christ.

VII. We note that the language of scripture and the names given to Christ indicate that he was the medium through or by which we are saved. Thus speaks Peter; neither is there salvation in any other; for there is none other name under heaven given among men whereby we must be saved. Paul says that there is one mediator; and that God, for Christ's sake, has forgiven us. John says, we have an advocate with the Father; and the author of the epistle to the Hebrews says, he ever liveth to make intercession for us as our great High Priest; and Jesus declares, without me ye can do nothing; I lay down my life for the sheep; if I be lifted up I will draw all men unto me; this is my blood which is shed for many for the remission of sins. John the Baptist cried, behold the Lamb of God which taketh away the sins of the world! Paul connects the death of Christ with the law and sacrifices; thus,—almost all things under the law are purged with blood, and without the shedding of blood there is no remission. He represents that it is impossible that the blood of bulls and of goats should take away sin, but that the blood of Christ, who through the eternal Spirit offered himself without spot unto God, purges the conscience from dead works to serve the living God. Thus the bloody sacrifices of the law are seen to be the foreshadowing of that blood which purges according to Paul, which cleanseth according to John.

And this mediation, and advocacy, and intercession, and propitiation, and blood-shedding, and life-giving, all indicate suffering; and suffering closely connected with man's redemption, restoration, reconciliation, and salvation. Yet, let it be observed, that all this work, or endurance, or suffering of Christ, was not to change God's disposition or character; for all this work and suffering are but the outgushing of that love which spared not his Son.

We come now to the question, Were the sufferings of Christ in the atonement vicarious?

Let us get at the signification of these words. Vicarious is thus defined. "1. Deputed, delegated. 2. Acting for another; filling the place of another; 3. Substituted in the place of another, as a vicarious sacrifice."

Atonement is thus defined. "1. Agreement, concord, reconciliation after enmity or controversy. 2. Expiation, satisfaction, or reparation made by giving an equivalent for an injury. 3. In theology, the expiation of sin made by the obedience and personal suffering of Christ." To this question we reply,

1. That, if by vicarious be meant substitutional, then, if Christ suffered the actual penalty due to sinners, his sufferings were vicarious.

2. If he suffered an equivalent for the actual penalty, *then* were his sufferings vicarious.

3. If his sufferings were a governmental expedient intended to show God's hatred to sin and satisfy public justice, as it is sometimes termed, then were his sufferings vicarious; being substituted for that purpose for the actual infliction of suffering on the offenders. *For that purpose*, we say, for this theory supposes that pardon might be bestowed on the condition of simple penitence, if it would not injure the universe thus to bestow it.

4. I do not see but we must also answer this question in the affirmative, even if we adopt Dr. Channing's

view, or even that of the Unitarians generally. Dr. C. says:—

"A difference of opinion exists among Unitarians in regard to the precise influence of Christ's death in procuring our forgiveness. Many suppose that this event [Christ's death] contributes to our pardon, inasmuch as it was the principal means of confirming his religion, and of giving it a power over the mind; in other words that it procures forgiveness by leading to that repentance and virtue which constitute the great and only condition on which forgiveness is bestowed. Many of us are dissatisfied with this explanation, and think that the scriptures ascribe the remission of sins to Christ's death, with an emphasis so peculiar, that we ought to consider this event as having a special influence in removing punishment, though the scriptures may not reveal the way in which it contributes to this end."

Dr. Dwight makes the agency of Washington, and of man generally, vicarious. He quotes James,—"Is any sick among you? Let him call for the elders of the church," &c.; and thinks the forgiveness of sin is made to depend on the intercession of others; and that this very agency will convert the world, instrumentally.— If this be a proper use of the word vicarious, then Christ's sufferings are certainly so, and so are the labors and sufferings of all good men.

The question however is still before us; What had the sufferings of Christ to do in procuring man's redemption? That they were needful, is seen in the fact that they were endured and that they are pronounced needful by the sufferer. But why needful? we ask. Was it to change the disposition of God, and make him placable? Was it to take the thunder from the Father's hand and turn his wrath to grace? So it has been sometimes thought. But this cannot be correct; for the mission of Jesus is the fruit of God's love, instead of God's love being a fruit of Christ's mission. The love of God was the same before as after Christ hung on the cross.

Why then, we ask again, did Jesus suffer? Was it to endure the penalty of the law? If this penalty be what it has been supposed to be—eternal damnation—then we certainly cannot answer in the affirmative; for whatever be meant by bearing our sins in his own body on the tree, Christ has not been eternally damned. Or if it be said that this penalty be moral death or alienation from God, none, surely, will contend that Christ endured this—he never felt condemnation, nor had any other than feelings of the deepest sympathy toward God. Besides, can our sense of justice fail to receive a shock, when a penalty, due to the guilty, is transferred to the innocent? And yet this seems to be the view of this subjet taken by many. Bearing our sins means, with them, suffering the penalty which would otherwise have been inflicted on us, and which we justly deserved. It may be asked again whether, if justice required its infliction on the guilty, it could be satisfied with its infliction on the innocent? And if justice demand that it fall on the guilty, will it not require the infliction of the *whole* penalty? This view of the subject is full of difficulty, and, in consequence, has been given up by many.

But the question returns, Why was it needful for Christ to suffer? Was it that God's law might be maintained? He had said, "in the day that thou eatest thereof thou shalt surely die." Now if that threatened penalty was eternal damnation, then as Milton says,—

> —— " die he or justice must ; unless
> Some other pay the dreadful forfeit."

That is, the sinner must be damned eternally, or some other one suffer an equivalent to that penalty. And as this has not been and cannot be done, we conceive this was not the import of the threatening. The threatening must have been moral damnation or its understood equivalent.

But once more the question returns, Why was it needful that Christ should suffer? Was it, as Paul says, that God might be just and the justifier of him that believeth in Jesus? This is without doubt the true reason of Christ's being a propitiation. But why could not God justify,—that is pardon and accept—a penitent and trusting sinner without this propitiation? Because, it is said, that justice demanded, not absolutely the damnation of some one, or the actual infliction of the full penalty of the law, but it had such a demand that God could not, in justice to the universe, pardon even a world of penitents without giving to the universe evidence of his displeasure against sin ; and that was done by the sufferings of Christ ; that in the bruised, marred, scarred, bleeding Savior, was seen that displeasure ; that in the tears, groans, and agonies, of God's well beloved, was seen, by the universe, the Father's hatred of transgression. And this, we believe, is the most popular view of the orthodox church at present. Fuller holds this view and calls it substitution. So also teach Dwight and Jenkyn.

Others there are, who see no need of such governmental exhibition, and find no such reason assigned for his sufferings in the scriptures. They find, or think they find other reasons which leaves nothing in his sufferings unexplained. They say, 1st. The work he had to do brought with it the necessity of suffering as preparatory and associative. They say that Christ learned obedience by the things which he suffered; and that he was tempted in all points like as we are to prepare him to succor us who are tempted; to enable him to be touched with the feeling of our infirmities. Thus it pleased him in bringing many sons unto glory, to make the Captain of their salvation perfect through sufferings.

2d. Christ was manifested to destroy the works of the devil, and this must be done by suffering. It is through death that he destroys him who has the power of death, that is, the devil, and hence it is urged that a large portion of his sufferings arose from his conflict with the powers of darkness,—a conflict involved fundamentally in his mission. The strong man armed must be bound, and this could not be done without suffering. According to these views, his sufferings were only what he must of necessity meet in being the light of the world,—an example to men, in removing the obstacles to his success.

Others again, dissatisfied with all these views, assert that it was needful for Christ, in his life and sufferings, to consecrate or re-consecrate the desecrated law of God, and give it a more exact and imminent authority than it had seemed to possess before, in order to make men penitent, and feel the need of forgiveness. Says Horace Bushnell :—

"My doctrine is summarily this :—that,—excluding all thoughts of a penal quality in the life and death of Christ, or of any divine abhorrence to sin exhibited by sufferings laid upon his person ; also dismissing as an assumption too high for us, the opinion that the death of Christ is designed for some governmental effect on the moral empire of God in other worlds ; excluding points like these, and regarding every thing done by him as done for expression before us, and thus for effect in us,—he does produce an impression on our minds of the essential sanctity of God's law and character which it was needful to produce, and without which any proclamation of pardon would be dangerous ; any attempt to subdue and reconcile us to God ineffectual."

"On one side it is affirmed, that God could not forgive sin without either an equivalent suffering, or an equivalent expression of abhorrence against sin made by suffering, in the place of punishment. On the other side, since this doctrine, in either form of it, seems to involve something offensive to our moral sense, or repugnant to our ideas of God, it is affirmed that God, out of his simple goodness or paternity can and will forgive every truly penitent sinner. Satisfied with neither doctrine, I venture to suggest, as the more real and reasonable view, that, in order *to make men penitent*, and so to want forgiveness—that is, to keep the world alive to the eternal integrity, verity and sanctity of God's law—that is to keep us apprised of sin and deny us any power of rest while we continue under sin—it was needful that Christ, in his life and suffering, should consecrate or re-consecrate the desecrated law of God, and give it a more exact and imminent authority than it had before : this too, without any thing of a penal quality in his passion ; without regarding him as bearing evil to pay the release of evil ; as under any infliction and frown of God ; and yet doing it by something expressed in his life and death."

Well, but what are your views? it will be asked. I answer, that I have held and now hold, as far as I know, the governmental theory. Yet I may hold some views which may be thought, and which may be, inconsistent with that theory.

1. I am satisfied that the sufferings of Christ did not make God placable ; because God in his attributes and character is unchangeable ; and because Christ and his mission and sufferings are the fruit of God's love.

2. I am satisfied that Christ did not bear the penalty or consequences of our sins actually and fully ; for, 1st. Penitent sinners suffer even for past sins ; which, if Christ actually bore them in purpose or in fact, would involve double punishment. And, 2d. As he died for all, then all have suffered in a substitue, and can justly suffer no more.

3. Although an innocent being may suffer on account of a guilty one—either voluntarily or involuntarily—yet our sense of justice and equity,—the voice of God in the soul, the man in the breast—is wounded at

the infliction of a *penalty* upon an innocent being which was due to a guilty one. We can look with admiration on a mother suffering even unto death for a beloved child; yet how should we be shocked at seeing a mother nailed to the cross instead of a guilty child! And the same objections lie against an equivalent. As there is no transfer of moral character, so there is no transfer of penalty conformable to our sense of justice. There may be a reason why the penalty should not be inflicted, but none why it should be transferred.

4. That whatever of substitution there may be in Christ's sufferings, the main object of them is to bring back a revolted and alienated world to God; or to make men penitent. And, further, I will say that, if all impenitent beings could have been brought to penitence, or if they would have been as likely to become penitent without as with the sufferings of Christ, I see no reason why he should suffer. And more still; that, if a sinner is truly penitent, the character and word of God teach us that he would be—must be—accepted of God.

5. And, finally, let it be noted that the terms Mediator, Advocate, Intercessor, Redeemer, &c., indicate the doing of something by him who bears these names, on account of which we obtain what we should not have obtained had not that something been done. And this something was done for the purpose of effecting a reconciliation between God and the sinner, or, more properly, of reconciling the world to God. "God was in Christ reconciling the world unto himself." And further, I would with gladness observe, that, as Media-

tor, Advocate, Intercessor, Redeemer, Savior, the work and sufferings of Christ are the great and only medium by which we are brought to repentance, are renewed, reconciled, made heirs of God and joint heirs with Christ. So that, adopt which theory we may, if we repent of our sins and believe on Christ as such medium, we shall at last heartily unite in the song, " Worthy is the Lamb that was slain!"

ESSAY.

MORAL OBLIGATION.

Christian Brethren:—In accordance with the appointment of your Committee at the last meeting, I would invite your attention to a few thoughts on Moral Obligation. The term Obligation is thus defined by Webster: " 1. The binding power of a vow, promise, oath, or contract, or of law, civil, political, or moral, independent of a promise; that which constitutes legal or moral duty, and which renders a person liable to coercion and punishment for neglecting it. 2. The binding force of civility, kindness, or gratitude, when the performance of a duty cannot be enforced by law. 3. Any act by which a person becomes bound to do something to or for another, or to forbear doing something. In law, a bond with a condition annexed, and a penalty for non-fulfillment."

The term Moral is thus defined:—" 1. Relating to the practice, manners, or conduct of men as social beings in relation to each other, and with reference to right and wrong. 2. Subject to the moral law, and capable of moral actions; bound to perform social duties. 3. Supported by the evidence of reason or probability founded on experience of the ordinary course of things. 4. Conformed to rules of right or to the divine law, respecting social duties; virtuous, just. 5. Conformed to law and right in exterior deportment. 6. Reasoning or instructing with regard to vice or virtue. Moral law,—the law of God which prescribes the moral or social duties. Moral sense—an innate or natural sense of right and wrong. Moral Philosophy—the science of manners and duty."

With these definitions before us, we proceed to consider, briefly, the *Nature* and *Extent* of Moral Obligation. Its Nature will be seen in what is implied in it.

I. The existence of moral beings; or of beings possessing a moral nature. Worlds of matter may exist in all the diversified forms given to them by wisdom, grandeur and beauty. Attraction, affinities, repulsions, light and darkness, cold and heat, tornado earthquake, volcano, all these may be about us; yet divide, and subdivide, combine and recombine, add or subtract, we search in vain among all these wonders for anything upon which we can predicate moral obligation. We see motion, but only as bodies are acted on by foreign powers; we see arrangement, but no arrangement taking place without extrinsic agency. We see nothing developing a moral nature in any particle of matter, or in any combination of its particles. We are forbidden to ascribe a moral nature to a stone or tree, to sun or stars. And why? Because we perceive certain elements to be absolutely needful to constitute a moral nature, and these elements are wanting to matter.

Again. We examine a world of sentient beings. Beauty, order, and skill are there; yea, more; sensation, feeling, life, are there; but we search in vain for a moral nature, a moral being, in all the vast variety of animated nature. We find that which seems to make some approach to a moral nature; there is instinct with its unerring guidance, and a measure of intelligence, sagacity, and discernment, which make an approach to reason. The approach is indeed so close that it is sometimes difficult to discern the difference. Still, among them all we fail to discern the consciousness of right and wrong, a sense of guilt, which indicate the presence of a moral nature. As we have said, moral obligation implies moral beings, and moral beings must have a moral nature; and, as yet, in the material and animal worlds such a nature is not to be found.

But what is a moral nature? is an appropriate and important inquiry. We answer, that a moral nature is that which has,

1st. The faculty or power of acquiring knowledge; the possession of the perceptive and reflective faculties by which the relations of things are seen. It is by means of this faculty that we perceive the difference between square and round, and angular, the relation between two and four, the relation between father and son, mother and daughter, &c.

2d. A moral nature is one that has what is sometimes called the *moral sense,* or conscience. In the possession of this faculty, there is not only ability to perceive the relations of matter, scientific relations, the relations which give rise to the grand, the sublime and the beautiful, but ability to perceive *moral* relations, and to feel impressed by moral qualities. There is a perception that some things are right and others wrong; and a feeling of approbation or of condemnation for things done or undone.

These two united elements will constitute a moral nature, and a moral nature is necessary to constitute a moral being. I know not as the perceptive and reflective faculties ever are or ever can be separated from the moral sense, but both are necessary to constitute moral beings, or to lay a basis for moral obligation.

II. Moral Obligation implies *law.* It is difficult, if not impossible, to conceive of moral beings, as above defined, without the existence of law. " Those having not the law, are a law unto themselves, which shew the work of the law written in their hearts." That is, the idea of law is inseparable from a being possessed of a moral nature. The scriptures make law essential to transgression; and where transgression cannot be, there can be no moral obligation. Law, which is a rule of life or conduct, is either human or divine ; either positive or moral. Human law rests on human authority ; divine law on divine authority. Positive laws are those which rests simply and solely on the command ; and obligation ceases when the command is withdrawn or superseded, as circumcision or baptism. Moral laws are those which are founded in the nature and relations of things, and can never be annulled or superseded while the nature and relations of things continue to exist. Moral obligation supposes that such laws exist.

III. Moral Obligation implies that there exists an *authority* to enact and enforce such laws. All laws imply a lawgiver; and moral obligation supposes that *rightful* authority exists to enact such laws. Moral obligation implies law. Law implies a lawgiver; and a lawgiver implies authority to enact law ; and moral obligation will hold only as the law is holy, just and good, and the lawgiver is possessed of rightful authority.

From these remarks we learn the nature of moral obligation.

1st. It can exist only among beings possessed of a moral nature.

2d. It can exist only where there is law,—and law holy and just.

3d. It can exist only where there is rightful authority to enact laws to bind moral beings. So far as we can see, take either of these elements away, and there can be no moral obligation. For, without law, there could be no moral obligation ; and without a supreme authority there could be no such law ; and without moral beings there could be nothing over which to exercise such authority.

Second. What is the *Extent* of moral obligation ?

I. It binds all moral beings ;—all beings who have a moral nature, or the moral sense. All beings who have not the moral sense or conscience, are not morally obligated—*all beings*, we say. The beast, the bird, the fish, are not under moral obligation, because they have not the moral sense. Nor is the infant, or idiot, or insane man, for the same reason. The last may have been under moral obligation, and may be so again, but is not, and cannot be, while insanity lasts. All else than these, thus deficient, are bound. It binds Jehovah, the Lord Jesus, holy angels, holy men, wicked men and wicked angels, and Satan himself. All these, unless their moral sense is destroyed, are under moral obligation; all being under law; all being under rightful authority; all having the perceiving powers; all having the moral sense: It may, perhaps, be thought that the Supreme Being should be excepted. But he acts in accordance with the infinite law of rectitude in his own breast. Others may say that Satan and wicked spirits should be excepted. If they are insane, perhaps they may, but not otherwise; for, unless they have lost the powers or the use of the powers which constitute a moral nature, they must still remain under moral obligation.

II. It binds them in all time. In whatever portion of time a moral being exists, there will moral obligation lay its claim upon him; and if such beings exist eternally, then will they be eternally obligated; unless, as we said before, they lose their moral nature.

III. It binds them in all places. Moral obligation is not graduated by latitude, or longitude, or altitude. Cold and heat make no changes in moral obligation, unless they change the moral nature of beings. 'From Greenland's icy mountains, to India's coral strand;' on earth's broad prairies or lofty hills, moral obligation remains the same. And, as in science, should another planet be discovered, we might know that the law which governed other planets ruled there also; so, wherever in God's vast universe families of moral beings shall be found, there also will moral obligation assert its claims. In a word, its nature shows its extent. When and where moral beings exist, then and there will moral obligation exist.

These views of moral obligation seem to us to be in harmony with God's word. Paul says, it is accepted according to that a man hath, and not according to that he hath not; that where no law is there is no transgression. And Jesus says, Where much is given much will be required; and he asks, "Why even of yourselves judge ye not what is right?" And in that rule called golden, he bases the command on that moral nature which perceives and feels what ought to be done. And, indeed, all God's commands, invitations, threatenings, and admonitions, imply the existence of a moral nature, of a standard of duty or law, and of a supreme authority.

But little time has been afforded for the examination of the sentiments of the various writers on this subject; but we think these views agree with those presented by Wayland, Abercrombie, Mills, &c.; and that they disagree with those of Hume, Hobbes, Paley, &c.

What has been said prepares the way for a few

REMARKS.

1. There is a difference between Moral law and Ceremonial or Positive law. Moral law is that which

binds in all places, at all times, under all circumstances, and on all moral beings. Being founded in the nature and relations of things, it is not, and cannot, while God remains the same, be suspended; the plea of necessity, of good to be done, or Dr. ——'s statement, that the golden rule may be sometimes suspended, to the contrary notwithstanding. Positive law or legal institutions, although there is a fitness in them, a reason for them, yet, not being in the nature of things unchangeable, but of a temporary nature, may and do pass away when the purpose for which they were introduced is accomplished. The law was a shadow of good things to come, but the body is Christ. He taketh away the first that he may establish the second.

But mark. Moral obligation asserts its claim equally under positive law and moral law, provided the existence and character of that law be equally clear and plain. And here we may see that the phrase, moral law, as applied to the Decalogue, is not strictly correct; that is, if our definition of a moral nature, and of moral law be correct; for some of the relations mentioned in the Decalogue may be, and some of them we are taught will be, abrogated. The Savior sums up the moral of the Ten Commandments in two, viz: "Thou shalt love the Lord thy God," &c.; and Paul condenses these two, in some sense, into one, when he says, "Love is the fulfilling of the law." The principle here is moral and unchangeable. The Golden *Rule* of Jesus is the same; the *act* to be done, may be, must be, what circumstances make it; that is, *it* is not strictly moral.

2. We may learn the place which Reason should occupy in determining duty. We have seen that, without the perceptive and reflective faculties, there can be no moral obligation, and that the moral sense is inseparably connected with them. The Reason, the judgment, or the understanding, then, must determine what is right, what is true, what is good, what is duty. It is not instinct, impulse, or propensity; not feeling or impressions arising from the emotional nature, but the Reason. It is by this faculty that we learn the existence of a supreme authority, of a law—the rule of moral action—higher than all other laws; of the claims which that law has on us, and on all moral beings. By it we decide what that law is, and what are its claims; and by it we expound and apply that law. By it we settle the claims of the Bible, the Shasters, the Koran, the book of Morman, the book of Nature. This is the faculty in which dwells the light that lighteth every man that cometh into the world; which made it appropriate for Jesus to say, ' Why even of yourselves judge ye not what is right?' and ' Whatsoever ye would,' &c. Reason is not God, but it apprehends a God. It is not law, but it discerns a law. It is not a Savior, but enables us to know a Savior. It is not the light, but the window which lets in the light, and without which moral light would do us as little good as it does the beasts that perish. This faculty, then, is that which makes man a little lower than the angels, and a little less than God; which stamps him with the divine image and superscription. Reason may and will receive trustingly, confidingly, and obediently, many

things which it may not comprehend, but will and must reject, as of no force, of no moral obligation, that which is clearly contradictory and absurd. All questions in morals and christianity come before this faculty in man; questions of belief and practice, and its decisions are final as to man's obligations. As that decides he must act, or feel the reprovings of his conscience.

3. If Moral Obligation has been correctly defined, then no circumstances can absolve from moral obligation, while the moral faculties remain. When it is proved that there is no God, or that he has no law, or that there are no moral beings, then it may be said that there is no moral obligation, but not till then. Human enactments cannot release from moral obligation which arises from God's law. Consequences, good or ill, cannot set aside moral law or moral obligation, and the Golden Rule can never be suspended. And it will be seen that the maxim which allows the doing of evil that good may come, is of Satanic origin; and that sin organized, framed into a law, is still sin, like the Fugitive Slave Law; only the more destructive and deadly for its organic and legal form.

4. We learn that Moral Obligation will exist in the future life; yea, eternally. As long as a moral being exists there will be moral law, as long as there is moral law there must be a lawgiver, and as long as he exists moral obligation will exist. Otherwise there would be no beauty in the future that we should desire it. Moral obligation carried out by all, constitutes the beauty and glory of heaven; yea, it *is* heaven.

*24

5. We see the foundation of human responsibility. 1st. There is a supreme authority. 2d. There is a supreme law. 3d. Human beings have a moral nature which enables them to see and feel the claims of that law, and the authority binding them to be holy, just and good. Hence they feel guilt when they violate that law and disregard that authority; and hence, too, the duty to repent and believe, as the conditions of salvation.

6. We add, finally, that it is of the highest importance that the minister of Jesus see clearly and feel deeply, and that he aim to make his hearers see clearly and feel deeply, the nature and extent of moral obligation,—both as to what they ought to have been, and what they now ought to be, and what they ought to do; so that they may sweep away those refuges of lies—Fatalism, Calvinism, and its twin brother, Universalism; and so that sinners may see that they are under a moral obligation to repent, because they have time and ability thus to do.

The following discourse was preached in New York City, on the occasion of the re-opening of the house of worship purchased by the First Freewill Baptist Church in that city, in September, 1851. Rev. Henry Ward Beecher, of Brooklyn, preached in the morning, while Mr. Cheney supplied his pulpit, and in the afternoon Mr. C. delivered this discourse to the Freewill Baptist Church and Congregation. It is a very good index to his views and feelings, respecting the subjects to which it relates, in the last years of his ministry.

SERMON.

NOT ASHAMED OF THE GOSPEL.

"For I am not ashamed of the gospel of Christ," &c.—*Romans*, i.: 16.

In calling your attention to these words of the Apostle, we remark ;

1. That the Apostle makes a strong assertion.
2. That the words strongly imply that some were ashamed of the gospel of Christ.
3. That the Apostle assigns a *reason* why he was not thus ashamed.

Shame is a feeling of the soul, and implies perception and a conscience ; or, in other words, rational faculties ; and it may well be doubted whether it can be found in any beings where the moral sense does not exist. It is a feeling of mortification and disgrace. All well instructed and well regulated minds feel this when they find themselves in a wrong position, when they are doing what is not becoming, or neglecting to do what is incumbent on them to do. True, there are those who, having seared their consciences and become past feeling, glory in their shame. This feeling may indicate either a virtuous or vicious state of mind. A virtuous mind might walk as did the first human pair in the garden, *naked*, and not be ashamed—their eyes not being open to guilt ; and yet, when their eyes were opened to see their own and the world's degradation, they might feel it to be a shame even to speak of those things which are done in secret. On the other hand, as we have intimated, there are those who have so long trampled on their convictions of right, that they are now ashamed of the true and the good ; " whose God is their belly, whose glory is their shame, who mind earthly things." And this feeling is manifested in treating those sentiments, things, or persons of which they are ashamed, with neglect or indifference, or with scorn and contempt. Such, doubtless, there were in the days when Paul wrote, who treated the gospel, its Author, disciples, and ambassadors, with scorn. Thus did they speak :—" Can any good thing come out of Nazareth ?" " He is a pestilent fellow, a ringleader of the sect of the Nazarenes." " He speaks against the law and Moses and this holy place." They were ashamed of the gospel of Christ.

Others there were, who, although not so violent, were still, through the fear of man or other powerful motives, unwilling to own Christ ; like Nicodemus who came to Jesus by night ; and others who believed, but, for fear of the Jews, did not confess Christ. At all events, the Apostle must have had in view those who, from some cause, were unwilling to own, to confess Christ, or who, in his strong language, were ashamed of the gospel of Christ.

We proceed to assign some reasons why none should be ashamed of the gospel of Christ.

But first let us define the term, and see how it is used in the scriptures. Webster derives the word from the

Saxon, *God-spell;* God signifying *good*, and spell *history;* and defines it thus ;—

"1 The history of the birth, life, actions, death, resurrection, ascension, and doctrines of Jesus Christ; or a revelation of the grace of God to fallen man through a Mediator."

The most simple and expressive development of the import of this term is, perhaps, that of the angel who touched his harp over the plains of Bethlehem. Hear him :—" Behold I bring you good tidings of great joy, which shall be to all people." The glad tidings of the advent of Jesus; this is the GOSPEL. The term is applied to the promise made to Abraham. " And the scripture foreseeing that God would justify the heathen through faith, preached before the gospel unto Abraham, saying, In thee shall all nations be blessed."—Gal. iii.: 8. Mark says, " The gospel of Jesus Christ the Son of God." Paul calls it the " gospel of God's Son."—Rom. i.: 9. And the " gospel of God."—Rom. i.: 1. " My gospel."—Rom. ii.: 16. " Gospel of salvation."—Eph. i.: 13. " Gospel of peace."—Eph. vi.: 15. The glorious gospel of Christ."—II. Cor. iv.: 4.

On that memorable day when, in the Synagogue at Nazareth, the carpenter's son stood up to read, there fell from his lips these startling words : " The Spirit of the Lord is upon me because he hath anointed me to preach the gospel to the poor, he hath sent me to heal the broken-hearted, to preach deliverance to the captive, and recovering of sight to the blind, to set at liberty them that are bruised, to preach the acceptable year of the Lord." And just previous to his ascension he said to his Apostles; "Go ye into all the world and preach the gospel to every creature." Another definition might be, "God's plan of saving sinners;" and still another, "The mission of Jesus;" or the principles, precepts, and doctrines, taught by Jesus Christ.

Such is a brief definition of the term, and an exhibition of its use. Its mighty meaning, its wide sweeping claims, its implications—embracing all moral relations—will be seen more clearly as we proceed to assign the reasons for not being ashamed of the gospel of Christ.

1. The first reason I would assign is the *origin* or *source* of the gospel. From whence did it come? Whence this mission of Jesus? these glad tidings of great joy? Who planned it? Who presided over its execution? Who had love enough, power enough, skill enough, to contrive and to carry out the plan of redemption. There is but one answer to be given to these queries. There is but one mind wise enough, but one arm strong enough, but one heart large enough, to originate the gospel of Christ. It must be from him who said, "Let there be light and there was light;" who spake and it was done, who commanded and it stood fast. It was the God who, in the beginning, created the heavens and the earth; and as the creation of the heavens and the earth displays his glory, and things that are made make known his eternal power and Godhead, so the gospel of Christ which proposes the re-creation of man in God's own image, makes known, by its sublime teachings, the source from whence it came. Says Christ, "I came down from heaven, not to do mine own will, but the will of him who sent me." "I must work the works of

him that sent me while it is day." " For God so loved the world that he gave his only begotten Son." " He sent his Son not to condemn the world, but that the world through him might be saved." These sayings teach from whence the gospel of Christ emanated. They show that it came from a heart of unbounded love, from a mind of infinite wisdom, from a hand of unlimited power. It bears all the marks of such a heart and such a hand. Well, therefore, might the Apostle exclaim ; " I am not ashamed of the gospel of Christ ;" and all the world should say, Amen. Alleluia.

II. The second reason which I would assign is the *object*, the *design*, the *purpose* of the gospel. That object is to open blind eyes, unstop deaf ears, heal wounded hearts, to bring pardon and forgivness within the reach of the perishing myriads of the human race, to seek and save the lost, to rescue man from slavery to his own lusts, to make him truly free, to renew within him and reënstamp upon him the image and superscription of his Maker, to make God's law supreme, to proclaim peace on earth and good will to men, and thus to bring the brightest glory to God ; to establish the universal brotherhood of man and the universal fatherhood of God. In the beautiful imagery of the scriptures, it is to make the lion and the lamb lie down together, and the weaned child to put his hand on the cocatrice's den, to introduce the reign of Christ when every knee shall bow, and the kingdoms of this world shall become the kingdoms of our Lord and of his Christ. Were the gospel allowed to have its legitimate influence, every chain and fetter and manacle would be broken ; war, intemperance, licentiousness, and oppression would cease, and one song would employ all nations. Has any one a heart to be ashamed of such an object, such a design as this?

III. We assign, as a third reason, the medium and instrumentalities through and by which this gospel was made known. He who was in the form of God, and thought it not robbery to be equal with God, made himself of no reputation, took the form of a servant, and became obedient unto death, even the death of the cross.

He who was David's Lord became David's son; he was born of a woman, made under the law, to redeem those that were under the law. The brightness of the Father's glory, veiled himself in humanity, that he might be touched with the feeling of our infirmities, and taste death for every man. Gospel redemption could not be by the blood of bulls and goats, by silver and gold,—only by the precious blood of Christ. In a word, "God was in Christ reconciling the world to himself." Christ is the grand medium by and through which God takes hold of fallen humanity, to restore and lift it up where it may anew receive his image. And around Christ, as a central sun, may be seen revolving the whole group of the Apostles. It is on Christ the Rock that the church is built, against which the gates of hell shall not prevail. And then through Christ we have the ministration of the Spirit, the mission of the Apostles and of the whole sacramental host of God's elect. From the day when it was announced that the seed of the woman should bruise the serpent's head, God, by angels, by prophets and apostles, moved upon by the

Spirit, has been crying, " Ho every one that thirsteth, come ye to the waters!" Here is dignity—One in the form of God ; here are riches unsearchable—the precious blood of Christ. Here are toil and sacrifice and death ; and all these mighty instrumentalities are brought to view in that gospel of which Paul says, " I am not ashamed." Surely we have no reason to be ashamed of such a gospel, unless we are ashamed of heaven and its agencies.

IV. The *Doctrines taught* in the gospel, we assign as a fourth reason for not being ashamed of it.

1. The being, character and government of God. The world has had Gods many, many of them cruel, contradictory, and licentious. But the gospel of Christ clearly reveals to us that there is but ONE GOD, and he without variableness or shadow of turning,—the same yesterday, to-day, and forever ; infinitely wise, powerful, and good, the true and living God ; the Father of spirits; making his rain to descend on the evil and good, and and his sun to shine upon the just and unjust ; more ready to give the Holy Spirit to them that ask him, than earthly parents are to give good gifts to their children.

2. The being, character and mission of Jesus ; his divine nature, his lofty position, his mission of love, the accomplishment of that mission, the going down to the grave, the bursting of its fetters, the leading of captivity captive, the abolition of death, and the bringing of life and immortality to light. This great central doctrine is clearly revealed in the gospel,—Jesus the Lamb of God, the Son of God, the Christ of God. To the ques-

tion, Whom say ye that I am? it replies, "Thou art the Christ, the Son of the living God." He is revealed as the Savior and Redeemer of the world; the only name under heaven given among men whereby we must be saved.

3. The condition of man is another thing contained in the doctrinal teaching of the gospel. The gospel teaches that Christ came not to call the righteous but sinners to repentance; that he is the propitiation for our sins; that he tasted death for every man; that if he died for all then were all dead; that all have sinned, and come short of the glory of God. And all this accords with history, observation and experience.

4. And there is another great doctrine, clear and bright as the river of life, full of hope to a perishing world, and bringing with it the breath of spiritual life when received. It is embodied in such expressions as these;—"The spirit and the bride say come; ..... and whosoever will let him take the water of life freely." "The Lord is ..... not willing that any should perish, but that all should come to repentance." "As I live, saith the Lord, I have no pleasure in the death of him that dieth." This soul-cheering truth—teaching God's compassion and anxiety for sinners—stands out in all its fulness, in the mission of Jesus, in his tears, and toils, and death. These great truths or doctrines are in the gospel of Christ, and, when embraced, will lead to the true God, the true Savior, and to true happiness. Well might the Apostle say that he was not ashamed of the gospel of Christ, when it revealed such soul-cheering and soul-elevating truths as these.

V. As a fifth reason we direct your attention to the *Precepts* of the gospel. Listen to them and see if there be anything of which to be ashamed. Hear Christ as he sums up the teachings of Moses and the prophets; " Thou shalt love the Lord thy God with all thy heart, and ...... thy neighbor as thyself." Listen to that world-embracing and world-blessing rule, which, on account of its priceless value, has been called golden; " Whatsoever ye would that men should do to you, do ye even so to them. Who can be ashamed of such a rule? Read in the gospel the story of him who fell among the thieves, the conduct of the Good Samaritan, and then listen to the precept of Jesus; " Go and do thou likewise," and be ashamed of such teaching if you can.

VI. We urge, as a sixth reason, the great *Principle* which pervades the whole gospel. That Principle is Love. The gospel is an emanation from God's great heart of love. It was born in love, cradled in love, baptized in love, and goes on its mission of love to men in the spirit of love. It is a great golden chain of love drawing all to the greater centre—the heart of God. " Love is the fulfilling of the law." " The love of Christ constraineth us," says Paul. " He that dwelleth in love, dwelleth in God and God in him." See it in its highest form, in the prayer of Jesus; " Father forgive them, for they know not what they do."

VII. We urge again the *Example* of Christ and his disciples. Behold their meekness, humility, zeal, patience, boldness. They are always true to the right, true to principle. Who have made glorious footprints on the sands of time? Not the time-servers, and compromisers; but the Elijahs, the Daniels, the Shadrachs, the Stephens, and, above them all, the Son of God, who loved not their lives unto death. The gospel of Christ presents for our imitation burning and shining lights, and especially *that* Light that lighteth every man that cometh into the world. With such examples before us we may well exclaim, " I am not ashamed of the gospel of Christ ;" and to those glorious ones revealed to us there, we may gratefully cry out; " Ye are the salt of the earth ; ye are the light of the world." Of such none need be ashamed.

VIII. Another reason is, that the teachings of the gospel are in harmony with the teachings of the inner man— with the law on the heart.—The gospel recognizes the reason, the conscience, the judgment in man, and makes its appeal to them. In the rule called, *golden*, he makes this appeal, " Whatsoever ye would," &c. That is, whatsoever, conscience, reason, judgment, tell you, you would have others do to you, do ye the same to them. And on another occasion it is asked ; " Why even of yourselves judge ye not what is right ?" God's voice even in the gospel, God's voice in his works, and God's voice in the soul are in unison. Not a discordant note in all God's dispensations. The gospel may be and is clearer, brighter, but is in perfect harmony with that " elder scripture" traced on rocks and hills, on rivers and streams, on suns and stars. The righteousness of God is herein revealed from faith to faith. God is in nature, God is in Moses, and God is in Christ.

IX. The gospel recognizes the important truth of human brotherhood.—It knows nothing of man's originating in an oyster or a monkey; knows nothing of one race as created merely for the service of another race. It knows nothing of any such curse as gives one man or one class of men the right to make property of another class of men. No. Its language is; "Who hath made of one blood all the nations of men that dwelt on all the face of the earth." Thomas Jefferson uttered the sentiment of the gospel when, in that memorable instrument, the Declaration of Independence, he said; "We hold these truths to be self-evident, that all men are created equal; and endowed by their Creator with certain inalienable rights,—among which are life, liberty, and the pursuit of happiness." It is self-evident, says Jefferson; that is, when the sentiment is announced it finds a response in every breast. The gospel teaches one common origin of the human race, one blood, one common Father. *Our Father*, is put into the prayer that becomes us all. We are in one common condition; "All have sinned, and come short of the glory of God." There is one common Savior; one common destiny—the grave and the Judgment; one common load of responsibility—every one shall give account to God. In a word, the gospel of Christ is a gospel of freedom, of equality, of right. It makes every man a neighbor and brother.—If any one is ashamed of such a gospel, it must be, we think, because he is either lording it over God's heritage, or wishes thus to do. He cannot, we think, have received the truth into his soul, for that makes free. It is such a gospel as the world needs, to purify and harmonize it.

X. We assign what the gospel has done, as another

reason. It has enlightened myriads and led them into the pathway of life; enabled myriads more like Simeon to triumph over death; and by its exceeding great and precious promises, it brings life and immortality to light. It is indeed the power of God unto salvation to every one that believeth.

XI. And, finally, we urge as a reason, the rich inheritance which is promised to those who receive and obey this gospel. "The Lord will give grace and glory, and no good thing will he withhold from them that walk uprightly." Thus does Watts versify the Psalmist;—

> "The Lord my Shepherd is,
> I shall be well supplied;
> Since he is mine and I am his,
> What can I want beside."

And such promises as these show us, in part, the heritage of those who yield to the gospel. "Fear not little flock; for it is your Father's good pleasure to give you the kingdom." "All things work together for good to them that love God." "All things are yours." "Henceforth there is laid up for me a crown of righteousness, which the Lord, the righteous Judge shall give me at that day, and not to me only but unto all them also that love his appearing." "They shall sit with me in my throne." "They shall hunger no more, neither thirst any more, &c." "They shall walk with me in white, for they are worthy." Here are sceptres, thrones, and robes, and crowns; but time would fail to recount a tithe of those exceeding great and precious promises. Suffice it to say in the language of scripture; "Eye hath not seen, nor ear heard, neither have entered into the heart of man, the things which God hath prepared for them that love him."

APPLICATION.

1. This is indeed a glorious gospel. Its origin, its object, its instrumentalities are glorious. Its teachings, its principles, its spirit and its examples, are brilliant with glory. In its power and influence it is full of glory. It is indeed the ministration of the Spirit which exceeds in glory, and, were it received in all the earth, then indeed would peace and love prevail, swords be beaten into ploughshares and spears into pruning-hooks. Then would one song employ all nations, and the great voice would be heard, saying ; " The Kingdoms of this world are become the Kingdoms of our Lord and of his Christ."

2. This gospel should be preached to all. The rich need it, the poor need it, the sick need it, the dying need it, the rum-seller needs it, the rum-drinker needs it, the slave and slaveholder and the slaveholder's apologist need it. The legislators and rulers of the land need it, so that they may feel when iniquity is framed into a law, and justice is violently perverted, that there is a higher than the highest among them who regardeth their work. Much needed is it in this great city, in its lanes, and alleys, and courts, and cellars ; and not much less is it needed, if we mistake not, in its splendid pulpits. Aye, would it not be cheering to have this gospel of universal brotherhood, of Christian equality, without respect of persons, uttered in all the pulpits of this city, in all its length and breadth, and

height and depth? Were this done, many, we think, would be found as in the days of Nineveh, sitting in sackcloth and ashes. Were this done, we should not be amazed at such astounding assertions as are reported to have been made by a clergyman of this city ; That if one prayer of his would liberate all the slaves in the land, he would not dare to offer it. O, friends, Paul was not ashamed of the gospel of Christ,—of any of it ; was not ashamed to preach it to all. No Governors or Councils, no Festuses or Felixes deterred him from uttering before them all, and to them all, the gospel of Christ.

3. The gospel should *all* be preached. Paul was not ashamed of a whole gospel. The gospel of Christ was not a one-sided, or a mutilated system. Its commands, requirements, obligations and duties, are to be made known, as well as its doctrines, privileges, and promises. Its penalties, denunciations, and retributions, are to be announced. Its conditions and applications are to be declared clearly and fully. There must be no shunning to declare all the counsel of God, under the specious but false plea ; " The people are not able to bear it ;" when the truth is, the people are able to bear, but not willing to hear the gospel in its stringent claims. Did Jesus refrain from uttering the claims of a whole gospel because Peter said,—" Be it far from thee, Lord ?" or because the young man went away sorrowful ? No, never. Nor did Prophets or Apostles or early Christians act on such a principle as this. Their language was; " Break off your sins by righteousness ;" " We cannot but speak the things which

we have seen and heard;" "I have not shunned to declare unto you all the counsel of God." To every creature should it be preached in its wide-sweeping claims, its soul-cheering promises, its lovely invitations, and its solemn admonitions. Nothing should be kept back that the people need.

4. There is danger of being ashamed of the gospel of Christ. That there were some in the days of Paul who were thus ashamed, we feel assured; it is implied in the text itself. And as long as human nature is what it is, and Satan's panorama of the Kingdoms of the world remains what it is, and the gospel remains what we have shown it to be, just so long may we fear that some will be ashamed of the gospel of Christ. And hence it will follow that, as there are Gods many, and Lords many, so there will be gospels many,—other gospels which are not the gospel of Christ; gospels made like garments, to order; gospels made to harmonize with the pride and luxury and oppression of man; a gospel that sanctions slaveholding and war; a gospel that sanctions the doing of evil that good may come; a gospel that makes Christ's law just what the powers that be make it; a gospel that makes it a Christian duty to trample on the Golden Rule and all Christ's precepts, by obeying that Covenant with death and Agreement with hell,—the infamous Fugitive Slave Law; a gospel that will not allow a colored man his equal rights in Church or State; that virtually denies the Fatherhood of God and the brotherhood of man; a gospel that breathes no prayer for the immediate emancipation of three millions of Slaves; a gospel that

would lead one, not to go himself, but to send a mother, son or brother—I know not which—into all the horrors of slavery, rather than see the union of these States dissolved; a gospel that repudiates the higher law—thus virtually condemning the Martyrs, Apostles, and even Jesus Christ himself—and substitutes the *lower law*, the law of man, the law of expediency, the law of compromise, as the law of God. This is the gospel of man, of the Prince of the power of the air, another, a perverted gospel, and not the gospel of Christ. Let all beware how they preach, or receive, or obey such a gospel, lest the anathema of Paul rest upon them; "Let him be accursed." Let all remember Christ's words; "He that loveth Father or Mother more than me, is not worthy of me; and he that forsaketh not all that he hath cannot be my disciple."

5. We see what high, deep, and wide reasons there are for not being ashamed of the gospel of Christ. It is just such a gospel as the world needs. It is needed in all lands; civilized and uncivilized heathen need it; the earth groans and travails in pain for the want of it. Slavery, War, Intemperance, and Oppression, tell how much a pure gospel is needed. Such a gospel is needed to bring men up to true manhood, women up to true womanhood. The very soil on which we tread needs it to free it from its curse; the beast of the field needs to feel its influence; and all human beings are to find their life alone here. What a world would this be if the gospel were everywhere received and obeyed! God would be glorified, Christ exalted, angels would rejoice, and man be saved. Then would earth's choir

and heaven's minstrelsy unite in one, their "Glory to God in the highest ; on earth Peace ; Good will to men !"

Finally. Brethren, you, a little band of Christ's disciples, are to preach this glorious gospel. Preach it in your lives, in your actions, in your spirit. Let me say in all kindness, keep this gospel pure. Be faithful to your high mission. Your Master, Christ, expects every one of you to do your duty. Take heed that Protestant Popery find no place among you. Crush the little Pope in your own bosoms. "All ye are brethren." Labor in faith, in patience, in zeal ; and, through this glorious gospel's power, you shall be permitted to say, "Thanks be to God who giveth us the victory." Amen.

CHAPTER XIV.

MISCELLANEOUS ADDRESSES, INCIDENTS, &C.

SEVERAL things, which seemed hardly appropriate to any one of the preceding chapters, have been reserved for the present place. Nothing like a full, outward history of Mr. Cheney has been given; both because the inner history seemed more important, and because it is not easy to gather up the external incidents in the order of their occurrence. He was constantly performing services in one and another department of labor, which arrested attention, and left his impress on the hearts about him. What have been selected may serve as specimens; and if they serve to give a just idea of his character and life, it is as well as though they had been greatly multiplied, and accurate dates assigned to them all. There are, however, some things which should not be denied a place in these memoirs.

Mention has already been made of the difficulties growing out of the political contest of 1842, and of the triumph of the Government party, as it was termed. There was framed and adopted a Constitution, extending the right of suffrage as widely as it had been extended in other States. That is, a convention of delegates chosen by the people at large, assembled, framed an instrument intended as a Constitution, and submitted it to the *people* of the State for their action upon it. It received a majority of the votes cast in the State, and so, by its framers and others, was regarded as the organic law of the State. The existing government, however, refused to sanction it, and declared and treated it as null and void. One party claimed that the Government could be changed by the direct action of the people ; the other party insisted that such change could be warrantable only when effected by or through the Government already existing. The first party proceeded to elect the officers prescribed by the new Constitution, and organize a Government under it. There were, therefore, *two* organized State Governments, each claiming rightful authority, and denying just power to the other. The old organization was, of course, *exercising* the authority, and the new one set itself to wrest it away. Then came the collision. A large proportion, however, of the suffrage party were opposed to taking the authority by force and at the risk of bloodshed, and so hesitated and gave back when the time came for the gathering of armed forces. Others, however, were ready to fight their way through to victory.

Mr. Thomas Wilson Dorr, who had been elected Governor under the new Constitution, was not inclined to abandon the cause, at whose head the people had shown their wish to place him. He asserted distinctly the right of the suffrage party to authority, and prepared, as he was able, to defend that right at the point of the bayonet. After a few warlike demonstrations in and about Providence, a small force gathered under his direction at Acote's Hill, in Chepachet, and commenced to throw up fortifications. The Government party immediately despatched a military force, with instructions to disperse the gathering at Chepatchet, and capture Mr. Dorr, if possible. The first part of the mission was executed; or, rather the company had mostly dispersed of their own accord, before the arrival of the military. Mr. Dorr being but feebly supported, deemed it unwise to make any attack or resistance, and left the State. Some time afterward he was arrested, tried, condemned, and imprisoned. Time passed on; the feeling grew more calm—Mr. Dorr still remaining in his cell. The Government had prepared a Constitution, submitted it to the people, and it had been adopted. Mr. Dorr's health suffered, and it was feared that his end was not far off. His release was petitioned for; and it was offered him on condition that he would take an oath to support the existing Government. This he refused to do, and so still remained in prison. He had no disposition to wage war upon the Government, was willing it should be tried as an experiment, but would not recognize its legality. Time passed on, and the feeling in favor of his unconditional liberation grew stronger and wider, and petitions were carried to the General Assembly, praying for his release,—signed by his friends, the clergy, the ladies, &c. All these details seem necessary to an understanding of what is about to be stated, regarding Mr. Cheney's effort in his behalf.

In January, 1845, such a petition was sent to the Assembly, and referred to a Special Committee. This Committee had a meeting in the Hall of Representatives, for the purpose of hearing any thing that might be said in favor of granting the petition. With two or three others, Mr. Cheney was appointed by the petitioners to urge it before the Committee. The day arrived, and the hall was crowded with earnest listeners. Mr. C. was full of his subject, and so had taken pains to prepare, in form, only a mere outline of his intended remarks. The speech, or plea, was regarded, on all hands, as one of the most able, impressive, and touching, that he ever delivered. A gentleman of some distinction in the city, pronounced it one of the best, if not *the* best speech ever made in that hall. The organ of the opposite party remarked, in substance, that it was the first time Mr. Dorr's cause had fallen into hands that did justice to it. The Herald thus spoke of it:

"Mr. Cheney's address was a beautiful specimen of easy, unaffected, pathetic eloquence, chastened by a sound judgment, and a correct perception of what belongs to the time, place, and occasion. His language, though extemporaneous, was so correct as to read handsomely if reported verbatim; yet the charm of his glowing, yet chastened pathos, can never be seen and felt on paper."

No full report of the plea, even in its verbal character, was ever made. An outline only appeared in the papers. The pencilled sketch which he took with him as a guide, is on a blank portion of the sheet containing the petition, and is simply as follows. It may not be wholly devoid of interest.

SKETCH.

1. Will the *Power* of the State be impaired? Mercy weakens no just power.

2. Will the balance of *Justice* be disturbed? The hand of Justice grows strong when *Mercy* is combined with it,—and especially in a free Government.

3. Will the Peace of the community be disturbed? Where are the men and means, even if the disposition remained, to carry on a war against the Government? Besides, the Prisoner has recognized the existing Government on trial.

4. And certainly *Revenge* should have no place. Mere political considerations should be laid aside.

5. Look at the man—his character—motives—the men who voted for him—the eminent men who agree with him in his views. Who prayed for his success? Will you impose a condition which to him shall seem degrading? Suppose him obstinate, if you please; should that prevent you from being magnanimous? Shall his Father, &c., plead in vain? Shall the festering wound in the community be kept open? and all because he will not say that which is against his conscience?

(Solitary confinement is an unusual thing. Shall he die there? That is now the question.)

Who am I addressing? Not the Court or Jury. Not those who simply dispense justice, but mercy. You have the pardoning power. I am not here to establish the People's Constitution. Not to demur at the proceedings of Court or Jury. This has been, and, perhaps, will be still, examined elsewhere. Who I am, I need not say. *I am a man*, and a brother. These petitioners are my brothers and sisters.

What a responsibility is resting upon you! On your report very much depends the hope of parents, friends, and thousands of petitioners. Multitudes of eyes will be turned here; and the peace and quietness of the community all call on you to grant the prayer of the petitioners. Be merciful, that you may obtain mercy.

The speech was concluded by the impressive recitation of these lines from Shakspeare.

> "The quality of mercy is not strained;
> It droppeth as the gentle rain from heaven
> Upon the place beneath: it is twice bless'd,
> It blesseth him that gives and him that takes:
> 'Tis mightiest in the mightiest; it becomes
> The throned monarch better than his crown;
> His sceptre shows the force of temporal power,
> The attribute to awe and majesty
> Wherein doth sit the dread and fear of Kings:
> But mercy is above this sceptred sway,
> It is enthroned in the hearts of Kings,
> It is an attribute of God himself;
> And earthly power doth then show likest God's
> When mercy seasons justice."

All the friends of Mr. Dorr, especially, were very desirous of securing a copy of the speech for general circulation; and this desire will sufficiently explain the following correspondence, which was published in the *Herald*—a city paper—and then issued in the form of an "Extra," and widely distributed.

*26

LETTER OF THE REV. MR. CHENEY, ON THE LIBERATION OF THOMAS W. DORR.

Copy of a Note from the Benevolent Suffrage Association to the Rev. Mr. Cheney.

REV. SIR:—The Ladies of the F. B. S. Association give you their unfeigned thanks for your fearless, able and eloquent Address on behalf of the Petitioners for the *Unconditional Liberation* of Thomas Wilson Dorr, and request a copy, if practicable, for the press,

Yours respectfully,
C. R. WILLIAMS.

Jan. 11, 1845. In behalf of the Association.

Reply of Mr. Cheney.

OLNEYVILLE, Jan. 14th, 1845.

Ladies of the Benevolent Suffrage Association:—Accept my sincere thanks for your friendly and favorable notice of the Address which I had the privilege of delivering in the Court House, in Providence, on the 11th instant, before a Committee appointed by the General Assembly, to consider and report upon the Petition of nearly four thousand citizens of this State, (including that of a Father) for the unconditional liberation of Thomas Wilson Dorr, from the State Prison in which he is now confined, in accordance with the sentence of the Supreme Court of this State to *solitary confinement at hard labor during his natural life.*

Believe me, Ladies, when I say to you, that the opportunity then afforded me, of pleading in behalf of my imprisoned brother, was one of the *choicest, richest, sweetest*, privileges of my life. I felt that my judgment, my conscience, my heart, and my God approved ; and I do most heartily thank you, for affording me such an opportunity. I feel grateful for the patient attention given by the Committee to my remarks, and those of my brethren, and also for the attention and interest manifested by a crowded audience. And above all, I feel grateful to my Heavenly Father, for the *feeling heart*, and ready utterance which he afforded me, on that (to me) novel, but deeply interesting occasion. I may be deemed presumptuous, but I have felt, and still feel it, as the deep wish of my soul, that what my *Heavenly Father* enabled me to utter, before a Committee of *three*, might have been uttered before a Committee of the *whole*, the *whole General Assembly* and if it had been practicable, the *whole people* of the State and Union.

You ask for a copy of the address. I wish I could give it you—you should have it with *all my heart*. But it is utterly out of my power. Who can copy *tone, manner, spirit*, when one is pleading for an imprisoned brother? Who can copy the *speakings of the eye*, aye of the whole human face divine, when the soul is on fire? when "out of the abundance of the heart the mouth speaketh?" Besides, I had no notes, except a few points, to which I proposed to myself to call the attention of the committee, with the exception of a few lines from Shakspeare.

I have hastily glanced at the report in the Gazette—

it seemed to me that the general outline was correct. True, the report in that paper is imperfect, is but a skeleton; and such would be any copy which I should furnish. There is a *copy* correct and true, on record I trust, where moth and rust will not corrupt, nor thieves break through and steal. No, Ladies, I cannot give you a copy, or any thing that would much resemble it.

But, Ladies, I can tell you of *some things* which I intended to say, as—That I was happy in being permitted to speak in that place in behalf of my imprisoned brother; this I think I did utter, and I *felt it*, and feel it still. I intended to say to the Honorable Committee, that I was not before them to affirm or deny the validity of what is called the People's Constitution, or to question the rightfulness of the present Government, or the means by which it has been established, or the authority or jurisdiction of the Court, or the partiality or impartiality of the jury before whom the prisoner was tried, and adjudged guilty, and sentenced. These questions have been, are being, and probably will be discussed elsewhere. This is not *my* errand here—but I am here as a man, to plead for my imprisoned brother. I am here as a signer of the petition you hold in your hands, and in behalf of the ladies who originated that petition, to urge you to report to the body from whence you came, in favor of granting the Prayer thereof.

I did intend to call the attention of the Committee to the high responsibilities which rested on *them*. That they occupied not the throne or seat of *Justice*, stern *Justice*, but that they, in connection with the body from whence they came, held in their hand the *pardon-*

ing power. That they sat in that most interesting and responsible of all places " *The Mercy Seat,*" and I did, I think, urge on the attention of the Committee the mighty responsibilities which rested on *them*, when it was believed by the petitioners, that as they reported so would the action of the Assembly be.

I did attempt to show that neither the requirements of justice, or the administration of the law, or the safety of the government, or constitution, stood in the way of granting the prayer of the petition, and that the Honorable Committee and the General Assembly might enjoy the luxury of dispensing mercy without sacrificing the claims of justice.

I did intend to call the attention of the Committee to some of the results of a refusal to grant the prayer of the petition : And, 1st, It will wear the appearance of revenge, of retaliation on the part of government. The question is being asked, through the length and breadth of the land—Why is Thomas Wilson Dorr kept in prison? Does the safety of the government demand it? Has not the majesty of the law been vindicated? Why, then, it will be asked from Maine to Georgia, from the Atlantic to the Rocky Mountains—why is Thomas W. Dorr kept in the felon's cell? This question will be asked in the land of the Metternichs, the Wellingtons, and the O'Connells, why, in Republican America—in the land of Roger Williams—is Thomas W. Dorr kept in the State Prison? Humanity will ask it—Philanthropy will ask it—Christianity will ask it—Freemen will ask it, every where, in tones of earnestness, louder and longer, sterner and stronger—and from you, Gentlemen of the Committee, and from the General Assembly an answer will be expected. Gentlemen, we hope you will put this agitating question at rest by a right answer, the opening of the prison doors. I did intend to say that if this petition be rejected, the verdict of the civilized world will be : That Thomas Wilson Dorr is kept in prison to gratify a spirit of revenge; and Thomas W. Dorr will be regarded as a Martyr.

2. I did urge on the attention of the Committee, that a refusal to grant the prayer of the petitioners would continue the *chief element* of strife, which has divided families, churches, and communities, and that such a course would crush the hope of the venerable parents of the prisoner, and cruelly disappoint the hopes of many, *very many*, of the friends of the present Government. I did intend to appeal to the Committee not to clog their report for liberation with *conditions* which the petitioners did not ask, and which they must know the prisoner could not, as an honest man accept. I did say, —Gentlemen, suppose in the recent struggle in this State, you had been the defeated party, would your defeat have been a sufficient reason for you to have renounced your principles ? You answer as *men*, no— never! Then ask it not of him, whose whole history shows him to be honest and true to his convictions of *right*, on this great question.

Should it be said, he holds dangerous sentiments, viz.: that the people are sovereign, above all laws, statutes, or constitutions ; be it so—thousands in this State, and others, believe with him, in this matter— and some of them standing high in the legal and political world. Shall all these be incarcerated in prison? I did appeal to them in the fulness of my soul, by the memories of their own loved mothers, to report in favor of the petition. I did ask: Shall the prisoner die in his cell? Shall the hope of his parents be crushed? Shall these tearful petitions be rejected? Shall bitterness and strife still continue, or shall we have peace?

And finally, for my heart is full, I did remind them of what we should be, if mercy was withheld from us. *Of Him* who sendeth rain on the just and unjust, and maketh his sun to shine on the evil and the good *without asking*. I did ask—do you not pray, and hope for mercy? and, O, forget not the words of the great teacher—" With what measure you mete, it shall be measured to you again; and he shall have judgment without mercy, who hath showed no mercy ;" and I did express a strong desire that they might so act, that they might hear from the lips of the final judge—" Inasmuch as ye have done unto one of the least of these, my brethren, ye have done it unto me—enter thou into the joy of thy Lord." " Blessed are the merciful, for they shall obtain mercy."   Yours,

MARTIN CHENEY.

It is sufficient to add that, though the unconditional liberation was not at this time secured, yet the prisoner was afterward set at liberty, and Mr. Cheney and he were warm personal friends. In the sickness suffered by Mr. D., a few years later, which threatened to be unto death, Mr. Cheney was solicited to visit him, and did so frequently, with much satisfaction to both parties.

In the autumn of 1850, Mr. George Thompson, of the British Parliament, paid a second visit to this country. It will be remembered that he visited here in 1835, at just the time when the mobocratic spirit was waking against the abolitionists. The lawless force, consisting of "gentlemen of property and standing," who were concerned in seizing, and leading Mr. Garrison through the streets of Boston by a rope, was organized for the purpose of doing violence to Mr. Thompson; but not finding him, they seized one of their own citizens. At that time Mr. T. travelled over different sections of the United States, and did not a little in calling public attention to the evils of Slavery, and the duty of Emancipation. He had labored arduously in the same work at home; and came, bringing his reputation and his scars of honor with him. His strong reasoning and powerful eloquence produced deep and lasting impressions on many minds; but few, probably, sat before him with more interest than Mr. Cheney, or remembered him with higher satisfaction. He had done not a little to kindle up the earnestness and the zeal which so often displayed themselves in Olneyville and its vicinity. And it was fitting that, when Mr. Thompson came back to revisit the theatre of his former toils, Mr. Cheney should be selected to give him, in the name and in behalf of the friends of freedom in Rhode-Island, the word and the hand of welcome. The meeting for his public reception was held in a large hall in Providence, which was most densely crowded. The address of welcome, delivered by Mr. Cheney, went beyond the highest expectations of his friends, in appropriateness, beauty, force, and effect. Few were unmoved, and Mr. T.'s tears flowed freely during the delivery of some of the passages. The following somewhat ample sketch will indicate its general character; though it must give but a faint idea of its actual impressiveness.

WELCOME TO GEORGE THOMPSON, M. P.

Mr. Chairman;—

The friends of emancipation, in this City and State, wished to extend to the Hon. George Thompson, M. P., of England,—the eloquent advocate of freedom—a cordial welcome on his reappearance among us, after an absence of fifteen years; and they have assigned to me the difficult, yet delightful task, of tendering it. It might easily have been put into abler hands; but to no one would it have given more heartfelt pleasure.

Sir, in doing this, shall I for a moment advert to my acquaintance with him, whom you would greet, and whom you delight to honor? I refer not to personal acquaintance, for as to that, my acquaintance begins to-night. But through the almost ubiquity of the press, I became acquainted with our honored friend while he was doing battle, side by side with Clarkson, and Wilberforce, and Buxton, against British Colonial Slavery, and urging on the people of Britain the duty of immediate Emancipation. Well do I remember reading with admiration those powerful arguments and appeals, with which he met, face to face, the paid agent of Slavery. Well do I remember the thrill which I felt, when Slavery's champion had declared that he could and would produce a certain law, and there broke from the lips of a young man upon the ears of the audience, the startling challenge, *"Read the law!"* Boldly did the agent of despotism declare he had the law and could present it; and then there rung out again the defiant words,—" READ THE LAW!" Then and there I became acquainted with GEORGE THOMPSON. I felt the pulsations of his mighty heart, as it throbbed against my own, and the acquaintance was complete. And when the Jubilee shout of freedom rose over the British West India Isles, then I could not fail to be acquainted with a man so intimately connected with that joyful event.

And then I became acquainted with him through the *patriotic* papers of New-York, as they levelled their artillery of abuse against him.

And then, for the first time in this city, we heard his eloquent pleading for the slave.

And then came the days of mobs, and Lynch Law, brick-bats, and bowie knives; and then, when the boldest held his breath, and the strong men trembled, our friend was true as steel; and here, if he did not shake the dust from his feet, it fell from his feet as a witness to the shame of this nation, as he returned to his native land.

SIR: Allow me to address you as the George Thompson of 1835, unabridged and unaltered. We have watched with deep interest your movements on the burning plains of India, through England, Scotland, and Ireland, till—strange to tell—we have seen you seated side by side with the Law-makers of the British realm. Yes, sir, we have watched you with deep interest; and forgive us if I say, almost with anxiety, while we beheld halting, faltering, and even open treachery and desertion. We have looked to see how George Thompson would meet success, and applause, and power. We knew how he could meet calumny and mobs, but we knew that flattery could often seduce where mobs could not terrify. We almost trembled when men who told us, that slaves could not breathe in England, found themselves unable to breathe freely in America. We knew how he stood in 1835, when his English friends failed him; but now the kingdoms of the world and the glory of them were passing in review before him, and we involuntarily said,—" *God help George Thompson!*"

Thank God; our friend, when weighed in the balance, has not been found wanting. For whom have we here? One from the high seats of power in that most powerful nation. And what is he doing? Why, pleading the cause of the poor and oppressed. It is the second edition of the "Old Man Eloquent." All honor to the Abdiels of Old England,—faithful among the faithless; not as the hero of the battle-field or of song, but as the faithful soldier in the moral battles for the redemption of the poor.

As Abolitionists and lovers of freedom,

We welcome among us the coadjutor and friend of Clarkson.

We welcome the man who silenced the paid agent of West Indian Slavery.

We welcome the man who detected the rottenness of that system of folly, deception, and cruelty—Colonization.

We welcome the man who was candid and keen enough to ascertain the name of that incendiary sheet, published in Boston, and the name of the madman who edited it ;—the name of the convicted libeller, the tenant of a dungeon, the companion of felons.* We welcome and honor the man whose instincts of humanity are so true that all the arts of Colonization could not deceive him.

We rejoice to give the hand of fellowship and welcome to the man who, whether on the plains of India, in the mobs of America, or seated in the British Parliament, has maintained without compromise and without concealment, the same great principles, the same unbending integrity, the same high and holy purpose ; the man who, in these almost superhuman labors, has planted himself on the rock of eternal truth—that truth which crushed to earth will rise again ; and with the sword of the Spirit he has conquered.

We welcome you, sir, among us, as of a kindred spirit with him who said ; *"I am in earnest. I will not equivocate ; I will not excuse ; I will not retreat a single inch. I will be heard."* Yes, we have seen that you was in earnest, &c., and that you would be heard ; and we opine you will be heard to-night.

* Reference is here made to Mr. Garrison and his paper, "The Liberator." Mr. Thompson gave his sympathy and aid to Mr. G. It is hardly necessary to say that Mr. Cheney speaks ironically here.

We welcome the man whose heart is so large that it cannot be limited in its action, by latitude or longitude or altitude; the pulsations of which are felt from isle to isle, from continent to continent, stirring the pulse of the world.

We are glad to greet you again, for we need you. Colonization is again attempting to raise its snaky head. Freedom of discussion is threatened. That wonder of cruelty, that legislative monster—the Fugitive Slave Law—has been enacted; and the pulpit, which has eschewed politics, is loud in demanding obedience to this infamous political statute. Yes, in these dark days, we need you to rebuke, instruct, and cheer.

Welcome then to the city of Providence, whose name is emblematic of the guardian care about thee. Welcome to the spot where Roger Williams found a refuge—to the asylum for all sorts of consciences,—to the spot where civil and religious liberty were first proclaimed. Welcome to our ears, our homes, our hearts. Not especially as a true Englishman;—not as the Hon. George Thompson;—not as the eloquent and accomplished orator;—not as the warm-hearted friend;—not even as the true Christian do we welcome thee *now;* but as the untiring, unfaltering, uncompromising advocate of universal emancipation,—as the eloquent advocate of the universal Fatherhood of God, and the universal brotherhood of man; as the incarnation of a spirit whose motto is, "My country is the world; my countrymen all mankind."

May God spare thee long, cover thy head in the day of battle, and give thee to hear another jubilee shout from the millions of American slaves, unfettered and free.

> "Go on!—for thou hast chosen well;
>   On in the strength of God!
> Long as one human heart shall swell
>   Beneath the tyrant's rod.
> Speak in a slumbering nation's ear
>   As thou hast ever spoken;
> Until the dead in sin shall hear—
>   The fetter's link be broken.
>
> I love thee with a brother's love,
>   I feel my pulses thrill,
> To mark thy spirit soar above
>   The cloud of human ill.
> My heart hath leaped to answer thine,
>   And echo back thy words,
> As leaps the warrior's at the shine
>   And flash of kindred swords.
>
> Have I not known thee well, and read
>   Thy mighty purpose long!
> And watched the trials which have made
>   Thy human spirit strong?
> And shall the slanderer's demon breath
>   Avail with one like me,
> To dim the sunshine of my faith
>   And earnest trust in thee?
>
> Go on—the dagger's point may glare
>   Amid thy pathway's gloom—
> The fate which sternly threatens there
>   Is glorious martyrdom!
> Then onward with a martyr's zeal—
>   Press on to thy reward—
> The hour when man shall only kneel
>   Before his Father—God."

With renewed thanks to the friends who assigned me this difficult though pleasant task, and to the audience for their kind attention, I present to you, as your guest and friend, the Hon. GEORGE THOMPSON.

Mr. Cheney was accustomed to meet the colored people of the city and vicinity, annually, on the first of August, to celebrate the anniversary of West India Emancipation, and to discuss the successive phases of the Anti Slavery enterprise in this country. This was always a privileged occasion, on many accounts, to him. It enabled him to show, publicly, his sympathy with the free people of color; to repeat a public protest against slavery and its appendages and supports; to encourage himself and others, by dwelling on the triumph of philanthropy over selfishness and distrust in West India Emancipation; and win over, if possible, to active, Anti-Slavery efforts, the opponents or the mere professed friends of the slave. Several sketches of the speeches delivered on these occasions are found among his papers; but they are probably not necessary to be presented, in order to give a just idea either of his Anti-Slavery feeling, spirit, or policy. He was always earnest and radical, and sometimes severe and personal.

He leaves, also, several outlines of addresses to children, delivered on excursion occasions, and Sabbath School Anniversaries and Celebrations. They indicate both his views and feelings in respect to the character and training of children. He always gave prominence to his doctrines of Peace, in these efforts. Henry C.

Wright's "Kiss for a Blow," may be said to be the text book from which he drew the materials for his efforts. He urged kindness towards each other in their intercourse; benevolence towards the suffering; and sought to attract them to Christ by the exhibition of his tenderness and love. These views were prominent in all his teachings, but especially so in his instructions to the young.

He was often called to the chambers of sickness; and, though he regarded himself as wanting in ability to make his visits in the sick room profitable, others felt that there was a singular appropriateness and beauty and value in his conversations and prayers. He had always words of comfort for the mourner; and over the pious dead his utterances glowed with chastened enthusiasm.

His public labors were so numerous and abundant, as to leave him little opportunity or strength for taxing, private labor. Some idea may be obtained of the amount of his public labors from the following abstracts, prepared for the Ministers' Conference of the Rhode Island Quarterly Meeting. At the January session of that body, it has been customary to examine the members, so far as to require a brief statement of their labors and experiences during the past year, and of their present views and feelings. The two tables which follow, were prepared by Mr. Cheney, the first being a record for 1845, and the second for his last full year of ministerial service —1850. They are fair specimens of his annual reports.

REPORT OF PUBLIC LABORS—1845.

Attended Funerals,	55
Funeral Sermons,	37
Other Sermons,	110
Whole number Sermons,	138
Temperance Addresses,	7
Addresses on Education,	2
Organization of Church,	1
Anti-Slavery Addresses,	2
Thanksgiving Discourse,	1
Peace Address,	1
Address before a Committee of the Assembly,	1
Essay on Moral Government,	1
Whole number of Public Addresses,	310

I have attended the most of fifty-two Sunday evening Conferences; most of the weekly Temperance meetings; most of the weekly enquiry meetings; most of the monthly Church and Covenant meetings; and some Special Church meetings. Have visited some on Committees; visited the sick somewhat,—how much I have no account. It has been a year of God's goodness to me. Have been prevented from preaching, by illness, only one Sabbath. It has been a year of liberty in preaching; a year of declension in the Church; a year of privilege with my ministering brethren.

REPORT—1850.

I have delivered one hundred and sixteen Sermons and public Addresses; attended sixty-one Funerals; with the usual amount of Church, Covenant, and Conference meetings, Sunday School, and Bible Class. I now meet a Bible Class once a week; and, a part of the time, on Sunday mornings, making, in all, about one meeting a day through the year.

My doctrinal views are, in some respects, different from what they were earlier in my ministry.

1. I do not now believe in Infant Depravity. I used to " kind o' believe it, and kind o' not" believe it.

2. On the Atonement my views are somewhat modified.

3. On the Trinity, I have never been very well satisfied; though called a Trinitarian.

4. On the Sabbath, views are changed. Do not see that any times or places are set apart by Divine command under the gospel, as holy.

5. Christianity alone a test of church membership, and the qualification for communion.

6. Life-taking forbidden under the gospel.

In the latter portion of Mr. Cheney's life he was obliged to husband his strength as far as practicable, but his public labors were still abundant. He lost nothing of his earnestness, however; parted with none of his decisive firmness, and still kept himself alive in the great causes of philanthropy, which had for so many years enlisted his attention. He was walking down to the end and goal of life, seeking to scatter the seeds of truth and righteousness as he went forward. Activity had always been his leading characteristic, and, in his latest years, he had nothing of inactivity. His eventful life was approaching its close, and it ceased not to be eventful, even when he was nearing the shadows of the grave, and the light of immortality.

CHAPTER XV.

ANALYSIS OF HIS CHARACTER.

We have followed Mr. Cheney along through the various stages of his life, until, worn with labors and with years, he stands near the mouth of his yet unopened tomb. Some of the striking events which marked his history have passed in review before us; and through these events may be seen, perhaps with considerable clearness, the various features of his character. Yet it seems appropriate, as we stand where his life stretches out before us, having made ourselves familiar with his history, to group together the various elements of his character, after having considered them in their separate existence. In this way we may be enabled to obtain a more definite view of the man, and be prepared to understand and estimate better the developments of his character in the statements already made.

Mr. Cheney had a character, definite and marked. His was a separate and independent existence. He was no mirror, reflecting the features of the life about him, changing the image as often as he changed his position. There was no danger of mistaking him for any other human being, or of supposing that he had ever moulded himself on the basis of any human model. He stood out before every beholder, never striving to be more, and never discovering himself to be less, than MARTIN CHE-

NEY. Yet he never affected eccentricity, nor was he at all what is usually termed eccentric. He was made up of striking individualities, yet few if any ever thought of calling him *odd*. He was simply natural; and in yielding to the laws and tendencies of his own nature, he never appeared as a second edition of any predecessor or cotemporary, and presented a character which rendered any person who attempted to copy it, simply ridiculous.

The formation of that character was, doubtless, somewhat affected both by his physical constitution, and by the circumstances which surrounded him. And, hence, it may be well to look for a moment at these outward things, before commencing the internal survey.

In person, Mr. Cheney was about five feet ten inches in height, with a well proportioned frame,—in the latter part of his life being rather thin than full. His organization was firm, close, compact; with a large amount of muscular and nervous energy. It was a constitution naturally elastic and enduring, with an active temperament sustained by high vital forces. The appetites and propensities, taking their rise in the body, were sufficiently strong and well developed to make his physical life an important and influential element to him. It was just such a constitution as is adapted to be the ally of courage and executive force. And that sort of courage which makes most of the heroes of war, he did possess largely. He was never accused of cowardice, even when he was enlisted in enterprises which his conscience refused to approve. He was very seldom cowed by threats, even when his antagonist had the support of a just cause. Opposition would rouse his resistance; the very fact that others had dictated, was apt to be a sufficient reason why he should rebel; and when thus roused, the presence of danger did but little to excite his fear. Nothing but opportunity needed to be added to his physical constitution to make of him a military hero. An incident will illustrate this. One of his warm personal friends speaks of having seen him, in the days of his wildness, at a military review, a few miles from Providence. The troops were drawn up, and the crowd of spectators had been pressing so hard upon one of the outside companies as to render the soldiery quite impatient, and they had made a flourish of their bayonets to disperse them. Just at this stage of affairs, Mr. Cheney, with two other young men, rode up to the lines, and drove along so near the ranks as almost to graze the persons of the company with the carriage wheels. Indignant at the intrusion, a cry was raised, "*Prick his horse with your bayonets;*" and a dozen sharp points were turned towards the intruders. With a sudden and decisive movement, Mr. Cheney drew up his horse, and, with a look in which there seemed to be a flash of lightning, he replied in a low, quick, defiant voice,—"*Let them do it if they dare.*" The narrator says he appeared as if ready to leap upon the very points of the weapons, if he had been provoked by a single aggressive movement. The soldiery quailed before him, and looked after him in silence as he proudly rode away. It will not be difficult to perceive the bearing of this physical constitution and its tendencies upon many of the facts already presented.

The circumstances surrounding Mr. Cheney were such as to *develope* whatever of courage and force might have existed within him. He encountered much opposition, and now and then his fears were sought to be excited by attempts at intimidation. He lived at the very time when the contests were going on over the moral questions that were agitating the world. Temperance, and Anti-Slavery, and Peace, were all presented to him in such aspects as aroused his feelings and gave a peculiar turn to his efforts. The suspicion with which he became accustomed to regard popular institutions and popular men, was more or less the result of his discovery of their unfaithfulness toward the causes which were obviously embraced within the objects of the gospel. The strong attachment which he always manifested for those causes, may have been partly created and preserved by his abundant labors in their behalf, and by the necessity imposed upon him to look into their merits and defend their claims. His early life had been spent, not in the halls of wealth or amid the temptations of power, but among the masses of the people and in the society of the vicious; and this had not been without its influence in quickening and strengthening his sympathies for the multitude, and making him a champion of the rights of the poor and despised. Men of wealth, talent, and influence, had encouraged and aided him when he was weak and unpopular; and so he was the more ready to recognize the nobleness of those who, amid strong temptations to tyranny and selfishness, had gone out into the needy and suffering world on an errand of benevolence and justice. His early outward life had brought trial and difficulty, compelling him to struggle or sink ; and in the struggle and the triumph which it brought him, he had learned to feel strong and independent in his ability. When he became a christian, he was where nothing would inspire confidence and sympathy but the boldest avowal of his change and the highest religious activity ; and these first decisive steps would naturally tend to make all his subsequent procedure bold and determined. The want of early study and mental discipline laid him under a kind of necessity for close observation ; and so would tend to make him specially familiar with, and interested in, the passing present. His own history had been crowded with striking and important occurrences; and so it was but natural that he should grudge the space occupied and the food consumed by a lymphatic, gluttonous, indolent mortal, and be satisfied with no life which wanted earnestness, energy, and efficiency.

In exhibiting the elements of Mr. Cheney's character, it seems proper to consider, first, his Intellectual, then his Moral and Religious, and finally, his Social traits. His moral and religious peculiarities were more or less determined by the structure of his Intellect, and his social qualities can only be understood when seen in their relation to the rest of his nature.

The first thing suggested by a view of his mental operations, was Activity of Intellect. His mental processes seemed to be carried on with very great rapidity. A whole troop of distinct thoughts would pass in review before him, while many others were seeking to get a clear view of the subject which had set them in motion. No impassioned hurriedness of speech, no condensation of ideas, no unusual fruitfulness in matter, ever enabled a speaker to outrun Mr. Cheney's capacity to follow him. In ordinary cases, he would anticipate a conclusion long before a speaker was prepared to state it.—And his intellect was not only rapid in its movements when acting, but it was always ready to act. There are many minds that are prompt, keen, and efficient when roused, and yet, under ordinary circumstances, are sluggish and dull. To develope their power they must be lashed, goaded, and stung into activity. It was not so with Mr. Cheney. His intellect seemed never to be taking rest. It seemed to be so accustomed to act as a sentinel, that it slept with its eyes wide open and its weapons grasped firmly in its hands. Start a topic of interest, and eye and face and form all told that you had one eager, critical listener. Open a new avenue of thought, and he was at the entrance, ready for an enthusiastic exploration. Hazard a statement which he did not believe, and you were almost certain of being laid under the necessity of setting earnestly about its defence. Make a strong argument in favor of a position which he regarded false, and he was instantly at work testing every link in the chain of reasoning, giving himself no rest till he had satisfied himself of its unsoundness, or given it an intelligent approbation. He carried this ready intellect with him every where, and it was continually kept at work. He would find an illustration of some important principle in the prattle of his children, frame a reply to some opponent while hoeing his garden, and arrange an impressive sermon for the next Sabbath while walking home from the city.

Nor did his mental forces wait for any foreign influence to summon them into action. He was perpetually stimulating other minds to effort. Few persons ever spent an hour with him without being set earnestly at thinking. Before they were aware of it, he had drawn them into a position where it was both a necessity and a pleasure to tax their powers of reasoning. The young and timid, who had thought it became them to listen trustingly to the words of age and experience, felt anew that they should have opinions and be able to give a reason for them. He did not set himself to puzzle them, and then laugh at their perplexity;—such a course would have increased their timidity and weakened the confidence in themselves; he made them feel at home and at ease, even when they felt obliged to retract opinions but recently avowed. He corrected an error so that the victim felt that he was less liable to fall into another. He reserved his logical traps for the pompous, self-willed egotists whom he sometimes met; and while they were writhing and vainly struggling to loose themselves from durance, he would sometimes encourage the laugh which their contortions excited. And this he did, not because he enjoyed the mortification suffered by his victims, but because, through mortification, he hoped to teach them the lesson of modesty and caution.*

* On one occasion he was speaking in the city on the subject of Peace. He alluded to the prophecy of Micah, that swords should be

It was this feature, blended with a keen perception and a power of close discrimination, which gave him the chief portion of his intellectual power. His mind was less comprehensive and philosophical than many others, and, in point of thorough discipline, the absence of early training had left him somewhat deficient. His mind was more analytical than synthetical; he could demolish better than he could construct. Phrenology marked his concentrativeness small; and, as a matter of fact, he did not seem able to dwell upon any one nice point in a subject for any length of time. When he sought to be critical, he often hurried over the

beaten into ploughshares and spears into pruning-hooks. At this point he was interrupted by a clergyman in the back part of the house, who expressed himself very decidedly to the effect that there was no such prophecy in Micah. Mr. C. knew his disputant, and says, "I confess I felt a little roguish." He replied with a little hesitation, that he certainly had the impression that there was such a prediction there. More strongly than before came up the denial from the back part of the house. Mr. C.'s eyes sparkled with rising fun; but he simply, in a half apologizing way, expressed his surprise that he should be mistaken, for he certainly thought he had seen the prophecy in that book. The third denial from his clerical disputant was more peremptory, decided and earnest than before; and an intimation was given that before the speaker came to argue such a question from the bible, he should be familiar enough with it to distinguish between Micah and Isaiah. Mr. Cheney's time had now come. His disputant had run himself into the snare, and all that remained to be done was to draw the noose. He calmly turned to a brother seated near him, and requested him to read from Micah 4:3. The passage was read, in a clear and distinct voice, and it was now the critic's turn to be confounded, as peal after peal of laughter rose from all parts of the congregation. Mr. C. said nothing, but went on with his argument.

distinctions and limitations which could only be understood and appreciated by being accurately marked and considerably dwelt upon. Owing to the same want of early training and of familiarity with philology and mental science, his language sometimes wanted precision, his definitions were not always exact, and his terms were not always happily chosen. He wrote but little, and what he did write was prepared with reluctance; and, as a result, his compositions lacked literary finish. These defects, however, if they may be called such, scarcely diminished his power in the estimation of those who knew him. What he saw he saw clearly; and what he attempted to say he made every body understand. Give him a premise, and his mind would bound forward to a conclusion almost before the statement was completed. You had to point his eye but once to an idea till now unseen, before his perception had grasped it. It was seen clearly in itself, though it may not have been always seen in all its relations. And as, under the telescope, the starry point separates into distinct luminous bodies, so beneath his discriminating gaze, what had been thought a single, simple idea, divided itself into several, wholly distinct from each other. He was never satisfied with seeing a thing in its outlines; he aimed to penetrate at once into its interior. It was this intense eagerness to get at the heart or bottom or end of a matter, that sometimes led him into the commission of an intellectual fault. Fixing his eye only on the heart, he did not always perceive how circumstances might modify its developements. Straining his vision to reach the bottom, he did not always thoroughly inspect the steps. Hurrying to the end of his inquiry, lessened his care to survey each point in the path which led him there. Accustomed to press a principle to its ultimate conclusions without fear of consequences, he sometimes found, in surveying the process, that some of his inferences, though seeming to be legitimate, were not necessary. Not to mention other things, his reasonings over the tests of church fellowship will illustrate this.

An idea seldom grew upon his mind gradually. A complex subject might do so; it usually did. But he never seemed to have any crude, imperfect, half-formed notions. He either saw a thing or he did not see it. And between the time of not discovering a point and laying hold upon it firmly, it was often difficult to make a mark. Shapeless objects in the mist, men as trees walking, seldom appeared in the field of his mental vision; and so, because he saw clearly, he made others see clearly; because things appeared so real to him, he made them realities to others. These qualities of activity, keen perception and close discrimination, made him a careful observer upon human life and character; and he seldom came into contact with a man without looking him through, and forming a pretty correct estimate of his abilities and character. He was not really suspicious, but he was seldom deceived. The same qualities rendered him a skillful debator. There, his mental activity was increased by pressure, and his perceptive and discriminative powers were wielded with the highest efficiency.

He was a close reasoner; but not alone because the mathematical or logical or metaphysical feature of his mind was very unusually prominent. The traits already indicated aided him largely. His logical processes were carried on by the combined activity of many powers. He had a very good ability to analyze and abstract; and,—but for the necessity of dealing so largely with actual life, with outward concrete things; but for being so earnest and practical,—he might have been greatly interested and successful in metaphysics. As it was, his reasoning power rested, to an unusual extent, upon his perceptive. He could sometimes see a fallacy when he could not clearly expose it; and so he was obliged to pursue the indirect method in his attempt to meet it;—that is, he would attempt to establish the opposite sentiment, without presenting any direct reply to the argument which he wished to overthrow. In the latter part of his life he came to place more and more dependence upon his reasonings and their results. Into new and hazardous fields of inquiry did he take his reason along with him, feeling that it was highly safe to lean upon its arm and follow its guidance.

Such a man could not have been very superstitious or credulous; nor, on the other hand, could he have been obstinately skeptical. He wanted rational evidence to support a statement before he was ready to endorse it; and, when this was found, there seemed to him the same folly in skepticism that there was in superstitious credulity. He dealt largely with facts and reason; and both of them convinced him that much held sacred was false, and yet many things held to be strange or unreasonable were yet both true and important. He kept his eyes open to every newly developed field of investigation, and his ears open to the words of every earnest and sincere teacher. He was not ready to accept every thing that had passed into society with the endorsement of men of great reputation, nor did he wait until a sentiment had become current and popular before he would take it to his understanding. If his reason pronounced it true and important, he bore it along with him openly, not caring to ask whether he and it were to be greeted with hosannahs or maledictions. A logical absurdity he could not be prevailed upon to swallow, whoever administered the dose ; he had rather be charged with being a skeptic, than be conscious of being insincere. He had faith in his reasonings on every topic. On some of the profounder doctrines of revelation he may have reasoned with too much confidence ;—may have trusted too implicitly to a guide whose inadequacy God has recognized in the bestowment of super-natural teaching. Certain it was that, in thus depending upon his reason, he did not unqualifiedly endorse all the doctrines of the usually received theology, and did sometimes lean toward sentiments which are held as heretical. By this is not meant that he wanted confidence in the bible, but that, as is always the case, his system of mental philosophy gave color to his interpretations of the bible. He thought independently, and gave his convictions a practical application. And, while he held the opinion, he seemed to regard himself as set for its defence. He would neither compromise nor push it out of sight, because it provoked attacks or exposed him to censure. You must either let him retain it and develope it when and where and as he pleased, or convince him that it was wrong; and when this last thing was done, it was unto him " as an heathen man and a publican."

His imagination was not remarkably vivid. He could not have written or conceived a very ingenious novel; nor would he ever have excelled as a poet. He was too busy and earnest with practical matters to leave much time, energy, or inclination for fanciful creations, such as he was able to originate. Yet he had imagination enough to give freshness and life to his exhibitions of thought, and enough to give him a high appreciation of the beautiful or the grand creations of others. A bold metaphor and a beautiful simile were treasured up as gems in the storehouse of his memory, and used to dignify and embellish his own productions.

His love of the grand and beautiful, whether appearing in nature, art, or life, was full of intensity and enthusiasm. He gazed upon the face of creation, listened to the music that swelled up amid its leafy temples, breathed the air made fragrant by the incense of the flowers, as one whose eyes had been anointed to behold the glory of God. His taste seemed instinctively delicate, and every where he was discovering something beautiful, half hidden in some niche of the temples of deformity.

In his studied efforts, he showed a strong love of system and order. The want of early mental discipline prevented him from systematizing his thoughts, if he was obliged to present them as they arose in his own mind.

And when his mind was set at work, without special previous preparation, it might exhibit the lowest or the highest specimens of his intellectual efficiency. Relying upon his ability to see within and through the topics presented to him, he sometimes failed to secure the needed insight; and sometimes a topic, almost wholly new, yielded up its hidden treasures under the intensity of his momentary mental gaze. But there are some of the discourses presented in the preceding chapters, which indicate that his mind was accustomed to act, in its calmer moods, in conformity to high principles of order. He had never learned these principles by study in search of them; if they had been prescribed by another, he would have deemed them spirit-fetters; but, being an outgrowth from his own tendencies, they were eminently natural to him. His system became the body of his thought, whose form and proportions were determined by the thought itself.

As a whole, his intellect was of a superior order. It must be remembered that it had but little early cultivation, and that subsequent circumstances were unfavorable to its growth. That, in certain directions, it had less force than though a liberal course of study had early put it on the path of progress, is obvious; but, with all its disadvantages, it was no common force. Of this, high testimony was furnished in the unabated interest felt in his preaching by men of learning and talent, and by the general reputation for power which he acquired and retained in the suburbs of the city, and among strong men. True, the force of his preaching did not arise solely from his intellectual energy;—that intellect had powerful allies, as we shall hereafter see; but without real mental strength he could never have held a leading position among the city ministry for twenty-five years. Fifteen years before his death, in conversation with a mutual friend, an eminent Baptist minister, said;—" There are many able ministers in the city of Providence, but none of them excel Mr. Cheney in intellectual strength and acumen." And there are probably few impartial and qualified observers who would hesitate to unite in this estimate.

In the Moral and Religious aspects of Mr. Cheney's character were seen the striking qualities of the man. There was something in his very look which seemed refusing all compromise with sin. To every form of selfishness and hypocrisy his eye seemed to be administering a perpetual rebuke. There was no half-heartedness in his religious profession. When he broke his league with Satan, he proclaimed open and uncompromising war with all his emissaries and works. The idea of his backsliding and weakening his protest against iniquity, was a thing which no transgressor dared to expect, after he had entered upon his public labor. Rumor once accused him of breaking his Temperance pledge. One of his former companions in sin was asked, whether he believed the report was correct. He at once replied,—" *No, but I wish it was true.*" So deep and general was the idea that the whole force of that nature was a pillar, supporting its religious faith.

This strong, firm, couragous adherence to what he believed to be right, was the regal element of his nature. Moral law ever appeared to him like the voice of God. Through all paths of perplexity, amid all forms of excitement, his eye was fixed upon the great principles of righteousness, as were the eyes of the wise men upon the star that guided them to the infant Savior. The claims of duty he saw with unusual clearness, and felt with uncommon force. The plea of expediency, when it tended to induce a sacrifice of what was abstractly right, was, to him, a new edition of Satan's discourse to Eve. What he thought was wrong he condemned, without stopping to ask who might be pleased or who might be wounded by his rebukes. His conscience was always active, and gave decided verdicts over almost every moral question submitted to it. To him, nothing that was right appeared unimportant. In his creed no note was taken of small sins. To violate a conviction willingly, to sacrifice a righteous principle knowing it to be such, even in the slightest matters, was, in his estimation, to do a terrible wrong. In little things as in great things, his course never deviated an inch from the straight line of perceived moral duty. Reputation, friendship, worldly interest, all were nothing, apparently, when they stood between him and his conscience. He not only refused to do what he thought was wrong, but would not refrain from doing what he thought was right. Not that he had no care for his reputation; few men were more naturally sensitive than he to the estimate put upon him by others; but duty was more sacred and precious in his eyes than the public hosannah. A friend's censure pained him not a little; but it was a pain he could bear much better than the cry of his wounded conscience. He did not always hurry to take a decisive position, especially on any new question; with all his activity of intellect, and his confidence in his logical deductions, he chose his ground cautiously; but when he had once planted himself he could not be stirred a hair's breadth from his stand-point, till he was dislodged by the conviction that he was wrong. Threats could wring from him no concessions, bribes only awoke his contempt, deprecating remonstrances only made him distrust the sincerity and value of the friendship which presented them, and the opposition that threatened to crush him, only petrified his courage into a rocky strength of resistance. He could die like Paul, taking as his heritage the crown of martyrdom, but he could neither betray like Judas or deny like Peter for the sake of security or silver. In the very foreground of his moral qualities stood this unbending integrity; it was the controlling agency of his mind, the captain of all his interior forces. Whoever accused him of indiscretions, no man suspected him of having compromised his principles.

His sensibilities were active. His mind may be said to have abounded in nerves, even more than his body. To be a stoic was, with him, an impossible thing. A truth never expended its whole force upon his understanding; his emotions lay so close to his intellect that the intercourse between them was both rapid and free. He was no cold, stern, soulless, statue of justice, no passionless incarnation of abstract righteousness. His intellect emitted no more light, than did his passions radiate heat. Indeed, not a little of his intellectual activity was the result of his emotional activity. He thought rapidly, because he felt deeply. The movements of his mental machinery were quick, because his soul supplied such an amount of motive power. His flashes of thought were often little else than the glow of his flaming feelings, and his words were the avenue through which the eye might look to discover them.

The bearing of this feature of his character upon every form of its development, was close and important. It created not a little of his outward greatness, and explains not a few of his defects. Without it he would have borne another character; and his biographer would have had to record another outward history, if, indeed, in its absence, his outward history would then have warranted any permanent record. His intellect was kept awake, not simply because it possessed in itself a powerful mainspring, but because it expanded, until it pressed against its outward environments, under the heat of emotion. His shades of feeling were nice and delicate, and so he was prompted to search after the delicate varieties of thought to which they corresponded. He adhered to a rational conviction, not only because experience had taught him that this was best and safest; but because he deeply felt the mortification and disgrace of being unreasonable. He debated earnestly with an opponent, not only because the moral sentiment advocated by his opponent wanted logical consistency to his eye; but, also, because his moral feeling revolted at a false principle. His high appreciation of the beautiful was not merely the result of perceiving fitness and propriety, but the going forth of his roused soul in joy and gratitude to pay homage at the feet of loveliness. His unbending Christian integrity, his firm adherence to what seemed duty, sprung, not only from the clear discovery that the law was holy, just and good, but also from the deep abiding reverence which he felt for truth ; from the deep feeling that God was abused and the soul disgraced, when it turned its back upon heaven-revealed duty, and paid its devotions at a sensual shrine.

This active and powerful sensibility explains the earnestness and vehemence of much of his effort. To be calm and temperate, when a great and good cause was in danger of a failure through human indolence and opposition, was not in his nature. He could not plead for it according to rhetorical rule, nor rebuke its foes with careful, tender mildness. His words came to his lips, glowing with the pale heat given them by the fused emotions which they had momentarily enveloped. He cared nothing for exact technical statement. He was as abrupt, perchance, as the fiery discharges of a volcanic crater, and as exaggerative as an oriental prophet. He saw, for the time, little else than a great interest sinking, and strong brawny men sleeping on the brink of the pit wherein it was disappearing, or quarrelling with those who were struggling to save it ; and whoever else might caressingly invite them to arise, and meekly ask them not to stand in the way of others, he was pretty certain to shake them with some violence, and utter some hasty and stinging words.

And when a giant evil was before him,—guarded by

law, custom, influence, and money, subsidizing talent, triumphing over virtue, stopping the mouths of men with bribes, and resolving to crush what it could not corrupt and buy,—he could hardly find rest by day or by night. It would mingle itself with every current of his thought, and ally itself with every topic he sought to develope. It was perpetually goading him into almost a moral fierceness. It seemed like a Nessus-garment enveloping his soul, and stinging every moral nerve into the agony that makes desperate. And he who looked, at such a time, for worldly prudence and timid moderation, must look elsewhere than to Martin Cheney. He analyzed the evil, held up its elements to view till each alone seemed worthy only of reprobation, developed the connected evils, dwelt on the aggravated circumstances, then, putting them all together into a monstrous unity, he held it up on the point of his terrible invective and demanded for it the curses of the world.

Nor was it enough for him to deal sternly with the evil. He never expended his whole force on abstract sins, or organic iniquities. A sin implied a sinner; moral evil always spoke of guilt. He never sought to atone for leaving a wrong-doer undisciplined, by a display of his courage in hurling verbal missiles at the head of the wrong deed. He lashed those who brought the evil to the birth; he lashed those who nursed it; he lashed those who gave it currency and reputation; he lashed those who bowed down before it; he lashed those who apologized for it; he lashed those who feared it; he lashed those who refused to lash it; and he lashed many of those who did lash it, because they would not lash it harder. And all this while, instead of using up his intense moral feeling that spurred him on, it seemed to be generated by the very process concerned in its expenditure. It seemed as though he could never be quiet until he had torn the evil itself to shivers, and driven every one of its supporters to the confessional of heaven with tears of repentance. This representation is strong; but it would be almost impossible to exaggerate this feature in his character and life.

That such a man should be constantly offending against the nice propriety of a compromising age, and shocking the fastidious taste and careful policy which are so much commended, was the most natural thing in the world. Indeed, that he should actually *be* imprudent, and defeat his object sometimes through excess of zeal and deficiency of caution, was a thing likely to occur;—a thing which did, doubtless, more than once occur. He did sometimes excite prejudice where he was not known, by the severity which he exercised; a prejudice which he never overcame. The development was taken as the index to harshness, censoriousness, and discourtesy; it was supposed to denote that the moral feeling was unusually dull, rather than highly intense. In warm debate with some of his dearest friends and brethren over an important moral principle, he would sometimes deal in a vehemence and severity which grieved their hearts, and made him appear at a disadvantage. At the State Peace Convention, held in Providence, in March, 1850, Mr. Elihu Burritt was making a plea in behalf of the Peace Congress to be held in Europe, and urging its claims in view of the highly successful effort made the preceding year, in the Peace Congress held in Paris. Mr. Cheney made a speech on the occasion, in favor of the object, but, during which, he took occasion to say that he hoped the Congress would submit to have no shackles put on their speech; that he would not have gone into the Congress at Paris under any such prohibition as that which required the members to be silent touching the state of France, or the French intervention in behalf of the papal power in Italy. It was uttered in Mr. Cheney's strong, earnest way; it was the spontaneous developement of his opposition to every thing which sacrificed freedom of speech. Mr. Burritt evidently felt chagrined. Two months afterward, at the annual meeting of the League of Brotherhood in Worcester, an intimate friend of Mr. Cheney who was present at the Providence meeting, was on a Committee with Mr. Burritt, to nominate officers for the ensuing year. For two years Mr. Cheney had been one of the Vice Presidents of the League. When they came to the nomination of a Vice President for R. I. Mr. B. hesitated. The friend suggested the name of Mr. Cheney. Mr. B. looked up in his peculiar, impressive, earnest, childlike way, and replied;—"Elder Cheney is a strong, able, advocate of Peace, *but don't you think he is rather bitter?*" and then referred to the incident already related. After a statement or two touching Mr. Cheney's character, his name was inserted; but it is probable that Mr. B.'s mind was never fully relieved of that impression.

This strong sensibility, in connection with his high

sense of justice, operated in another and much more amiable form;—it made him a champion in behalf of the rights of the weak, when they were in danger of being awed by the terrors or crushed by the power of the strong. He could not bear tyranny; both because it was opposed to his convictions of right, and because it did fearful violence to all the deep moral feelings of his soul. He could *see* why the weak and necessitous had a claim upon the guardianship and help of the strong, and all his emotions combined to make their claims appear sacred. And so when power was employed to wrest rights away from those who had not the ability to defend them, he felt summoned forward to protest against the injustice, and to give the tyrant the alternative of restitution, or exposure and conflict. This explains his uncompromising warfare against Southern Slavery, and especially his restless, constant, determined, and almost fearful warfare against that latest developement of Slavery—the Fugitive Law. But the same thing, in principle, appeared every where. With him, equality of rights had a meaning. To him, the opening sentences in the Declaration of Independence were simple statements of fundamental truths, however they might have seemed "a rhetorical flourish" paving a way for what was to follow, to Southern statesmen. And, so, whenever he saw an earnest and sincere spirit crushed or tethered by the hands to which nature or accident had given a higher measure of mere force, he was at the side of the sufferer, lifting his arm in his defence. The speakers at the Anti-Slavery Convention in Providence, *might* have been spared that conflict with Mr. Cheney, had they not done violence to his sense of justice, and excited his indignation by their attempts to silence a brother, whose only alleged crime was his profession, and whose self-respect made him comparatively inefficient in a controversy whose weapons were coarse epithets and wholesale denunciation. And in the Conferences, he was always careful to insist most strenuously upon the rights of minorities, and of young and modest brethren. To treat them with marked disrespect, was to draw flashes from his eye and stern protests from his lips. Any ministerial dictation to churches, any undue attempt to have the ruling preëminence over private brethren, any tendency to lord it over God's heritage, came within the same category of sins which were every where to be resisted.

Another feature in his religious character, was his freedom from affected sanctimoniousness, from every thing that savored of false dignity and cant. He had no pulpit mannerisms, never made any parade of his professional badges, or claimed for himself any professional privileges or courtesies. He regarded his rights as springing from his manhood; not at all as imparted by the hands of the ordaining council. He never looked to his post to give him dignity; he rather sought to increase the estimated importance of his own functions, by uniting to them a lofty character, and discharging them with faithfulness and success. Few, perhaps, would think him a minister as they saw him in the street; not because he looked and appeared as a minister should not, but because there was nothing about him that seemed to indicate his profession; because *the man* stood out so prominent that the accidental appendages were seldom thought of.

And, in dealing with religious truth, there was the same freedom from every thing artificial. He spoke in his usual familar tones, and with the same natural, rational earnestness that distinguished him every where. There was never any attempt to appear reverent and awe-struck and impressive. He had, by virtue both of his constitution and his experience, a mortal abhorrence of all Pharisaical sanctity and officious egotism; and so he never pretended to a religious state which was not his own. In the discussion of theological questions, he exercised the same freedom of inquiry, the same determination to look through a subject, and demanded the same logical consistency, which marked his investigations elsewhere. He approached God with his questions, not through the thick darkness and amid the quakings of Sinai, but with the quiet familiarity of the disciple who leaned on the bosom of Jesus. His devotional enthusiasm never carried him an inch farther than his reason warranted him in going. Amid a tempest of excited feeling, or surrounded by a group of weeping penitents, his intellect was still on its throne, and his critical eye was inspecting every developement about him,—measuring and testing it by the truth acquired through the calm study of the past. This was more fully true of him during the last years of his life than before; but he always wanted a rational basis for his faith, and a scriptural justification for his hopes. Being in Boston at the Anniversaries, in the Spring of

1849, in company with a friend, he attended the morning Prayer meeting at the Winter Street Church, at which were present some one thousand persons. The exercises were conducted chiefly by aged and eminent ministers, some of them returned missionaries, and were characterized by a chastened and solemn interest. At the close of the meeting, Mr. Cheney passed out with the friend, and walked along the street some little distance in silence, and apparently in deep meditation. Suddenly he looked up and said, with his calm earnestness;— "I sometimes think that I have no devotional element in my nature." Why ? it was asked. "Why," he replied, " I have been occupying myself all the morning in criticising the theology developed in the exhortations and prayers of those reputable ministers, and trying to form an estimate of their characters for real moral courage and fidelity to christian principle in an unpopular cause."

To some minds, this free, daring, unawed manner of dealing with the things held particularly sacred, seemed to savor strongly of irreverence. He was deterred from laying hold of nothing and subjecting it to the severest logical tests, simply because it had been laid away in the Holy of Holies in an ancient Cathedral, or stood as a prime article in the creed of a hoary orthodox sect. He thought God had desired to be known, and had revealed himself for that purpose ; and that, as he had given us only human eyes with which to see, and a human understanding with which to study, it was both our right and duty to learn of him whatever was within our reach. He regarded the barriers about Horeb as broken down, and the veil of the temple rent that all might gaze freely upon the Shekinah which it had hidden from the vulgar eye for ages. He was certainly daring in his speculations, assertions, and denials, when tried by the usual standards of religious conservatism. He would criticise some portions of the bible, apply principles of interpretation to some of its passages, lay sweeping deductions of philosophy side by side with its statements, riddle the dogmatic propositions of venerated and canonized creed-makers, insist upon the authority of reason and conscience in religious matters, and apologise for much that was branded as infidel, in such terms as to make cautious men hold their breath and tremble, lest he should finally topple over into skepticism. Even some of his warm friends and brethren felt an uneasiness and anxiety on this subject, at times, which they made no effort to conceal from him. He always received the cautions kindly, but deemed them unnecessary; thought, instead of parting with his christian faith, that it was gradually losing itself in glorious visions over which unbelief had no power. He deemed himself ever learning, ever coming nearer and nearer to the central light and truth; and so his eager spirit struggled up the hills of difficulty where the fields of knowledge were to be spread out more vast and glorious beneath his eye. Speaking familiarly to some friends on the subject of his differences in opinion from some of his brethren, he said, he knew they were tried with him; and added, that it was only because he was nearer the summit of the mount than they, and so saw some things more clearly than they; that when they came to occupy his position they would see as he did, though now they deemed him almost a heretic and infidel.

This feature grew more and more prominent up to the time when he was laid aside from labor. Point after point in his early Confession of Faith was either laid aside for another, or, what was more usual, it was modified, both in its spirit and in the form of its statement. He quarrelled more and more with the prevalent theology in some of its features, and defended his own views with fresh earnestness and skill. No formal statement of his theological sentiments or of his usual modes of preaching is needed here, for both are sufficiently indicated in the Sermons and other Discourses found in the preceding chapters. He grew more guarded in his statement of some sentiments, and less so in the statement of others; he laid down important limitations where there had been none previously, and withdrew some that had been carefully stated and earnestly insisted on in earlier years.

Notwithstanding what has been said, and in spite of his own remark in Boston, he was a man of devotional piety. If he might *appear* to have less devotional feeling than others, because he never assumed it, he certainly did possess more than many who display great and uniform fervor in their exercises of worship. His veneration for God was deep, though it was the veneration that admitted of sympathy and invited to a familiar intercourse. His reverence was most deeply excited by those very views of God, afforded by his sympathetic tenderness and stooping condescension. Power, knowledge, and wisdom, expanding into infinity, seldom awed him to prostration of soul or body; superadd to them Justice and Love, and then his soul hasted joyfully with its offerings to the feet of the Deity. The result was, that he studied God chiefly through Christ. If he would give definiteness to his conceptions of Jehovah, he did not go back to the splendid imagery of the prophets, or to Moses' picture of the smoking mount; he turned rather to the graphic delineations of Matthew, as he sketches the features of the Son of Mary, or to the artless narratives of John, as he tells of the Master on whose bosom he had leaned unrebuked. He remarked, on one occasion, that, when he prayed, he sought to bring before his mind the spiritual image of Jesus of Nazareth, and to speak as he would have spoken if he could have gone and preferred his request at the time when the blind man was restored to sight, or when Lazarus was called back from his tomb. His devotional expressions were usually just what they might be supposed to be, when determined in their character, largely, by this habit of mind. He felt that Christ was great, glorious, sympathetic, calm, just and wise; conditioning his gifts upon the conscious necesities and reverent humility of the applicant; and so his prayers were calm, meditative, devout, simple, direct, comprehensive, and, usually brief. They probably affected different persons differently. Some, doubtless, thought them cold and spiritless; lacking in fervid earnestness, because they had little noise or vehemence; but to most pious Christians they were deeply impressive and highly profitable. A true spirit of devotion in the heart of the hearer, was almost sure to be borne up to heaven on the wings of his petition.

The same trait of character gave color to all the developements of his personal piety. It was never ostentatious, always humble. He never boasted directly or indirectly of his spiritual goodness. He made no profession of usual or of unusual sanctity. Of having a good conscience, and of his settled purpose to adhere to his convictions, he made no scruple of speaking plainly; but in respect to what is usually implied in the word *spirituality*, he rather seemed to regard himself deficient. In personal conversation with inquirers, he ever sought to fix their attention upon the plain truths and duties revealed by the gospel; never seeming to regard his own individual experiences as any standard by which they were to try themselves. His allusions to his phases of feeling were seldom and modest; his applications of christian principle to the heart and life were earnest and frequent. Like Paul, he wished that the faith of Christians might stand, not in the wisdom of men, but in the power of God. When he condemned impenitent persons or indolent professors of the Christian faith, his censures were usually mingled with the recognition of whatever there might be that was praiseworthy, and they were tempered with discrimination, until he had reason to believe that they wilfully sacrificed principles which they knew to be sacred and duties which they knew to be binding; after that, he spared neither plainness nor severity. True penitence and real sincerity forever commanded his sympathy, and made the guilty or the erring one feel that they had found a friend whom it was safe to trust.

His Benevolence and Charity might be considered large or small, in proportion as they were viewed from one or another stand-point. Not every suffering applicant for alms, for the body or soul, carried off either his gifts or his blessing; and not every high pretender to honesty or goodness received his endorsing 'God speed.' He steadfastly refused to bestow on many causes that aimed at good results, and that were suffering from the want of assistance; and sometimes strongly condemned distinguished and zealous portions of the church, for the sentiments to which they subscribed and the policy which they had adopted. Of political parties, in spite of their lofty pretensions and the good he acknowledged they might have done, he always had suspicions; and his condemnations were strong and many. He was once strongly solicited to be a candidate for a seat in the R. I. Senate. He at once positively declined, on moral grounds. His friends sought to reason with him. "Suppose," said they, "that all men of worth and moral principle were to keep aloof from the Government, what sort of society should we have?" "A good deal better than it is now, probably," was the reply. "And so you wont consent to be a candidate." "No." "Well, do you know of any one who will consent to run?" "Yes, there will be no difficulty in finding men enough who will jump at the chance." "But we mean a man who is well fitted for the post, a good, able, honest, worthy, high-principled man." "It is *very doubtful* whether you can get *such* a man as that."

Still, whether his benevolence and charity were or were not wisely directed in every case, both were prominent in his character. His heart was full of sympathy for the distressed, and his earnest desire to relieve them often found the most reliable and substantial expression. Many of his alms were done in secret, and he was never known to boast over his benefactions and sacrifices—seldom indeed was he known to allude to them. Whenever he withheld from an enterprise or an object, few doubted his conscientiousness, if they did not always approve his reasons. In his early days, while his income was small and his economy rigid, a brother, with whom he subsequently labored many years in the ministry, was dismissed from his father's door because he had persisted in entering the ministry. Mr. Cheney, learning of the fact, promptly came forward and offered him a home in his own family. The independent and couragous young christian declined the offer, but his gratitude was no less fervent, and the act was no less noble and generous.

Mr. Cheney's views, as they have been developed, can be explained only on the ground that his charity was very broad. He asked no endorsement of all his sentiments as a condition of gaining a passport to his confidence and heart. He loved to see opinions held decidedly, and the reasons for them at hand, even when opposed to his own. He thrust no man from him because he had one more or one less article in his creed than himself. There was scarcely a theoretical doctrine in the gospel but might be rejected, and he would not treat the rejector either as a heathen man or a publican. He believed that men might err sincerely; and he believed also that truth was not so weak but that it might be safely risked in every fair conflict. Strong as were his convictions on those subjects, he would have had no objection to allowing a defender of War or Slavery to argue the case in his own pulpit,—provided he might be allowed to reply. Among the members of the Olneyville Church, were those who differed widely from each other on more than one point of doctrine usually regarded as fundamental; but that was, with him, no reason for complaint, and no reason for hostility among themselves. He believed and taught that there might be unity of the spirit amid diversities of belief.

This must be proof, sufficiently ample, of his high Catholic liberality. And yet, more than once, he was accused of being uncharitable; and, no doubt, often really appeared so. The explanation is not difficult. He could give his christian confidence to no double-dealer, to no moral coward, to no ministerial aristocrat, to no temporizing conservatist, to no ingenious demagogue in Church or State, to no one whose life was radically inconsistent with his profession, to no one who did not give evidence of being deeply sincere. And so far as any of these characters acquired influence and popularity, were his understanding and his moral feeling set against them. They might be talented, zealous, might seem to be doing great immediate good, his eye was perpetually fixed on what to him appeared their treachery. Into this catalogue of insincerity, varying in the degrees of guilt, he put, either justly or unjustly, a large proportion of popular churches, eminent ministers, successful politicians, &c. The consequence was, he suspected these classes of the community, and his treatment indicated his suspicions. When others praised them for the good they seemed to be doing, he could not join in the eulogy; but, instead, he sometimes uttered the words of doubt and wielded the lash of rebuke. That this should wear the aspect of uncharitableness in the eyes of the general community, was a thing which could not have been otherwise. And that, with his strong moral feeling and peculiar experiences, he should have been sometimes too hasty and unsparing in his condemnations, was a thing to be expected, and a thing which occurred.

And then his strong, stern, sharp, earnest way of dealing with his opponents in controversy,—a method which was prompted by his tendencies, which was the most natural, if not the necessary mode of developing his spirit's forces,—often had the appearance of uncharitable severity. He would sometimes thunder down upon his disputant with a fiery force that made a stranger regard him as wanting in kindly sympathies, if not in justice. He would sometimes become warm, and, in his warmth, would sometimes sacrifice courtesy, and fail to give a very high application to his catholic and liberal principles. But whenever his heat betrayed him into any such indiscretion, it served to exhibit his frank, manly, conscientious spirit in a new and endearing form. In the meekest manner would he acknowledge his fault, without the least disposition to extenuate it, ask the forgiveness of the wounded brother and of all who had witnessed the scene, and put himself upon his guard against a similar offence in the future. The confession was so free and hearty, that every body was put into a sympathy with the man, more deep, if possible, than before. It showed that justice, benevolence and charity were deeply seated principles, and that they were never sacrificed,—save as his strong impulses sometimes buried them in the surges of feeling; but when the storm had passed, they were still seen anchored to the base of his nature, like the ocean lighthouse resting on the enduring rock.

From what has been stated, it may easily be inferred that Religion and Morality were never divorced in his mind; and that whatever was operating to render the private and social morals corrupt or lax, was regarded as the greatest foe to Christianity. He could have confidence in a person's religion just so far as it led to a rigid practice of christian morality, and no farther. Bigoted sticklers for a creed, fervid and impassioned exhorters in a prayer meeting, seers of heavenly visions telling them with immoderate rapture or with tearful solemnity, gained his confidence just so far as they dealt justly, and loved mercy, and walked humbly before God. He was forever applying the testing principle, furnished by Christ, to human character,—" By their fruits shall ye know them." With him, religion was an all-controlling principle, seated in the heart; not a gush of occasional feeling, or a mantle for Sundays and other special occasions thrown loosely over the shoulders of a worldly soul. He who, in any sphere of life or department of action, made religious obligation of no account, or put it into a secondary or subordinate position, he thought needed yet to be taught what were the first principles of the doctrine of Christ.

He could not, therefore, confide in great men or small men, however high or low might be their profession or standing, who crowded their religion out of their politics, their business, or their social intercourse. An eloquent sermon on christian self-denial or the necessity of repentance, would never atone for ministerial aristocracy or inhumanity. The plea of a great statesman for the sanctity of religious truth, or his impressive public compliments paid to a wise and guiding Providence, made him look with no complacency upon his political jugglery or his personal vices. The benevolence which ostentatiously gave a thousand dollars to replenish an exhausted Missionary Treasury, and then allowed the donor to oppress his poor tenantry and consent to the oppression of millions, he regarded as essentially defective in the christian element. No extent of power, no elevation of functions, no dignity of office, exempted the possessor from the claims of that law which requires all men to be perfect. Indeed, vices in high life, corruption in places of power and influence, sin invested with the robes of honor, seemed to him to be more wicked and more dangerous, and so requiring the stronger condemnation. He had no faith in the papal doctrine of Indulgences, purchasable by wealth or guaranteed to station. If a rigid code of practical morality was given to the poor and weak ; he insisted that wealth and power were not to be treated to more lax statutes. He could forgive a petty crime committed by the beggar, whose necessities impelled and whose training had done little to restrain him; but for a rich boaster of wisdom to project or aid in perpetrating a mighty public wrong, was to leave a stain of guilt on his soul, effacable only by the bitter tears of a public confession and repentance.

And hence he labored earnestly to bring public and civil, as well as private and individual life, into subjection to the gospel. He bewailed public and organic sins, and prayed and toiled for public and organic virtues. He wished to put a conscience within corporations, and give the Sermon on the mount a place in civil Legislatures. He longed to see the marts of commerce become the temples of integrity, and the Judge's ermine free from the stains of bribery. He longed to see Law give proof that it came from the bosom of God, and Government become the just and benignant Schoolmaster of Society. He could conceive of no Millenium but Satan's, till the Rulers feared God, and the people loved to have it so.

It hardly needs to be said that such a moral and religious character attracted attention, both by its unique individuality, its sharp, distinct, prominent features, and its intensely active outward force. It became an element of life in a community that must be recognized; that was constantly giving every body the amplest proof of its presence. Other lights might be hidden, but his always burned where it could be seen. Sleepy as the souls might be about him, they were kept conscious of one thing, and that was that Martin Cheney was among them. Nobody had need to ask who he was, or what he was. His influence penetrated every corner of the community, and was felt in every circle, public and private. Whether he excited pleasure or dissatisfaction in the minds about him, he was almost certain to excite emotions of some sort in every heart. To feel perfectly indifferent toward him, to pass along day after day just as though he was not there, was a thing not easy to be done. Religion uttered a voice through his lips that fell on all ears to startle, and developed a power through his life that pressed on all hearts to rouse them.

The Social department of Mr. Cheney's character was in perfect keeping with the intellectual and moral traits which have already been developed. He was as far removed as possible from being a misanthrope, both by his tendencies and habits. He enjoyed society, he sought it, and was sought by it. There he unbent himself from the defiant and defensive attitudes which his public warfare with evil had made necessary. He never shrunk from the conflict; whenever the trumpet sounded for a charge, he was in the van of the forces, and he was also the last to leave the field; but when his work there was done, he welcomed the genial, social afterpart, with a relish that seemed to have been made keen by the fierceness of the strife.

Yet he never parted with his dignity, or compromised his radical principles, in the most genial of his social moods. Whoever followed him or invited him home, from a stern public controversy with an opponent, a principle or a custom, hoping to hear him retract in his calmness or his humor what he had maintained in his firmness, had mistaken their man. His compliments were not his principles, and he never laughed away his integrity. Any attempt to take advantage of his merry and apparently careless moods to gain from him a compromise, once refused on moral grounds, would change the relaxed humorist into the rigid expounder of moral law. "Leviathan was not so tamed." His watchful intellect did not thus let in an enemy without warning. He was not thus thrown off his guard. He seemed to recognize that as the hour and point of weakness, and so doubled the number of sentinels. And he loved society, not only for itself, but because it was a means of training him better for his battles with iniquity,—of nurturing the christian fidelity he deemed it his special mission to illustrate and enforce. And he who was not ready to endorse the same integrity in private which had been seen in his public life, or was unwilling to exercise the same courtesy and respect toward him in the social circle which were conceded in the presence of the world, would soon find that rebuke could be administered as well to a colloquist as to a crowd. He was the same man in the parlor of a friend as in the pulpit; and they who took it for granted that he was otherwise, and treated him accordingly, would very soon learn the mistake into which they had fallen.

Still, while thus unbending in respect to his principles, he was easy, familiar, and talkative in the social circle. Save as certain topics were introduced, his courteous, conciliatory, cheerful demeanor, almost forbade one to think of him as the stern, fearless, severe reformer. The only exception to this remark occurred when he was thrown among strangers, and especially among strangers somewhat distinguished or somewhat sensual. In such cases he usually said little. This was owing in part to his modesty, in part to his caution, in part to his habit of trying to read character ; and, in the case of meeting with a group of sensual beings, he was repelled by the grossness for which he could have no sympathy. His conversation never flowed briskly, except when meeting those who could somewhat sympathize with him. He could have preached a sermon to a crowd of worldlings or conservatists, but that his sense of propriety seldom allowed him to do without the consent of the audience. But when he was social, there was nothing of dogmatism,—nothing which savored of the lecturer. He would never monopolize the time or the conversation, and nothing but the most evident wish of the company would reconcile him to the idea of doing the chief portion of the talking. He sought to make his inferiors feel at home, and usually succeeded ; to send them away pleased with themselves and others, and so they were apt to go.

His mental activity and his serious views of life combined to make his conversations instructive and profitable. Frivolous chit-chat, neighborhood gossip, seldom satisfied or pleased him. His mind was always fruitful in topics, they were usually selected with a judicious reference to the company and the circumstances, and so made interesting to all. Many of his happiest things were uttered in these social circles. There was a sparkling vivacity peculiar to himself, and especially in his genial moods. And here, too, he would develope his subtle powers of analysis, and exhibit the nicety of his perceptions of thought and of character.

He loved fun. There was a large fountain of humor in his nature. His conscience was scarcely more fully awake to the wickedness of vice, than was another portion of his being to its supreme folly and ridiculousness. He could not only denounce a sin, but caricature it. He could not only mourn over Milton's picture of Satan, despoiling Eden of its divine beauty and man of his Godlike glory, but could shake himself with laughter as he saw him " squat like a toad," troubling the dreams of Eve, and stung into his devilish shape again by the sudden prick of Ithuriel's spear. He enjoyed the ludicrous with a high relish, and could be somewhat ludicrous himself. In the circle of a few confidential friends, after becoming weary with close thought and taxing business, he would sometimes discharge his jets of wit in constant succession, until the room seemed to blaze with merriment; and rehearse the wild, frolicsome adventures of his early life with a skill and a zest, which made care and weariness alike to be forgotten. And yet, through it all, no one felt that he had demeaned himself—that he was any thing less than the Martin Cheney of their previous conceptions.

His friendships were strong. He probably had but few intimate friends,—few of whom he made confidants. But when he formed a real personal attachment, it was fervent and deep. He made no professions of peculiar regard; he left the proof of its existence to its fruits. These attachments were usually formed on the basis of similar features of character, and of their confidence in him. He repaid sympathy and kindness and approbation, with confidence and gratitude and reciprocal kindness. And, as in most other cases, it was not so easy for him to see the faults of these personal friends, or to measure their excellencies accurately, as it was for him to perform the same work for others. Their virtues, doubtless, seemed sometimes more numerous and striking than they really were, and their defects fewer and less worthy of notice. But if his partiality did make it more difficult for him to discern their errors, it made him if possible more prompt and faithful in seeking to correct the errors which were visible.

In his family he was a bright shining light, a perennial fountain of joy, an high priest of chastened gladness. Even strangers who came and shared his ready and generous hospitality, were at once enveloped in an atmosphere of home feeling. Dignified and yet condescending, manly and yet tender, exercising decisive authority and yet ever dealing in gentleness and love, combining order with freedom, at once the head and the companion of the group, he seldom produced a happier impression upon an observer than when seen in the bosom of his home. He treated his wife like a husband, and his children like a father; he sought to lighten the burdens of the one, and directed and shared in the sports of the other. And they who became members of his family, for longer or shorter periods of time, found it in many senses and on many accounts, a pleasant and interesting home,—always left with regret and returned to with pleasure. His children, as, one by one, they went out from it into the world of temptation and responsibility, remembered its experiences with tenderness, felt chastened and guarded by the influences which it had thrown about them, and went back to its fellowships, as opportunities were afforded, as Noah's dove went back to the ark.

His pastoral visiting, so far as time and opportunity allowed him to carry it on, was always a source of high gratification to those who enjoyed it. That there might have been some of the feeling which makes a minister's calls desired because they who receive them are thus noticed and made to appear respectable, is highly probable; but there were other and higher reasons for esteeming his visits. He was regarded as a friend of his people and of all,—one to whom they loved to confide their deepest and dearest interests, with the assurance that he would endeavor to sympathize with and aid them. They felt encouraged to throw off their reserve in his presence, and open their hearts before him. He put himself, courteously, on familiar terms with them, and so they felt at home with him. He used to say that he had no talent for visiting; but others deemed themselves authorized, for once, in differing from him in opinion.

The sick and sorrowful found him a comforter. He did not, could not, multiply words in such places, because he would only say what he believed and felt; and sometimes he could think of no consolations for

*31

such sufferers as he met, and sometimes he could give no adequate expression to his feelings. But all this made his words appropriate and full of meaning. What he did say was to the purpose, and so was felt and remembered the better. His sympathies were keen; and, hence, he was not inclined to seek suffering which he could not relieve, to talk where words were but a mockery, to tarry where he could not profit. But his visits to the sick room made many a passage to the grave and to heaven clearer to the departing spirit, and made the spirit itself stronger and firmer to walk through the shadowy valley. And as he lifted up his voice over the dead in tenderness and in hope, many a bereaved circle grew calmer, and learned anew to look upon its affliction as the work of wisdom and of love, capable of leaving behind the choicest blessings for the soul. Nothing could be more touchingly beautiful than some of his remarks and prayers on funeral occasions. They were highly appropriate, and often left behind the most grateful and lasting impressions;—simply because they were the natural expression of his deep social sympathies, chastened and made powerful by his religious faith.

Yet his fondness for society never led him to seek a place in any circle where he could not be admitted as an equal, even when bringing all his peculiarities and radicalisms with him. He would accept no compliment paid to the half of his nature, while the rest was disgraced. If he could not be welcomed as he was—as the veritable unabridged Martin Cheney—he chose to go or stay elsewhere. He made no attempt to conceal an opinion or a trait if it was passing under a scathing criticism; indeed, this was usually the very surest way to bring on an avowal. He would pass under no yoke so low as to forbid his standing erect; walk through no door not wide enough for his full proportions. There were paths sufficiently broad for his own convenience, and, if he could walk with none of his neighbors, he could walk alone.

He seldom, if ever, courted admission to any grade or quality of society. He usually waited for invitations, or for the proof that he would find a welcome. His life having been spent among the masses, it is not strange that he should feel more at home in their cosy sitting rooms, than in the magnificent parlors of the aristocracy. He had such an independence that he went his own way, feeling that he was abundantly able to take care of his own reputation, when he discovered that the higher circles were disinclined to take it under their guardianship. So far as they curled their lips at him, he turned away pitying their want of good breeding, and half merry and half indignant at their pompous assumptions of merit. He would have preferred being a man alone, rather than a cringing sycophant in a palace.

In short, his social qualities were such as to develope nearly all the gentler, finer, tenderer elements of his nature; to show how deeply seated were his religious principles; to make every body feel that he was a man, with all the human sympathies in full play; to give him an easy access to the hearts of the masses; to chasten his analytical intellect and temper his impetuous feeling ; to correct the unjust impressions produced by his frequent severity, and to hold him back from the excesses into which his roused forces were ever in danger of hurrying him.

Such were the chief elements of Mr. Cheney's character; modified in their action by circumstances, and by their reciprocal influence. It had, of course, its sharp points, and its strong antagonisms. It was not so balanced as to make either the interior or exterior life calm and even. The various forces were so strong and so susceptible, that, when circumstances combined to rouse any one of them into its highest action, it would move with a controlling energy before the great regulator could be put into successful operation. He was, hence, in constant danger of overaction,—of falling into excesses ; and, looking at his character in its elements, the chief wonder is that his excesses were so few, and his prudence so great. This liability was, doubtless, in some sense, a defect ; but it was a defect necessarily incidental to his power and excellencies. Without this ready strength he could never have been the bold, prompt, vigilant, efficient reformer that he was. The very qualities that distinguished him,—that made up his power and gave him his usefulness,—exposed him to danger, excited the fears of his friends, and laid him and his cause open to the apparently just censure of his foes. So he himself used sometimes, in his frank way, to tell his brethren. He knew, he said, that he must often have tried them, that he sometimes tried himself; but that it would spoil him, make him good for nothing, if those things—sometimes unpleasant in their developements—were wanting to his character. He was conscious of tendencies to imprudence; often said, when his soul was calm, that he knew he had been imprudent when his soul was heated; that his hasty, earnest movements, when necessity seemed to be laid on him to act at once, were not always wisest or best. Still it was not in him to do nothing because he could not be sure of doing the wisest thing. And so he is to be judged, not before the tribunal of a cold, stern, passionless, stoical, indolent nature, seated calmly on its study cushion; but judged in view of what God had made him,—in view of his constitutional temperament and tendencies, and in view of the circumstances which surrounded him. An indifference to Slavery in a child of a dozen years, brought up in the family of Senator Foote of Mississippi, is not to be set down as denoting the same traits of character that would be recognized in connection with a similar indifference in a son of William Lloyd Garrison, who had spent two years in setting type for "The Liberator." And, judging Mr. Cheney thus, he must be set down as no common man, and as having no common merit.

Uneducated, in the usual acceptation of that word, he nevertheless compelled the highest scholarship to sit delighted at his feet to learn; and his reasonings and opinions were received with deference even on the subject of mental education. Subjected to no other systematic culture than that which he was able to develope and apply, amid the constant pressure of heavy cares, crowding duties, and a perpetual open moral warfare, he grew in mental force, even after his head was hoary; and was a more and more enthusiastic student of nature, philosophy, science, government, morals, and the bible, until disease cut short his labors.

For years a reckless leader in vices terribly corrupting, he became specially distinguished for a strength of moral and religious character that had few equals. From being the terror of all good men who knew him, and the champion on whom the worst sinners relied for a defence of their cause, he became the scourge of wickedness, and a pillar for the weak faith and trembling hopes of gray-headed Christians.

With no reputation but for evil doings, in an immoral community which he had aided to corrupt, allied to an unpopular sect, and surrounded by popular and educated ministers, he established a character for integrity and ability which made him to be hailed as a leader and a champion in the great causes of christian philanthropy; and for twenty years he was perpetually winning fresh laurels on fields of conflict covered with giant hosts.

With a soul full of strong passions, a sensibility like a magazine, and surrounded by circumstances that acted like torches flung into its heart, he still managed with a prudence that made him a respected counsellor among cool and sagacious men, and led a church and society along, through troublous times, up successive steps of growth and progress, to high influence and power.

These are significant facts; not to be explained without conceding both greatness and goodness to him of whose history they make a part.

CHAPTER XVI.

ESTIMATE OF HIM AS A PREACHER.

The sphere in which Mr. Cheney chiefly distinguished himself was the pulpit. He was known, to be sure, as the philanthropist and the platform advocate of the great moral enterprises of his time, but in all these places he was known as the minister of Christ,—preaching and illustrating the very gospel which he preached at home. It might be possible for one to infer all the interesting peculiarities of his pulpit life from the sketches of his Sermons and the various traits of his character. Still, there seems to be a high propriety in devoting a single chapter to the presentation of him in the character of a public religious teacher. It will aid in giving a fuller view of the man, and may not be without its benefit to others who occupy the same sphere, and who covet the highest possible efficiency there.

High pulpit power is seldom wholly the gift of nature or accident. Nor yet is it alone dependent on moral goodness, or deep religious consecration. Without these last elements no one is fully qualified for the pulpit ; no one can ever honor its functions, or rationally expect a real and large success. This deep sympathy with the truth which he is to utter, this abiding faith in God, this earnest solicitude for the salvation of his people, is a fundamental qualification of a minister. Whatever else can be spared, this is indispensable. But deep piety is not the only thing needed in the pulpit. There are other qualities, both of a moral and intellectual sort, in whose absence the purest hearts would act in the pulpit but feebly. And they who have been distinguished for large efficiency in the pulpit have, usually if not always, reached that distinction through much labor. That some must toil more arduously than others to reach this goal, is true. Efficiency of every sort offers itself to some hands at lower prices than to others. But no strong man ever found his strength in his possession without being able to explain how it came to him. It has been gathered up by the slow accumulations of time and effort. Men who stand on the heights of greatness as quietly and calmly as though they had inherited the station as a birthright, and never could be made dizzy, have climbed there by steps many and wearisome, whether the eye of the observer is able or unable to discern the long, difficult, dangerous path which led there. And to this, pulpit efficiency presents no exception.

Nor does the efficiency which belonged to Mr. Cheney in the capacity of a minister, present itself to us as the product of accident. It was not alone his genius or his native talent that gave him the eminence which was conceded to him here on all hands. His exhibitions of power were not all the sudden gushings of a perennial fountain, which needed only an outlet to disclose its wealth. Whoever thought otherwise, Mr. Cheney was a close and earnest student. He knew what mental application was. Over the subject which he discussed with ease and confidence and clearness, he had spent, perchance, weeks of the most wearing thought. The principles which an unexpected emergency called suddenly forth, and the strong, close, compact reasonings by which they were sustained—though their novelty might lead his hearers to suppose that they were the new offspring of his fruitful mind—were only the exponents of that close, patient investigation which he might have been carrying on for months previous by day and by night. They who were coveting his readiness knew not, perhaps, always, that he was ready chiefly because the past had borne so high witness to his diligent preparation. His active intellect was a great helper without doubt ; but not a little of his ready force consisted in drawing from the storehouse of his mind what previous study had carefully labelled and deposited there, for just such occasions as those which witnessed its coming forward to the light.

Mr. Cheney had a method of making every thing appear fresh ; and this, in part, may explain the impression which he so generally gave of unstudiedness and spontaneity. But whoever will look over his manuscripts, will find abundant evidence of the fact that he made very few random efforts in the pulpit or on the platform. He very seldom spoke in public, unless called to do so without warning, without devoting time, with pen or pencil in hand, to specific preparation ; and what he prepared he kept, that it might be ready for future reference. He probably preached few sermons in his life without preparing a sketch of them ;

and he probably prepared very few sketches which were not faithfully preserved. And in preparing many of his discourses he would sometimes draw out two or three plans; then sometimes condense them into one; sometimes select one in preference to the rest; but the whole of them would be carefully preserved. An address on the subject of Peace is found among his papers, marked as having been delivered ten times; and, packed up with it, are not less than ten loose papers, each of which contains an expansion of some thought in the address, some new argument or illustration, some emendation or appendix, a reply to some anticipated objection, or an enforcement of some position not likely to have its desired weight. If he trusted for some sort of inspiration to aid him when the excitement of an effort was on him, he evidently trusted it after he had done all that he could to remove or lessen the necessity for securing it. He had no carelessness in regard to what he should say on ordinary or extraordinary occasions. He had too much prudence and felt too deeply the weight of responsibility to leave willingly either his thoughts or words to the influence of the occasion, or to the miserable guidance of caprice. He never seemed to feel that the promise given to the disciples, that the Holy Ghost should teach them how and what they should speak, had any such application to himself as to save him from imprudence and error, if he carelessly refused to take thought beforehand what he should say. He did not probably take any very special pains to conceal from others the preparation which he was wont to make; it was, however, less apparent to most who knew him than it is made by an inspection of his manuscripts and papers. And his not having so strong a sympathy with the operation of Theological Seminaries, as many others, might have given many minds the impression that the systematic study of theology did not appear very important to him. But his own success as a private and unaided student, doubtless aided to give him the impression that private study would do for most men; and the creed-fetters which he saw keeping down the free and manly spirit of not a few young men trained in the Schools of the Prophets, raised the query in his mind, whether their real benefit warranted the outlay required for their support. Education had few firmer friends than he, and upon ministerial education he earnestly insisted; but demanded that it should be such education as would aid in making strong, efficient, consecrated men.

So much it has seemed necessary to premise, in order both to disabuse some minds of the impression that Mr. Cheney owed his greatness in the ministry to something entirely different from mental application, and to encourage others situated similarly to "go and do likewise." Instead of being an exception to the rule that requires study in order to mental force, he is a high and striking example of it.

Mr. Cheney's preaching and other public speaking, like his character, was marked by a strong individuality. He was no copyist, and he could not be copied. It appeared peculiar both in its matter, its manner, and its impressions. When heard, he was singled out from any number of associates as a distinct person, having something distinct to say. Few who listened to him soon forgot either the man or his discourse. Some thought or some expression would be almost sure to make its mark and leave it. The impression might be a pleasant or an unpleasant one, but an impression of some sort there was almost sure to be. He was not a model preacher, if, indeed, there can be any such thing. Minds are differently constituted, and so must find various modes of developement. Some general rules may be furnished by both Logic and Rhetoric, but any one might as consistently expect to write a "Paradise Lost" by studying Iambic, Spondee and Hexameter, as to rise to the pulpit efficiency of any able minister by copying his outlines, noting down his arguments, recollecting his metaphors, and repeating his gesticulation. Tried by almost any standard, Mr. Cheney sermonized defectively; and, in his manner, sometimes set at naught every ideal which a human imagination could create or a human taste justify. And it may not be amiss to note a few of what seem to be defects in his pulpit labors.

And a fault into which he was very apt to fall when speaking on a special occasion, and especially if abroad, was that of explaining, in a sort of apologetical way, the details of the circumstances under which he was called to speak. It was no index to his unwillingness to speak, no indication of a wish to lower the expectation of the audience that he might be surer of their impartiality and approbation, no assumption that whatever related to him and his present work was important, no wish to call attention to himself before it should be arrested by his subject. It was not in him to be over anxious about these things. It was, perhaps, somewhat the fruit of his scrupulous conscientiousness, that bade him let the audience understand all the relations between himself and them; but probably more the result of a habit, formed in his youth when he felt that his ministry needed explanation and apology, and afterward adhered to without any distinct thought regarding the impression it was likely to give. These explanations, sometimes long, seemed unnecessary, they curtailed his sermon or his speech, and, of course, were much less interesting than so much said on the topic in hand.

And, as if to atone for this defect, he sometimes developed another. In his own pulpit, on ordinary occasions, he began his sermons often with what seemed a hasty abruptness. Almost without introductory remark of any kind, he would commence the critical examination of a passage, requiring perhaps closer and more careful thought than any thing which followed. Into the very heart of his discourse he would sometimes seem to have penetrated before the expiration of five minutes after naming his text. Before the attention of his hearers had become fairly fixed, he would have gone over much ground, familiarity with which was more or less essential to a full apprehension of what was subsequently developed. His mind would appear like a panting race-horse pressing forward with its eye on its goal, and so to follow it, when it had started at the top of its speed, was a task full of difficulty. It was hard work enough to keep at its heels when its rapid running was expected and provided for; and his hasty beginnings often made that difficulty too great to be overcome.

And then he was more or less accustomed to define the terms in his text or subject by simply copying and reading, without note or comment, all the definitions found in Webster's Dictionary. Examples of this will be found in the discourses inserted in the preceding chapters, and especially in the Essays on the Atonement, and on Moral Obligation. Instead of selecting one of these numerous definitions and using the term as its equivalent, or of deducing from the whole a general one which was included in each and embraced all, he was very apt to crowd the multitude of definitions all undigested before the mind of the hearer, leaving him to do the work of analysis or generalization without stopping at all to afford time for its performance. It was probably all plain to him; but if it interested his audience enough to secure their close attention, it must have sometimes mystified rather than elucidated his subject.

His tendency to multiply divisions was somewhat excessive. As they appeared in the form of primary and secondary and remarks, they sometimes numbered from twenty to forty. Professor Finney, of Oberlin, perhaps surpasses him in this, but it is very hard to commend it even on the basis of such a precedent. His distinctions were so nice, his shades of thought so slight, that, to common eyes they melted imperceptibly into each other; and hence he seemed to be often repeating himself. Fewer and more general heads would have left him all the opportunity to exercise his discrimination, and he would have been less liable to confuse his hearers and overtask their memory. Besides, his discourses lacked the unity which they would otherwise have had. They seemed too much sometimes, like a numerous series of propositions, expressing a collection of independent truths. There was not the great central idea to whose force every subordinate one contributed; instead, the collateral truth might make the deepest impression, by seeming to be the most prominent.

And then the suddenness with which he would develope his ideas, and the rapidity with which he made his transitions from one thought to another, were not always the most favorable to a deep impression. As an idea seldom grew upon his own mind gradually, so it was seldom developed gradually to others. He bounded into the heart of a thought at the first spring, and sought to teach others to do so. An idea would be thrown out at once, on the bosom of some condensed expression, without the least warning of its approach, and while an audience were recovering from the surprise and preparing to inspect it, a second was blazing in their very faces, warning them to prepare for the approach of an equally abrupt successor. All this was highly favorable to *strength*, but hardly so to *depth* of impression; minds would be kept excited, but not put into the state most favorable to having thoughts melt into them and become a part of themselves. There was, therefore, a tendency to carry away the image of the man and a conviction of his high power, quite as strong as to bear off a deep impression derivable from the truths he had been uttering. This resulted from the excess of an excellence, and from the weakness of a faculty; the excellence was the abundance of instruction crowded into his discourses, the feeble faculty was what phrenologists call concentrativeness. And to these might be added, perhaps, an over-estimate of the mental activity and perceptive power of the audience; because a half dozen words disclosed a thought readily to him, he did not think perhaps but it might be so with others.

And another defect still was his habit of throwing out what chanced to lie uppermost in his mind, without consulting the highest propriety or the requirements of circumstances. His discourses were almost sure to indicate the moods of his mind,—not in spite of himself, but with the consent of himself. His audiences were pretty likely to know what topics were specially interesting to him, both because they had prominent places in his public efforts, and the pains which he took to make them appear, whether importantly related to the subject in hand or not. In the last years of his life, his discourses were almost sure to have some place for the presentation of the subject of Slavery. Either in the form of a deducible doctrine, an illustration, an inference, or an application, would some feature of that abomination appear. For a time after the passage of the Fugitive Law, his sermons, even on funeral occasions, were likely to be marked by stern condemnations uttered over the head of that enormity. His convictions and feelings were a pent up force; he had always been accustomed to utter his convictions freely, and so no special effort was made to repress them. And, hence, on not a few occasions, his hearers, while holding his pulpit freedom sacred, regretted that he should seem to be lessening the moral weight of a discourse, by introducing some features that were foreign to its nature. If there was any thing which he wished to rebuke, it was always easy for him to spring aside from the path along which his subject was taking him, deal out the blows of severity, and resume the beaten way. They were episodes which showed his ingenuity and his faithfulness, but they neither showed his moderation nor added to the finish of his discourse. A nice taste would be tried by such methods of dealing with whatever he wished to condemn, and by the unceremonious way in which he sometimes brought all sorts of incidents to set off his points. To him they seemed forcible because he was interested in them, while they lacked force to others because they wanted appropriateness.

Add to this the stern way in which he would oppose a theological sentiment, the fierce war which he carried into the hoary creeds which he deemed false and mischievous, and our bill of indictments is made out. There was little in his manner to conciliate a believer in the sentiment he was combating, especially if he chanced to be a stranger. His war was unrelenting. He used all sorts of weapons which a Christian man might use. He carried on no guerilla warfare; he made no secret thrusts; he had no masked batteries. He took the open field; but when he had taken it, it was to use all his forces. And the severity of statement which he indulged at times, was certainly not the most likely to make at once friends or converts of his opponents. This method resulted from the discovery that there was so much shuffling, double-dealing, and low policy in other pulpits and by other men. It was, in some sense, a natural re-action, and could very well be tolerated in view of the circumstances which gave it birth; but, though natural and tolerable, it was still an excess and a defect.

So much respecting Mr. Cheney's pulpit faults. They may all be regarded as little things, and some of them are the results of his constitutional tendencies; but it seemed proper that they should be noticed.

The subject matter of Mr. Cheney's discourses was ample and varied. His view of the functions of the pulpit contributed to make it so. To reiterate a few theological common-places from Sabbath to Sabbath, did not at all meet the idea of preaching which had grown up in his mind. All sins of which his hearers were in danger, he deemed himself set to disclose; all duties which moral obligation prescribed, he felt bound to devolope and enforce. He lived among his people, he knew their wants, their perils, their susceptibilities, and their lives; and so sought to make his preaching applicable and practically important to them. His audience felt that no monk was muttering to them mysterious sayings, in a dialect half obsolete, from an antique monastery, but that a living, earnest man was standing in the temple of their present life, and speaking to them of the things with which they were every day conversant. He was not enough of an antiquarian to occupy himself with the study of the tomes of the past, nor enough of a prophet to live amid the fancied glories of the future ; and so almost his whole heart and his whole forces were reserved for the significant present. And so in exposing present wickedness, and in exhibiting the present work assigned to the hands of men, he manifested the depth and the constancy of his interest.

CHRIST was specially prominent in all his preaching. Both his understanding and his heart were strongly attracted to Jesus of Nazareth. He never grew weary in his communings with the Son of God. He loved to dwell on his character, to narrate the touching incidents of his life, to repeat his words, to sit with his audience at the feet of his wisdom, to gaze tearfully at the gushings of his love, to climb the hill and listen to his dying prayer, to follow his gospel on its march of triumph, to dwell on the brighter world where he reigns, and anticipate the higher teaching which he waits to give the spirits that rise up to his presence. He met a deduction from Moses' law, authorizing a wrong, by quoting Christ ; he rebuked a low-principled expediency by pointing to Christ ; he proved the safety of virtue by opening the forsaken tomb of Christ ; and he demonstrated the efficiency of moral truth and influence by pointing to the victories of Christ.

As already intimated, he crowded his discourses with instruction. He attached importance to his weekly or more frequent religious addresses to the people, and so prepared himself to profit them. Few ever compressed so much into the same length of time as he. A text or a topic which seemed barren as it was announced, grew into importance under his developement of it. And, usually, when he had done with a subject which he intended to discuss thoroughly, it was felt to be exhausted—his work had the aspect of completeness. Nothing but a capacity too small to comprehend him, or a carelessness which forbade the hope of improvement, could sit under his ministry without gaining both knowledge and strength. He both helped his hearers to think, and taught them to think without help.

His distinct references to the Scriptures were frequent and pertinent. A point in theology he supported by proof texts as well as by argument. He had studied his bible much and closely; for it was the large part of his religious library in his early ministry, and he consulted it with confidence. Dr. Messer's presence also contributed to make his references to the bible frequent and careful. He felt not a little timidity in respect to preaching before so distinguished a man, and, for a time, hoped that he would discontinue his attendance.

After he found that he was not likely to do so, he concluded that he would hazard as little as possible;—that he would have chapter and verse for as many of his statements as could be thus sustained, feeling that he should be safe so long as he was supported by the written word. This habit, thus formed, became invaluable to him, and a kind suggestion now and then from Dr. M. encouraged and strengthened him not a little.

He never appeared as if he had merely undertaken to go through with a required service. He uniformly gave his hearers the impression that he felt that he had something important to say to them, and that he was earnestly desirous of having them sympathize with him in his feeling and efforts. He never suggested religious formality; every occasion and every sermon seemed to be a special one; and when it was over he did not appear satisfied till he was assured his object had been gained. He watched for the fruit with the same interest that had marked his preparation of the soil and his scattering of the seed.

His style or manner of preaching it is very difficult to describe. It was peculiarly his own; as unartistic as nature, and as unique as his character which it developed with singular clearness. In his earlier efforts he displayed great strength and depth of feeling, and his discourses and his style told powerfully on the sympathies and emotions of his audience. He then warned even with many tears; frequently recounted with a choking voice the scenes of wickedness amid which he had revelled; deplored and bewailed his early influence; pleaded with others not to follow in his footsteps; and dwelt with a grateful, humble, adoring joy on the mercy that had reached and saved him;—and then would he urge, with the eloquence of his own deep and overpowering emotion, the impenitent to go in submission and faith to the same glorious gospel and Savior. In later life there was less of this feature apparent. He remarked that he had wept the fountain of his tears dry, and used up his sympathetic power. He might have said more appropriately, that the intellectual element of his nature had become more prominent, and that he had hence put himself under its guidance, and depended on it more fully to exhibit and impress the truth. His earlier preaching, therefore, was adapted to produce more immediate effect, but to be less powerful in moulding the characters of those who sat under it.

He seemed to enjoy preaching with his whole soul and body. His whole demeanor indicated the pleasure which he found in his work. He seemed to be in his true element when he stood up to preach the unsearchable riches of Christ. If he had felt that wo was unto him if he preached not the gospel before he entered upon the work, he indicated afterward that blessing was unto him while he did preach it. He never seemed cowering under the threatened visitation of divine chastisement, but was rejoicing under the light shed from heaven upon his heart and labors. The gospel had brought life and peace and hope to him, and while he saw about him those who had neither, his soul yearned to carry them up to the feet of that same Savior who had brought him salvation and waked his adoring love. He seemed to be preaching a *gospel*,—that is, imparting the good tidings which he himself had so gratefully received from heaven.

In much of his preaching he was highly colloquial. He never appeared to be preaching *before* his audience, but talking *to* them in the most familiar and natural way. He never seemed *trying* to be eloquent,—he was too earnest to secure his object, for that; nor did he ever seem to be making an effort to maintain a pulpit dignity;—he had too much *real* manly dignity in himself, to give him any interest in such an object. He talked there just as he would talk to an individual neighbor whom he should meet in the street. He put on no clerical airs. He would now and then indulge an innocent playfulness in the choice of his illustrative anecdotes, and especially in his attempts to make a custom or a vice appear ridiculous. Some there were, no doubt, who thought him too careless in regard to his pulpit demeanor, and sometimes deemed him more than half irreverent; but he would there, as elsewhere, give the freest expression to his joyous and humorous moods of mind. Speaking of Christ's skill in replying to the questions intended to puzzle him, by proposing searching queries to his catechists, he says it might have been thought, at first view, that he was brought up in Yankeedom. Speaking of the habits of prayer, and of the practice of some persons who made it a point to pray for every body and thing in general, and for nothing and nobody in particular, he said they reminded him of Benjamin Franklin when a lad, who, after assisting his father to fill a barrel with pork, asked why it would not save time and labor to say grace over the whole barrel at once, instead of doing it over a few slices at each meal. Speaking of the equality of rights and the unity of the human race, during the war with Mexico, he said the practical reception of the doctrine of human brotherhood would speedily revolutionize society, and change the positions of men at once. "Why," said he, "the President would betake himself to his closet, and even old Rough and Ready would be down on his knees." If these jets of playfulness had not obviously been perfectly unpremeditated and spontaneous, they would have been intolerable; but breaking forth like momentary flashes of sunlight through the mantle of cloud, they seemed to detract scarcely at all from the seriousness of the impressions produced by the general discourse. His keenest, sharpest, richest, and most remarkable thoughts and expressions often came unexpectedly forth in the midst of his argument or his appeal. They were like a brilliant stream of light suddenly flashing half way across the heavens from the arch of the Aurora Borealis. Those who did not know him might have felt that all this was exceedingly unbecoming; but they who did know him, though they may have felt no disposition to imitate, never thought him less fitted for the pulpit, or as having weakened his influence there.

That he was sometimes vehement, stormy, and rapid in his pulpit developements, has been more than once impliedly asserted. When his moral indignation was roused by the view of some great injustice upon which he was commenting, when he was dealing with the treachery to righteousness and the poor found among the leaders in Church and State, he seemed the ideal of a moral avenger,—the incarnation of a roused conscience busied in its executive functions. His manner, no less than his words and thoughts, contributed to make his work a fearful one to the transgressor. He never seemed to be restrained from doing the highest work of censure of which he was capable, but to be goaded on to perform it by the whole force of his convictions and impulses. Few hearts, at such a time, were cold enough to be unroused; the blood of stoics would chill and curdle, and men of courage would shrink into the corners of their pews as if from the presence of danger.

Mr. Cheney's physical man, too, was eminently one to become a strong ally of his spiritual. Mind and body had numerous and striking correspondencies. The bodily attitude would generally indicate the mental state. Tenderness would relax it in an instant, defiant courage would nerve it to an inflexible firmness, and impatient indignation would make it quiver in its restlessness. Almost every mental state had some natural language for its expression.

More fully than of almost any other man was it true of him, that his face was the mirror of his soul. Few countenances were ever capable of so great a variety in expression. It would develope the subtlest shades of feeling, and change its manifestations as rapidly as his mind could change the phases of its thought. Benevolence would overspread it with the sunniest of smiles, and moral indignation never failed to impart to it an expression which conveyed stronger censure to the transgressor than the most fiery words of some earnest men. He would have conveyed to the mind of a deaf man, through his aspect and action, quite a distinct notion of the general character of his discourses. He would create a conviction that he was eloquent by his address to the eye ; while to those who could both see and hear, it often appeared marvellous how even common thoughts assumed interest and importance as he developed them. He appeared all interest himself, and so excited more interest in others. Every thing with which he grappled wore an importance to him, and so others felt a measure of the same importance.

There was a varied power too in his voice, that contributed to his pulpit and platform efficiency. Its tones were clear, rich, musical, and silvery when speaking on his ordinary key; it was mellow, soft, and subduing when he was dealing with the more touching views of truth; and it was sharp, keen, and ringing, penetrating every corner as if searching out offenders, when the inspiration of his fierce energy was on him. And, in this last case, his flushed face, showing that the heart and head were in sympathy, and his abrupt, decisive, rapid and impassioned gestures, all combined to augment his power. These were the moods which, to most minds, revealed the highest force of the man.

But the most efficient outward agency which he employed was his eye. To *hear* Mr. Cheney simply when he could not be seen, was to lose the half of his effort. His look often did as much to give a thought distinctness and power, as all other agencies combined. His eye could preach a sermon. It was small, deeply set, keen and piercing. When arguing closely it would be half closed, and often suggested the idea of his attempting to look through the intricacies of a complex and tangled subject. When he was animated and joyful, especially under the glory of the higher truths of the gospel, his eye would be lighted up with a radiance that seemed born from above; and when administering his rebukes, it flashed as though there were thunderbolts behind it, waiting to leap out and smite the offenders. His eye never rested on vacancy. He saw every thing and every body before him. Every person was made to feel that that eye had singled him out, and that he was no more lost among a crowd of listeners. And in his roused moods he was wont to conclude every argument and finish every appeal by fixing that piercing eye on some conntenance belonging to a person whom he wished to impress, and holding him spellbound for a few seconds, as the serpent holds its charmed victim. It was hard for a courageous man to return that look for five successive seconds, or feel calm and easy under it, and yet it was scarcely less difficult to look away; and when the speaker had withdrawn his gaze and resumed his speech, the soul felt relieved of an uneasiness which it had been difficult to endure.

Such were the chief characteristics of Mr. Cheney in his capacity of preacher. And, having before us the traits of his character, it will not be difficult to estimate his power. An interesting, impressive and animated speaker he always was. He filled his sermons with thought, and his delivery with the life of animation. Prosy, dull and heavy as a preacher he could never be. And so few persons, in the capacity of hearers, were tempted to sleep or to be occupied with any thing else than the subject which was being developed before them. They were made to feel that the gospel had the most important bearing upon their interests, and that it was having to do with their every day business and life. They felt it to be no mere theory calling for their speculation and criticism, but a great system of practical law, developed by the highest wisdom and sustained by the largest authority. They never felt themselves treated to a graceful reproof of abstract sin, but every member felt that the inner and outer vices of his own life were laid bare, and the call to repentance was made to break on every ear.

He had no ambition to appear learned or profound. He determined to be understood, and set his heart on the moral instruction and improvement of his congregation, rather than on making additions to his own reputation. He used no ambiguous language, but sought to render every idea definite, every truth clear, every duty plain. The result was, all his hearers grew in religious knowledge. They made definite and available acquisitions. They were taught to be critical, to receive no statement unchallenged, to give themselves up unqualifiedly to human guidance. He aided them to hold their religious convictions intelligently, and to be ready to give to every man that asked a reason for their hope—a reason which should be recognized as such by others as well as by themselves. He made God's character appear glorious to worldly men; God's government was a scene of grandeur and a work of perfect justice even in the eyes of sinners trembling before its penalties; and when his love and mercy were the theme of remark, all souls ceased to wonder at the angelic song which announced its incarnation. All forms of sin were revealed in the light of that obligation which they had despised, and penitence and love felt newly encouraged to trust and rejoice in the soul's great Saviour and Helper. The guilt and danger of sin were made clear, and the certainty of redemption, when the heart committed itself in obedience to Christ, appeared a precious reality under his labors. He made the thunders of Sinai to be heard distinctly in attestation of the sanctity of law, and the prayer of Calvary fell soothingly on the soul of the penitent as a mother's lullaby on the ear of a timid child.

He was no faultless sermonizer or model orator.—
Every teacher of Homiletics would have complained
and corrected, criticised and protested, and yet, while
finding the most fault, he would perhaps have been
most deeply impressed by the power of the discourse
and the effectiveness of the delivery. He had always
the merit of being natural, fearless, independent, sincere,
earnest, and enthusiastic; and, in being so, he often
disarmed prejudice and made the critic forget his objections in his veneration for the man and his sympathy
with the discourse. It was not hard to find fault with
his speaking when one sat down alone for that purpose,
but he who tried to do that when the speaker was before him, sweeping on in his rapid majesty, was apt to
find no time or inclination for any such tasks. He was
a strong man, and the pulpit would reveal his strength;
he saw grandeur and beauty in the gospel, and his
pulpit efforts were perpetually revealing its grandeur and
beauty to others. He thought closely and felt deeply
over the subjects which he was wont to treat there, and
he had ability to rouse thought and awaken feeling in
others that, in some measure, corresponded to his own.
He could put himself into sympathy with his audience
so that, for a time, their intellects and souls would reflect the features and correspond to the workings of the
master mind before them.

That he must have possessed no ordinary measure of
pulpit and platform power, is sufficiently evinced by
facts—facts that lie even on the surface of his life.
That he should acquire and retain such a hold upon
men of thought year after year; that the masses of the

people should increase in the confidence and veneration inspired by his abilities; that in such a position he should always be regarded as decidedly in advance of his congregation and of the ministry about him; that a strong and influential society should continue to recognize him as a reliable leader; that a ministry of nearly thirty years in the same field should attract a wider and deeper interest even to its close; that some eight hundreds of persons, from every rank in life, should recognize him as the instrument of their salvation in his own immediate vicinity; and that his departure should be mourned by all classes and sects of christians, as the exit of a strong and leading champion from among the hosts of God's elect;—that all these things should be, on the supposition that Mr. Cheney was only an ordinary preacher, would be to admit most striking effects, and yet deny the existence of causes which are alone adequate to their production.

CHAPTER XVII.

THE PASTOR AND HIS PEOPLE.

The relation between the pastor and his people is one to which there are attached various degrees of importance under different circumstances. It is sometimes treated by both parties as a mere secular thing, to be created like any pecuniary contract, and to be modified or annulled according to convenience or caprice; and sometimes it is accepted as a permanent feature of life, with which no hand but God's has the right to meddle. Both these are extremes, perhaps equally pernicious. Both parties should evidently have a voice in the procedure which is to ally them to each other, and form the connection under a conviction of the responsibility belonging to the relation, with eyes open to the real objects which are to be gained, with a mutual understanding of each other's character and rights. And having thus formed a union, for no slight cause should it be dissolved. Permanency, as a general rule, is the condition both of the pastor's efficiency and the highest religious profit of the people. That sort and degree of christian confidence which are essential to the free intercourse of a minister with his people, are usually the growth of time. And where there is faithfulness and prudence on the part of the pastor, and sympathy, charity and appreciation on the part of the people, the relation will grow dearer and more sacred with the lapse of time, the bond will be cemented by more tender and hallowed experiences, and the calamity of separation will seem more sad and fearful.

All this finds an illustration in Mr. Cheney and the Olneyville Congregation. There were very many things—some ordinary and others peculiar—that contributed to attach both parties warmly to each other. Mr. Cheney was the first, and, for nearly thirty years, the *only* pastor. He was widely known before his conversion, and his name especially was familiar in every one of the twenty dwelling houses at Olneyville. He was intimate with nearly all its youth, and sympathised with them as, in his love of sin, he was able. He became a changed man, and at once sought to use that confidence which had been reposed in him, to reach and save others. He stood up in the Hollow, as the first striking illustration of what the gospel could do for a human soul, and let his light shine clearly into the places of moral darkness. From the circles of its corruption he had broken loose, and started off on a mission of purity, calling on his companions to follow him up to virtue and heaven. He proved his friendship, and demonstrated his solicitude for his associates, by braving their jeers with a true heroism, and staying in their very midst for the sake of their salvation. The few christians who had been wont to meet in their private dwellings for prayer, half trembling lest Martin Cheney should appear among them as Satan did among the sons of God, could do no less than hail his christian faithfulness with gratitude, and feel a reverence for his courage and his consecration. They felt, doubtless, somewhat as did the men and women of apostolic times whom Saul of Tarsus was seeking to drag off to prison, when they heard his impassioned eloquence supporting the doctrines of the Cross. And then when some of his former associates had been led by him to the Savior, it was but natural that they should feel toward him the deep affection of a christian's first warmth, and lean on him for support in their christian feebleness, as if they were safe so long as he was present with his strong arm uplifted in their defence. And when he began to preach, if many hastened to the hall from curiosity, it may well be supposed that there were some who went there with a gratitude to God which they could hardly express, and with an interest in and an affection for the speaker which it was difficult to conceal. It was not only because they felt that they needed better and ampler religious accommodations, but also because they felt that he deserved a wider theatre and larger encouragement, that the various members of the community set about the erection of a house of worship, and would be satisfied to have none but himself to occupy it. He had allied himself with their interests with a generous self sacrifice when they had little reputation or money with which to assist him, and they appreciated the service by giving him what they had to bestow—their small dignities and their large confidence. And when the church was organized—a little band of eleven disciples, some of whom had prayed *for* him with much earnestness but with little faith, and then prayed *with* him in their gratitude, and then afterward had felt stronger because he prayed for them, and some of whom felt that they should have never learned to pray but for his assistance—whom could they choose for pastor but him, and how could they do less than give the whole heart's sympathy and love and hope with the vote which declared him elect to that office? And when, as often as the month came round, others still were added to their number, who had felt equally indebted to the man who bade them welcome to the church of Christ, it was but natural that the ties should seem both tenderer and more precious.

Nor were the struggles through which he passed a few years later, in his advocacy of the cause of the slave and in his faithful rebuke of prevalent sins, without their influence in binding him to the people who stood by him in his perils. They who approved his courage and his zeal, (and these were the great body of his congregation,) were attracted more warmly to him by the discovery of his readiness to sacrifice in their behalf as well as in behalf of the truth, and their ready help and strong sympathy, given just when he must have been crushed without it, awoke his own gratitude and wedded him still more firmly to their interest. His ministerial reputation and pulpit freedom the people had undertaken to guard when surrounded with perils; and in proportion as they had taken an interest in them, did they increase in apparent value. There was a double tie uniting him to their hearts. He was their dear christian friend, and he was also the embodiment of some great principles which they had learned to hold both dear and sacred.

And thus he had continued to live and labor among them. He had always been a prominent and leading agency in building up all the social and moral interests which successively arose. In the growth and improvement of Olneyville his influence was felt to have largely contributed. Year after year he had stood in their pulpit, and instructed and roused and blessed them. He had been among them in their varied experiences, sympathising with them in all. He had rejoiced with those that rejoiced, and wept with those that wept. He had presided at the marriage altar, and given his blessing to the cemented hearts, as, in the warmth of love and the glow of hope, they went forth to their life-work, leaning trustfully on each other ; and when bereavement was spilling its tears over its recent dead, he had been wont to approach and speak of the immortality lying beyond the tomb, and of the perpetual fellowships of the pure in the presence of God. Almost every family had passed through some experience to which he had been intimately related ; and thus he had been bound up closely with the community's life. And many there were who had been enlightened by him to see their own lost condition, and who, putting themselves beneath his guidance, had been led to behold the Lamb of God who taketh away the sins of the world. They had sat down with him in the circles of prayer and meditation and conference, and talked familiarly together of the christian life on earth, and of the higher, richer, better life in heaven. He had spoken words of comfort in their distress, words of warning in their danger, words of peace in their anxiety, words of hope in their distress, words of encouragement in their despondency, and words of cheer in their faithfulness. He had never betrayed their confidence; but, in his character and life, had been constantly suggesting fresh reasons for their respect and love. So long and so constantly among them, they had come to feel that he was almost one of the real elements of their life—as an important integral part of Olneyville, which they could never think of sparing in response to any summons but God's.

It is not to be supposed that such a man as Mr. Cheney would be left without solicitations to go to other fields of labor. Such solicitations he did receive, and both moral and pecuniary arguments were brought to bear on him. He probably never felt very strongly inclined to go, and yet it is probable that he felt much less reluctance to listen to such proposals than did the society. Several years previous to his death he was strongly solicited to take another important pastoral charge. The request he consented to lay before his people, and a meeting was appointed to consider the subject. A general attendance was invited, that all phases of the public feeling might be indicated. The meeting was crowded and enthusiastic. Men who seldom or never entered the place of worship, and had very slight religious tendencies in any direction, members of other denominations, all alike seemed to feel that they had a personal interest in the matter. It was moved, after the subject had been freely considered and discussed, that Mr. Cheney be earnestly requested to remain at Olneyville; and, on calling the vote, *every person* present voted for his stay. He was growing old, and must soon be so enfeebled as to be laid aside from labor, or be carried to his tomb, abundance of younger men could have been obtained to take the vacated post, but not a man woman or child would consent to his departure. This new proof of his people's affection touched him deeply, and anew he gave himself to abundant labors in their behalf.

Mr. Cheney's sympathies were strong, and his gratitude was always roused by kindness. And the testimonials which he was almost perpetually receiving from his people, made them very dear to him. He reciprocated their kindness by rendering them the very highest services of which he was capable. They had never guarded his reputation with more care than he guarded theirs. He appreciated his flock not less than the flock appreciated the shepherd. He never praised them abroad; he had too much prudence and too pure a love for them to do that; but he would sooner suffer an impeachment to rest against his own character, than hear in silence an insinuation against theirs. He loved them as a body, with an affection similar to that which attached him to his few personal friends.

The following extracts from his auto-biography will indicate his own feelings toward his people, better than any general or specific statements from others. So far as they are testimonials, they are such as justice to his own feelings required him to write, and such as he would be unwilling should be excluded from these memoirs. After speaking of the heartiness and firmness with which he was sustained by his people in the days of peril, he says;—

"Does any one ask why I am so much attached to that people? and so unwilling to leave them when higher station and larger salary have been offered?— Among other reasons they may find one in such acts as above noted."

Again. "For the first sixteen months after the church was formed there were additions every month, either by letter or baptism. The church has had its seasons of coldness and declension, but on the whole it has increased in numbers till at the present time, (1850) it numbers from three to four hundred members. It has numbered over four hundred, but has decreased for the seven or eight years past—the dismissions, exclusions, and deaths, having exceeded the additions.— Many have been dismissed to other churches since the organization, quite a number have been excluded, and very many have died in the triumphs of faith. I know not the exact number who have belonged to the church since its organization, but suppose it may be from seven to eight hundreds—perhaps more. There have been, from time to time, seasons of peculiar religious interest. At one time I baptized fifty-three persons; at another time sixty-three. The last of these seasons of unusual interest was enjoyed about eight years since, when about one hundred were added to the church in a few months—a number of these being members of my own family. Beautiful green spots are these— delightful to look back upon.

"With tearful joy I've often seen
 The healing waters move;
And many round me, stepping in,
 Their efficacy prove."

Then was seen the power of truth and love.

I have been the pastor of this church from its organization till now. I have wept with them and rejoiced with them, and they have sympathized with me in my trials and afflictions. They have sat down with me in the house of mourning. While with them I have lost by death a father, a wife and four children. I have not been the faithful pastor which I might have been or ought to have been in all respects. Yet I have loved them and labored for them, and am laboring for them still; and notwithstanding my short comings, I rejoice in the assurance that they love me and that I have their prayers.

The church are strong and decided on the subject of Temperance, and are decidedly Anti-Slavery; and, if I mistake not, have made some progress in the noble principle of thinking and letting think. They are now engaged in sustaining as interesting and flourishing a Sabbath School as can be found in Rhode-Island. Thanks to the Giver of all good."

It has already been stated that Mr. Cheney was chosen Moderator of the General Conference of Freewill Baptists, which assembled at Providence and Olneyville, in October, 1850. He presided over it with dignity and ability, and found himself, at the close, warmly attached to many of its members whom he had met as strangers. As it was about to close, several of its members addressed a few words of christian sympathy and counsel to each other. Mr. Cheney was one of the number. In the last years of his life he seldom became so affected in speaking as to be forbidden to proceed. He arose on that occasion in a spirit calm and tender, thanked the Conference for the confidence implied in his appointment, expressed his satisfaction at the general spirit which had pervaded its sessions, spoke of his pleasure in meeting and becoming acquainted with so many christian friends, alluded to the approaching separation as likely to be final on earth wth many of them, then gave utterance to a most hearty and sympathetic assurance of the joy he had felt in welcoming the gathering at Olneyville, and then added in substance ;—" Nor does this feeling attach alone to me ; it is shared by this whole people. No differences or peculiarities in sentiment or policy which may be entertained here, have repelled you. You have been among this people ; you have formed for the time a part of their families ; you have seen them in circumstances calculated to give you an insight into their real spirit ; and if you have not met a cordial, generous, christian welcome, if you have not been made to feel that you were at least among warm-hearted and large-hearted friends, then I kno nothing about the people among whom I have labored, in my imperfect way, for twenty-five years." . . . . . As he struck this tender cord his emotions overpowered him ; and, sitting down, his silent tears completed and sanctified the tribute of respect and affection which the Pastor wished thus to pay to his People.

Such a picture of permanency in the pastoral relation is rare among us, but less rare than we hope it will be hereafter. It may not be best that all who preach the gospel should seek to realize such permanency in their position ; but there is no need of insisting particularly upon the exceptions now; they are so frequent as almost to make us forget that there is even a theoretical rule. But while other churches, seeming at times to have more prosperity than the church at Olneyville, have faltered, and, at times, have seemed at the point of death, it has ever held on its way, and its light, sometimes more or less eclipsed by trial and declension to be sure, has beamed forth steadily like the stars of heaven.

Mr. Cheney's relation to his ministerial brethren of the same denomination, especially to those situated near him, was scarcely less important or interesting than his relation to his flock. He was one of the earliest Freewill Baptist ministers who settled as a pastor in Rhode Island, and was one of the oldest at the time of his death. A large number of the churches about him were formed with his advice, and a large proportion of the ministers he had assisted in ordaining. Step by step he rose up gradually to high influence in the Quarterly Meeting and Yearly Meeting. He rose by dint of his own energy—and it was energy expended not for the sake of rising, but for the sake of the truth. When, in his earlier years, his unanswered reasoning was overpowered by the overshadowing influence of men who had acquired a reputation, he would writhe in spirit and bite his lips with determination, but he patiently bided his time, and it came to him. His younger brethren in the ministry looked up to him as a father, but he always welcomed them simply as brethren. So far from being jealous at the discovery of talent and promise in them, nothing pleased him more than when he saw public confidence turning towards those who had given proof of ability and worth. How much he did to inspire confidence in themselves and put them on the road to success, neither himself or they, probably, could perfectly know. That he did much he must have known, and others must have felt. In his intercourse with them he was ever on the alert to find out their peculiarities and state, that he might aid them; and yet he usually carried on the study and imparted the benefit without making them aware of the work he was doing. If he was chairman of a meeting, and there was present some young, timid, trembling brother, who needed encouragement and yet who had hardly a disposition to confess his necessities even to himself, he was almost certain to invite him to pray; or, in some other method, equally delicate, he would manage to inspire the very confidence which was so much needed. Thus he was perpetually doing something to add to the efficiency of his young associates in the gospel, while, at the same time, he never *appeared* to be conscious of the debt of obligation under which he was laying them. And so they seldom thanked him for the work he was doing for them, simply because it did not seem as though it would be pleasant for him to be told of his unconscious benefactions. But if the lips spoke less, the heart felt more; if the gratitude was repressed, it burned more strongly within. His brethren in the ministry all felt the strong attachment of a warm personal friendship for him, and felt that all their gatherings were wanting in one of the important elements of interest and value in his absence. They conceded superiority to him as a matter of course, and listened with the deference of children, even when they felt obliged to dissent from his views.

And he, too, seemed to prize his association with them, as one of the choicest privileges of his life. Their reputation was dear to him, and though he never humored their foibles, and seemed forever determined to make them independent and lean on themselves, still they felt, not without reason, that, in their deserved prosperity he felt the liveliest interest, and in their unavoidable embarrassments and trials they were sure of his sympathy. Faithfully dealing with them all and teaching them to deal faithfully with each other and with himself, he united them strongly to his own heart, and aided to create many of the bonds that held them to each other in fellowship.

CHAPTER XVIII.

SICKNESS AND DEATH.—FUNERAL SERVICES.—TESTIMONIALS.

It is not simply a conviction that it must be so, but a submissive acquiescence in the wisdom and love which appoint it, that gains our christian consent to the departure of goodness from its earthly sphere and labors. If our earthly affection would detain it, our christian faith can bid it a God-speed as it soars up higher. The question, "If a man die, shall he live again?" met its answer from the lips of Him who said, "I am the Resurrection and the Life." We do not feel now that the glorious light which has burned about us is to be quenched in the grave, but kindled to an immortal glow. We can take our leave of the christian friend at the portal of the tomb, assured that all is brightness beyond it; and then come back to life, confident that the affection which we treasure up shall find a still better theatre for its exercise hereafter. It is fitting that we walk calmly to the grave, for God's appointment has opened it for the rest of the wearied body; and it is fitting even that joy should kindle up in the soul of faith, for a voice from heaven breaks musically there, saying of the spirit, "It is not here, but risen." So Mr. Cheney has already been followed to the tomb in fact, and we have now to follow him in history.

For at least fifteen years previous to his death, he suffered more or less from a cough, sometimes attended with hoarseness. The cough was more or less the result of a catarrhal affection, aggravated by the exposures and severe labors incidental to his profession. Sometimes this affection would be serious, and sometimes it occasioned very little uneasiness. He was satisfied that it would eventually become the immediate occasion of his death. He and others were alike unaware that a disease, dating back probably in its origin to the period of his early manhood, was at last to develope itself suddenly and hurry him to his tomb. For several of the last years of his life his health was not really firm, though he was almost constantly enabled to perform a large amount of ministerial service.

He returned from his tour to New York in September, 1851,—mention of which has already been made—considerably prostrated. Indeed, while remaining in the city, he suffered more or less from illness. He remained in New York and Brooklyn among his acquaintances nearly a week, and, on his return, spent a little time with some friends in Connecticut. He was absent from his home and pulpit two Sabbaths—a thing which had very unfrequently occurred before. He seemed not quite as well as usual for two or three weeks following, but his state failed to arrest particularly the attention of himself or of others. He preached in his own pulpit as he had done, and some of his hearers seemed then struck with what seemed to them an unusual interest and impressiveness in his development of the fundamental evangelical truths. On the first Sabbath in November, he preached at Taunton, Massachusetts, on exchange with Rev. T. H. Bacheler, the pastor of the Freewill Baptist Church in that place;—preached what proved to be his last sermon. Some of his friends were struck with his apparent feebleness, as they saw him preparing to leave home. He suffered much from dizziness in the afternoon,—so much as to find it exceedingly difficult to go through the service. He returned home on Monday morning, really ill; and, yielding to the advice of his friends, sought medical aid. On Tuesday he spent an hour in attendance on an Anti-Slavery Convention in the city, but his pain of body compelled him to return home. A day or two more elapsed, and he was confined to his house and mostly to the bed. His disease was at once pronounced to be Chronic Liver Complaint.

After being attended for some three weeks by the physician whom he at first summoned, another was employed by the advice of his friends, though he himself seemed to expect very little relief or benefit from their prescriptions. In the mean time he had requested the Deacons of the Church to act as a Committee in securing supplies for the pulpit. The new physician concurred with his predecessor in regard to the nature of the complaint, but somewhat modified the treatment. He attended him a week, during which Mr. Cheney seemed to be growing weaker; and suffered extremely from nausea and a violent pain in the back portion of the head. Both these physicians had adopted the Homeopathic method of practice. At this stage an eminent Hydropathic practitioner was summoned from Boston to attend him, and immediately put him upon the course of treatment usually prescribed by that school of medical men,—withholding all nutriment. Mr. Cheney's friends were encouraged to look for his recovery. The physician spoke hopefully. How far Mr. Cheney himself shared in this confidence is not known, as he said very little respecting his prospects. He had seemed to suffer during nearly his whole life more or less from a natural shrinking in view of the grave. Death seemed naturally to inspire him with a sort of terror or dread— a result of his constitutional susceptibilities. The temple of life beyond the tomb was glorious to the eye of his faith, but the cold dark portal was not without its horrors. Still, he expressed himself as fully willing to leave the question whether he should live longer to the disposal of God's wisdom. Rather than suffer long and seriously with sickness and pain, being apparently of no service to the world, he would prefer to die at once and be at rest, but was cheerful to wait patiently God's own disposition.

After he had been kept under this treatment for two or three weeks, he seemed improving. His pain abated, his appetite seemed more natural, he began to receive nourishment, and his physician predicted his restoration at no distant day. But few visited him, and even with these few he conversed but little—exercising a prudence which he felt was demanded by his circumstances. He continued in this state till Saturday, January 3d, 1852, when he seemed to grow worse. His strength failed, and his pulse seemed weaker through the day. His son-in-law watched with him during the night, and his increased illness was regarded as only a temporary relapse, until toward morning, when he seemed to be fast failing. He sank rapidly, though remaining apparently perfectly conscious of his state, and of what was passing about him. Toward morning, as his attendant bent over him, he gave a feeble utterance to his last earthly words,—"I HAVE A HOPE THAT ENDURETH TO THE END." His breath grew shorter and fainter as the tide of life ebbed away, until about half past five o'clock, on Sabbath morning, January 4th, when the body quietly sank to its rest, and the spirit soared to its God, to begin with the dawn of the Sabbath the worship of the upper temple.

> " So fades a summer cloud away ;
> So sinks the gale when storms are o'er ;
> So gently shuts the eye of day ;
> So dies a wave along the shore."

With what feelings Olneyville arose from its slumbers and learned its bereavement, it is not for words to tell. It was well nigh smitten dumb with astonishment and grief. Not alone in the cottage which his delicate taste had selected and beautified, and where his form lay—already growing stiff and cold,—were there sadness and tears ; nearly every family circle was a picture of sorrow, and every person a mourner. And as the message flew abroad, many, very many bowed down their heads and wept, feeling that they too were sharers in a great and sore affliction.

His Funeral services were attended at the Meeting-House, on the following Thursday, January 8th, at half past ten o'clock, A. M. Business was generally suspended throughout the community, and the temples of trade were closed. The tide of worldly life stood still in reverence before the bier of the dead. His remains were borne close by the hall where he had commenced to hold forth the word of life, and set down in the house of worship which he had dedicated twenty-five years before, and under the very pulpit where he had stood so long and so faithfully in defence of the gospel. The organ, and the pillars on either side of the pulpit, were shrouded in mourning drapery. Four of the members of his church were bearing his pall, and, as immediate mourners, appeared his widow and five children, some of them with their families—his only son being detained by the death of a member of his own family. More than twenty ministers of the same denomination were in attendance; and they, with most of that vast congregation, packing every corner of the house, felt that they too were there, not as spectators, but as sad and sincere mourners. Rev. James A. McKenzie offered a prayer full of the most touching allusions, and powerful over the hearts of the assembly by its spirit of fervor and resignation. He had long been an intimate friend of the departed, and they had labored much together in their calling. Rev. M. J. Steere delivered a most appropriate discourse, setting forth the glory of the gospel as it had appeared in the character and life of Mr. Cheney—a task for which his long personal familiarity with the deceased eminently fitted him. During its delivery that crowded house was scarcely less silent than the tomb itself, save as now and then the sighs that would not be suppressed, and the sobs that defied all effort to restrain them, told how deep were the wounds inflicted by the bereavement.

The services concluded, the assembly were permitted to look once more on the face with which most had been so long familiar. One by one they pressed up to the coffin, and then turned away feeling as they had not done before what a desolation had been left in the heart. Writing to a distant friend, one present thus describes the sleeper :—" He lay gloriously in his coffin. He did not simply look *natural*,—a word often used to describe the face of the dead,—*he looked just like life.* It seemed almost as though he could be only resting from the toil of some moral battle, and already to wake at the first tap of the drum. Or, rather, he appeared just as you have seen him in conference meeting, with his eyes closed, a calm, half developed smile on his features, as if communing in spirit with the high truth and glory of God." The last view had been taken, the last eyes had grown tearful above his face, the lid of the coffin was adjusted, and, through the winter's cold and storm, a large sad company followed all that was mortal of the christian man and hero to its narrow bed in the dust.

The place of Mr. Cheney's earthly rest deserves a little detailed description ; for it promises to be a spot of no ordinary interest in the future, and it may prompt others to good works similar to that which has created an humble Mecca for the pilgrimages of christian faith and love.

Two miles south-west from Olneyville, in the town of Cranston, is a large and beautiful Nursery for the culture of trees, shrubs and flowers, called 'Mulberry Grove.' It is owned by the family of Deacon Daniel P. Dyer, who has been both a member and an officer in the Olneyville church for many years. On the west side of the Nursery is a plot of ground, laid out in the form of a semicircle, simply yet tastefully decorated, and appropriated as a family Cemetery. A few years since the idea occurred to Mr. Dyer of laying out a similar plot, contiguous to this, as a Cemetery for the convenience of his Freewill Baptist friends more particularly, and especially for the convenience of his friends in the Freewill Baptist ministry. The work was undertaken and most happily executed. It is shut in on every side by trees, commanding however, a view of varied scenery, presenting at once to the eye the graceful blending of artificial and natural beauty, and the sympathetic fellowship of life and death. None of the lots have been *sold*, but *given* to the proprietors, and, with a very few exceptions, have all been taken up.

Mr. Cheney had buried his first wife in Foster; his second wife, his father, and three children in Johnston. In the autumn of 1849 the remains of them all were removed to the spot already described, and interred side by side, and a space at the head of the lot reserved for himself. After the removal had been effected he seemed to think of it with much satisfaction, and visited the spot with new interest; and, on one occasion, remarked in his pulpit respecting his feelings in view of his own prospective sleeping place. To that place of beauty, where the sun shines mellow amid the forest trees, where the winds sigh in gentleness through the dark green Firs, and where the unscared birds sing lovingly over the dead, gentle and affectionate hands bore Mr. Cheney and left him in his rest. Few spots there are, more suggestive of sanctified thought and chastened religious feeling, to those who have lingered among its graves, than 'MULBERRY GROVE CEMETERY.'

The following testimonials to Mr. Cheney's worth will indicate the views entertained respecting him by his acquaintances. They are the independent utterances of various persons, differently related to the subject to which they refer, and they may aid in bringing out more distinctly points of character which the preceding pages have failed to reveal. The discourse preached at his Funeral has been reserved for this place, that the thread of the narrative might not be broken. The following extracts are taken from the "*Morning Star*," where it appeared soon after its delivery.

DISCOURSE:

AT THE FUNERAL OF THE REV. MARTIN CHENEY.

BY REV. MARTIN J. STEERE.

"I have fought a good fight, I have finished my course, I have kept the faith :
Henceforth there is laid up for me a crown of righteousness, which the Lord the righteous judge shall give me at that day."—II. *Tim.* iv: 7, 8.

" This is a solemn hour; this is a solemn auditory. This is a time for solemn meditation. Whether I look forth upon this throng of people, or turn to my brethren in the ministry, I am assured that something solemn has occurred. Alas! it is too true! our brother, our venerable brother, our beloved brother, our brother in the ministry, with whom we had so often taken sweet counsel, and to whom we were so much indebted, is dead! He, the long tried pastor of this church, and minister to this society, endeared to all his parishsoners, and respected by all who knew him, is dead! We are in his funeral! O how dreamlike it seems—how unlike anything we had known before! Yet it is true he is dead! Last Sabbath morning about three o'clock, his spirit went forth to meet, not his usual congregation, but the congregation that never breaks up in a Sabbath that never ends. He has gone. And now the tears with which we follow him are not the tears that would call him back—they are but the burst of affectionate recollection. They only show how we loved him. We would not—no, we would not, if we could, call back from the abodes of blessedness, to endure over again the trials, to fight over again the battles of the Christian warfare, one glorified spirit—no, not even that of our brother and father in Israel, whose funeral we to-day solemnize! So may we all feel, and not least this afflicted family circle, now the object of so strong a sympathy, and so many prayers. May they, may we all, have the spirit of Christian resignation, which he, whom we to-day mourn, was accustomed so vividly to set forth in the numerous families to whom he was called to minister consolation."

* * * * * *

[After speaking of the Christian warfare of the Apostle, the various features of which he specifies as original strength and vigor of mind ; an ardent temperament ; great firmness and moral courage ; an uncompromising fidelity in dealing with the foes of the gospel ; activity ; faith in God, in the Holy Spirit, and in the cross ;—he thus dwells on the character and memory of the departed.]

" Without saying more of the many things that might be said of Paul as a Christian warrior, here let us pause. The warfare of another demands our present attention—that of our brother—*O God, is he dead*—that of our brother, who last Sabbath morning "finished *his* course with joy." " He, too, had fought a good fight." His warfare, too, was substantially, though not circumstantially, the same as that of the apostle Paul. In a different age, and under far different circumstances, he followed the same standard with him. The same blood-stained banner waved over St. Paul and the Rev. Martin Cheney. From the former, we turn for a few moments to the latter. For he, too, had warred a good warfare. And we institute no comparison invidious to the apostle, or flattering to our deceased brother and father in Israel, when we say there were not a few points of marked resemblance between them.

The last sermon our brother preached to his own people was on Sunday morning, Oct. 26th. The last sermon he preached any where was preached in Taunton, Mass. Nov. 2d, 1851. From about that time till near the time of his decease, his friends had been alternately agitated with hope and fear, [although hope was generally in the ascendant] with regard to his recovery. But our feelings alternate no longer. He has left us, and left with us the the savory influence of his life. He has left us indeed to mourn, but not as those who are without hope, and not, we trust, without the spirit of true christian resignation. Such was the nature of his sickness, that he could talk but comparatively little. And as he was at last taken away at an hour when the hopes of his friends, and his own, were strong for his recovery, he did not leave the *much* dying counsel which might otherwise have been expected of him. But his mind was calm and clear, his confidence in the salvation of Christ confirmed. His death was the sun at its setting. And, as if to throw behind him light to cheer those whose who should feel their firmament darkened by his departure, and to encourage those who should thereafter be disposed to run up the steep way by which he passed to God, he spoke with his expiring breath, and said, "*I have a hope that endureth to the end!*" And having said this, "he fell on sleep," and his spirit glided sweetly and softly away to its everlasting rest. He died—but not till he had served well his generation. And now many people are going, and saying, "Know ye not that there is a great man fallen in Israel to-day." And not a few are crying, "Help Lord, for the godly man ceaseth, for the faithful fail from among the children of men." Many of us would like to have gone to the bed-side of the deceased and received his last blessing. But this, in the inscrutible providence of God, was doubtless for *wise* reasons denied us. We can only come to his bier and look upon what is not he! Yet a blessing we may there receive, as valuable as we could have received at his dying couch, if we will but imagine his lips to part, and utter the words of tenderness and love and persuasion, which we have so often heard him utter while he was yet with us! This is indeed a trying hour, but above all its agitation I hear a voice saying to this afflicted people, to this sorely afflicted church, and to this most keenly afflicted family, "Be still, and know that I am God."

Let us now compose ourselves again to briefly notice a few points in the character of this fallen pastor. And for brevity's sake, we shall condense what we have to say as much as possible. And here perhaps as well as elsewhere we may remark, that,

The change wrought in his spirit and life, which resulted in his enlistment as a soldier of the Cross, was scarcely less remarkable than that under which the persecuting Saul was transformed into the Apostle Paul. He had wrought the will of the Gentiles, as Saul had that of the persecuting Jews. *After* his conversion, he as faithfully wrought the will of God. Like the Apostle, he, at his conversion, lost sight of flesh and blood, and bent all his energies in the direction of eternal salvation. At once, he commences his plea with sinners to be reconciled to God, and after but about two years is publicly recognized by the church as a minister of the Gospel. This was all apostolic. But we proceed to remark that,

As a minister of the gospel, the deceased had the advantage of a naturally strong and vigorous mind. This was well understood by all who knew him. Had he been blessed with an early and liberal education, some might, perhaps, have attributed the talent his life exhibited to that cause. But such was not the case. His education was very limited, even for the age in which he grew up. It therefore afforded no possible shadow of ground for hope of such things as the world has realized from his life. And the fact that right *here*, under the very turrets of the city, he, uneducated, and single handed, established himself as he did, as a minister of the gospel, and that here he maintained himself as he did, shows clearly that he must have had a large share of native mental strength and vigor. In his mental organization, the perceptive faculties decidedly predominated. They were most thoroughly acute, and acted with the rapidity of lightning. This made him a mighty champion in debate. He could thereby throw so many arguments together, in the short time during which a sinner would be disposed to listen, as would work conviction upon his soul. This consideration, too, connected with the ardency of his temperament, made him, as a christian warrior, resemble the general who prefers carrying cities by assault, rather than by the slow progress of a regular siege.

We have alluded to the ardency of his temperament. This was indeed remarkable. His heart was ever warm and deeply in earnest.—He, like Paul, knew nothing of indifference, and ideas lying latent in his breast. What he loved, he loved much, and what he did, he did with his collected might. His soul, like Paul's, knew no rest. It was forever flashing in his eye, and giving it that expression of deep penetration, which not a few of us have marked and felt, as we have shrunk before its earnest glance. To look into its depths, when his whole soul was in motion, was to be conscious of an awful presence, and to feel yourself looked through. While, on the other hand, its smiling and sympathetic beam, all lambent and easy, gave the fullest assurance of sincerity and love.

But with his ardency of temperament was joined a firmness of purpose, which gave him that stability of moral character for which he was so remarkable. His possession of this quality is clearly indicated at almost every step of his life, and, especially, of his ministerial life. From the time when he began to preach in that little hall yonder, across the way, down to the solemn moment when he said, *I have hope that endureth unto the end*, he was the subject of one single purpose, too firm to be shaken by all the smiles and all the frowns of the world through which he pressed. What the younger Pliny, writing to Trajan, pronounced *obstinacy*, in the persecuted Christians of primitive times, was characteristic of his life. He was as obstinate as are *facts*. His purpose was as solid as a pyramid. In this he was like Paul,—like Jesus. For his purpose, like theirs, was a glorious one. His deep settled conscientiousness, under God, forbade that it should be otherwise. It constantly secured him against wilfulness. His sanctified firmness and conscientiousness, acting in unison, were invincible. We have heard him talk of the Lions' den and of the fiery furnace, when we have felt, that however it might be with us, he would shrink neither from the growl of the one, nor from the red glare of the other. And yet, he was cautious. Of the spirit of caution, he had a very large share. Combined with his naturally low view of himself, it often made him appear timid, especially among strangers. But how necessary was this humble quality, to one possessing such mental activity and propulsion as he did. How necessary was this, too, to one whose whole life was to be watched as his, and who, without Education and single handed, to break in upon the reigning wickedness of a village, to establish there a church and be himself its pastor for life, rebuking sin in high places as well as low. Without cautiousness, how quickly would his career have been run. But he was not without it, and hence he never entrapped himself, nor suffered himself to be entrapped.

He approached the sinner earnestly and cautiously. Earnestly, because his whole soul glowed with love to him ; and cautiously, lest by injudiciousness he should defeat the end at which he aimed. But his cautiousness never made him afraid to declare the whole counsel of God. He could not restrain the free course of the the Spirit of God in his heart. To do so he knew to be neither safe nor expedient. His *active* boldness, as a minister of God, was, so far as it could in the premises, ever confirming the truth of a remark made by him in General Conference some twelve or fifteen years ago. " If," he said, " I am conscious that I ought to utter a truth in the pulpit, I will utter it, though a man stand over my head with a drawn sword, ready to take it off." Such a remark might seem egotistic, and boastful, to one by whose whole life its sentiment, was not, as in his, fully certified.

We have spoken of his Christian cautiousness. This, for he was only human, sometimes, for a moment, failed him. In an hour of ardency, when his whole soul was in motion, it occasionally left him to speak things unadvisedly. But this occurred only to give him opportunity to show his readiness to confess a fault, and seek forgiveness. How many times have we heard him request, at the opening of some one of the sessions of conference, the privilege of making a remark not with direct reference to the business before it. Leave being granted, he would proceed to say, "On reflection, I have thought that some remarks I made yesterday may have injured the feelings of certain brethren. I intended no evil, but I spake unadvisedly, and humbly ask their forgiveness. To this, the reply would generally be, Brother Cheney needs no forgiveness. We regarded the remarks to which he refers, as being perhaps rather *warm*, but kindly intended. Thus was the deceased both the lion and the lamb. They could lie down together in his great heart.

His benevolent feelings were very strong. Nor was his love of approbation weak. These two feelings acting together, would afford some ground to infer that he was time-serving and compromising, if we knew nought else about him. But as we all know, he was neither. He, like Paul, knew no compromise with sin. He, too, repudiated the idea of doing evil that good might come. His high moral sense, his sincere love of truth, held his soul like an anchor. His benevolence led him not to please men, so much as to do them good. It was this, that made him a champion for suffering humanity. His ear was first to catch the sounds of distress coming up from the wretchedness and squalor of the haunts and homes of Intemperance, and his voice was first to be lifted up, and his hand first to be stretched out, for the relief of its victims. His soul was among the first to feel for the millions whose deep wails of anguish come up from the cane fields and rice swamps, of petty, but terrible despotism. Nor could he be indifferent to the horrors of cities sacked, and fields all gory, in the terrible tread of war. Wherever was human suffering, thither his sympathies were flying. Had he been on his way to Jericho, following hard after the priest and Levite who passed by the sufferer on the other side, he would *himself* have been *the* good Samaritan. He was *a* good Samaritan. And you know, at least many of you, that as the philanthropist plunges into the stream to save the drowning man at the hazard of his own life, so Martin Cheney was ever ready to hazard his reputation and his earthly all as a Christian minister, rather than be recreant to the spirit of Christian Philanthropy that burned in his heart. But this is a point upon which I need not dwell. It has been dwelt upon by thousands of tongues along all the streets and by all the firesides in this region. Nor will it be forgotten, or cease to be talked about, while the grave of the deceased is visited, his name remembered, or independent virtue respected.

As the deceased lived *for* the world, so also he lived in it. He knew little of abstraction. He was a constant observer of the times, choosing to know every thing, affecting morals or religion, which was occuring around him. The past and the future were to him, in a sense, less important than the present. To use his own language in reference to himself, he lived only in the present. He lived a man among men. Every thing around him had for him a doctrine, out of which arose a duty, which he was never afraid to find out and practice.

He was eminently the Lord's freeman. He felt free himself. He *would be* free himself. And he sighed for those who were not so. Christian Liberty was a theme over which his soul ever kindled. Nor was the remark of one who passed to God a short time before him, " that he had done more for Christian Liberty in Rhode Island than any man since the days of Roger Williams," very extravagant. How often have we seen his soul grow hot with shame and pity and indignation, as he has been speaking of others of his own profession who had basely submitted to the fetters and the chains, which his own soul had spurned.

I have said he was free. Not however like some men the world affords, free abroad simply, and among strangers! *He* was free at home in his own pulpit. Some of you have sometimes, and *for his sake*, trembled at his pulpit boldness, while others, perhaps, felt indignant at it. But there it was, and you could not help it. There he stood and you could not move him. Feeling that he was the Lord's freeman, it was impossible for him to become a human slave. He died a FREEMAN, bearing with him down to the grave, the respect of all, both friends and foes.

We have said of the Apostle Paul, that he ever evinced a strong faith in God through the cross. The same we may say of our departed brother. It was the sanctifying influence of the Spirit of God which made him what he was. From the time when God met him in the way of his wild career, and wrought in him so mightily, that he gave up his heart to Him, down to the glorious end to which his hope endured, he is sanctified to God. A heavenly influence spreads itself over his whole being. Henceforth, Christ and his cross are all his theme. The virtues of Christ he will every where inculcate, while their opposite vices he will every where denounce. The example of Christian piety given by Christ is the pattern upon which he would have all men form their characters. The atonement of Christ, and the necessity of redemption through Him, are things which he every where urges upon his fellow-men. He would have them not only virtuous but pious; and not only pious but virtuous. His christian character was alike removed from cold morality and rationalism on the one hand, and from spiritualism and superstition on the other. And it is probably owing to this fact, joined with the fact that his instructions to young Christians were ever remarkably clear, that conversions, and the results of revivals, were, in his congregation, remarkably permanent.

But time fails us now, as it did in preparing for this occasion. But should we spend any length of time here, we are assured we could tell to most of this congregation little that could to them appear new. A residence of forty-two years among you, about twenty-eight of which were spent in preaching the Gospel to you, under circumstances fitted to develope his character as a man and a minister most thoroughly, has made you, at least many of you, better acquainted with him than even the speaker at his funeral. You have not come together to-day to learn about him. You have come *because you knew him*, to pay your deep settled respect at his bier. May you remember, O remember, the words he spoke to you while he was yet with you! He did you good by his life. O consent to have him do you more good by his death. Imagine him to speak on the present occasion. What would you not give to hear him once more. Would that he could preach his own funeral sermon to this people, whom he so dearly loved, and to whose welfare his life was so sacredly devoted. But the wish is vain. We have thought that he might have preached ours, but certainly not his own. O how much indebted to him are not a few of us! How much this place! What changes since he first opened his mouth for God and your souls, in that little old hall, where a few gathered to hear him, moved perhaps, more by curiosity than anything else. How different that little room into which he went to *build his own fires*, from this goodly temple; and how different the music in that place—his own voice perhaps single, yet musical,—from the solemn notes of your mourning organ, rolling along these aisles. How different that congregation from this. Little did any of you think that he who was then opening his mouth with trembling was to be the future champion of virtue and religion in this place,—that under his influence such changes were to be wrought—that he was to gather such a church, and at last to die thus lamented.

No, you did not dream of all this. But thus it has been, and thus it is. He has done for Olneyville, for Rhode Island, for the world, a glorious work, and God forbid that we should be ungrateful for it. But he has now gone. The sheaf was ripe and ready, and the angel of death took it and garnered it up for God. He has gone and left his society, church and family, ah yes! and not least, his brethren in the ministry, to linger yet in this cold, "earthly world." But

>'Twas not darkness gathering round him
>That withdrew him from your sight,
>Walls of flesh no more could bind him;
>And, translated into light,
>Like the lark on mountain wing,
>Though unseen, we hear him sing.

And his song is that of "Moses and the Lamb" for ever!

Having already consumed so much time, my concluding remarks must be few.

1. To all those who were accustomed to hear the deceased preach, let me say, take to yourself in this hour of sorrow the spirit of Christian resignation which he has so often urged upon you. He often talked of HEAVEN. He sung of HEAVEN; now cheerfully resign him to rest there. He had labored long, he needed rest. God has given it, even the glorious rest that remaineth for the people of God. Do not murmur that he will no more walk among *you*. He walks, and shall forever walk, among the saints in white. But you can never forget him. Whoever shall succeed him here, his feet will seldom touch those stairs, but you will

think of the venerable one who will tread them no more. But to forget his *words* were worse than to forget *him*. O *remember his words*, the words of sober earnestness with which he was accustomed to address you from this holy place,—a place seemingly more holy, because he once and so long occupied it. O, remember, *remember*, REMEMBER his words.

2. To this mourning church, I would gladly speak a word of comfort. He had been with you so long and so regularly, that some of you had perhaps almost ceased to distrust his continuance, as the world long since ceased to distrust the rising of the next sun. Alas! how mistaken! He is even now dead. You are in his funeral! Your loss may justly seem to you great, irreparable. But while you speak tearfully of *loss*, he sings cheerfully of *gain!* We have compared him with Paul, and found some points of marked resemblance. Nor does that resemblance cease at death.—As for Paul to die was gain, so for your beloved pastor. Nor shall he, more than Paul, lose his crown. Paul departed, according to his desire, to be with Christ. So has your pastor. He under whose banner he fought, and the trophies of whose victories are ye, has at length called him from the field in which you are to remain yet a little longer. And O! if saints in heaven hear of what takes place on earth, let your glorified pastor, "*hear of your affairs, that ye stand fast in one spirit, with one mind, striving together for the faith of the gospel.*"

3. And to this afflicted family—O may Heaven give them consolation. But to you, the very remembrance of the deceased is consolation. To have had such a

husband and father, is itself a solace. Well may you say with the poet of the footprints of angels,

> "O, though oft depresssd and lonely,
> All my fears are laid aside,
> If I but remember, only,
> Such as he has lived and died."

I would not step between you and the spirit of God. I can but direct you to the seat of mercy and consolation at which he so often knelt. And here let me say to the audience, that no where did the character of him whom you mourn, shine more conspicuously than in the bosom of his own family. His children all in lovely subjection, and forming a circle for the morning devotion. O, it was a scene in which angels might delight to mingle. But I have no time to go back and gather up forgotten things. But in that family he will mingle no more. No, you will hear his voice no more at the family altar. Well do I recollect a prayer of his for you, when a few years ago we were together in another State, and a snow storm was out in its strength. "O thou that temperest the wind to the shorn lamb, bless our wives and little ones at home." Be assured that prayer will be answered,—the winds will be tempered to your condition, now he is gone. You have the abundant sympathy of both earth and Heaven. God is schooling you in the severity of his Providence, preparatory, we trust, to meeting again with him who has gone so little before you to his reward. O may the blessing of him rest upon you who is now hiding his smiling face behind a frowning Providence.

4. Did the time permit, I would like to say a few words

to my brethren in the ministry.—But it does not. We shall talk of our brother and father in Israel by the way, and as we meet in Conference. We had known him long.—We shall always remember him with the tenderest emotions. May we be as faithful as he was; useful, like him, and close our eyes in death, saying, We, too, have hope that endureth to the end.

> " Would ye bewail our brother ? He hath gone
> To Abraham's bosom ! He shall no more thirst,
> Nor hunger, but forever in the eye,
> Holy and meek, of Jesus, he may look,
> Unchided, and untempted, and unstained !
> Would ye bewail our brother ? He hath gone
> To sit down with the prophets by the clear
> And crystal waters; he hath gone to list
> Isaiah's harp and David's, and to walk
> With Enoch and Elijah, and the host
> Of just men now made perfect. He shall bow
> At Gabriel's hallelujah, and unfold
> The scroll of the Apocalypse with John,
> And talk of Christ with Mary, and go back
> To the last Supper, and the garden prayer
> With the beloved disciple ! He shall hear
> The story of the incarnation told
> By Simeon, and the triune mystery
> Burning upon the fervent lips of Paul !
> He shall have wings of glory, and shall soar
> To the remoter firmaments, and read
> The order and the harmony of stars;
> And, in the might of knowledge, he shall bow
> In the deep pauses of arch-angel harps,
> And, humble as the seraphim, shall cry,
> Who, by his searching, finds thee out, O God !
>   There shall he meet his children who have gone
> Before him, and as other years roll on,
> And his loved flock go up to him, his hand

MARTIN CHENEY.

Again shall lead them gently to the Lamb,
And bring them to the living waters there!
Is it so good to die! And shall we mourn
That he, e'en now, is taken to his rest?
Tell me! Oh mourn ye for the man of God!
Shall we bewail our brother—that he died?"

This discourse which, by request of the church at Olneyville, was published in the Morning Star, was prefaced by the following obituary notice, written by Rev. Mowry Phillips, pastor of the Second Freewill Baptist Church in Smithfield, R. I. The statistics are omitted in both the sermon and the notice.

REV. MARTIN CHENEY.—The much esteemed pastor of the Free Baptist church in Olneyville, R. I., calmly fell asleep in Jesus, on the 4th of January, 1852, in the 60th year of his age.

As a minister, our dear departed brother in Christ possessed those characteristics which rendered him extensively useful. To a remarkably clear and vigorous intellect, he united a keen sensibility, an ardent temperament, an unshaken faith, and a consecration to his work which placed all upon the altar of God and humanity. To him the gospel was no abstraction, but a code of morals and a system of faith adapted to the wants and woes of the world—hence he applied it to all the great moral questions of the age, with a discrimination of judgment, and a power of eloquence, which could not fail of producing an impression as lasting as eternity. This made him a reformer in the true sense of that term. No time-serving policy could quench the generous impulses of his large heart, or check the utterances of his firm convictions. When the wail of the bondman fell on his ear, his tender spirit wept over the wrongs of outraged humanity. Nor was this all. Commissioned of God—clothed with the authority of an ambassador of Christ—sustained by the law of Jehovah—and armed with the majesty of truth, he uttered soul-stirring words of honest indignation and merited rebuke against the oppressor.

He was one of the earliest and most efficient laborers in the temperance reform, and many still live to bless his memory, through whose instrumentality they were enabled to break the chains of a depraved appetite, and to enjoy the blessings of a redeemed manhood.

The peace question found in him a warm friend and a powerful advocate. With him *all* war was opposed to the spirit and teaching of Christ—to the doctrines and principles of the gospel. Having been baptized into the spirit of religious freedom himself, he was the uncompromising foe of all intolerance. Probably no man in Rhode Island, since the days of Roger Williams, has done more than he, to develope and illustrate the principles of true religious liberty. Christianity with him was a deep, permanent principle of love to God and man, which shed a benign influence over his entire life. His devotion was eminently spiritual, knowing no distinction in times or places. He seemed conscious of dwelling in the presence of an all-pervading spirit—an omnipresent Deity, before whom his soul bowed in the deepest adorarion.

His social qualities, which were of the highest order, constituted him a warm friend, a kind husband, and an affectionate parent.

He bore his sickness, which was severe, with Christian fortitude. For the sake of others, he desired to live; but for himself, he preferred to depart and be with Christ, which is far better.

His reason was unclouded until the last moment; and his faith in Christ, and the great principles which he had advocated, remained firm as he approached the portals of eternity. His last words were, "I have a hope that endureth to the end." And then silently bidding adieu to earth, he entered the valley and shadow of death without a struggle; and his triumphant spirit soared away to mansions in the skies.

Our loss is his eternal gain.

> "He sets,
> As sets the morning star, which goes not down
> Behind the darkened west, nor hides obscured
> Among the tempests of the sky, but melts away
> Into the light of heaven."

May the consolations of that religion, which he so well exemplified in his useful life, and peaceful death, be the support of his widowed wife and fatherless children, of the church of which he was so long the honored pastor, of the religious associations so long blessed with his presence, labors, counsels and prayers, and of the community for whose welfare he so earnestly labored.

M. PHILLIPS.

January 28, 1852.

[From the (Providence) Evening Telegraph, January 7th, 1852.]

DEATH OF MARTIN CHENEY.

Elder Cheney, whose decease took place on Sunday last, 4th inst., after about eight weeks' illness, caused by an organic affection of the liver, was in the sixtieth year of his age. He was a self-made man, of strong mind,— a really good preacher—a man who had been the stated preacher at Olneyville, twenty-eight years. He died with his harness on, battling for God, truth and righteousness. The many and severe trials he experienced during his ministry, and attempts made by certain of his parishioners to eject him from his place as Pastor, only gave him more faith and courage to be a true Minister of Jesus Christ. He could not be bribed or bought, (as too many are in similar situations,) but always had stirring words of rebuke for sinners in high life, as well as in low. The cause of God and humanity has lost a noble champion. Temperance, Anti-Slavery and true Peace, or Christian Non Resistance, were subjects which often received his attention in the pulpit, as well as out of it, being as he averred, important parts of the Gospel of Jesus Christ. Though his tongue is now silent in death, his earnest and truthful words so often reiterated in that pulpit will be remembered. May his mantle fall on some courageous soldier of Jesus, and his place be filled in some good degree by a true disciple of Jesus Christ.

MARTIN CHENEY.

[From the (Providence) Republican Herald, Jan. 7th, 1852.]
WRITTEN BY MR. THOMAS W. DORR.

A GOOD MAN DEPARTED.

The death of the REV. MARTIN CHENEY, of Olneyville, will be learned by many with deep regrets. He departed this life on Sunday, December 4th, aged sixty years. He had long been afflicted with a chronic complaint, which had recently brought him very low. He was supposed to be recovering, but the strength of his constitution had failed. Elder Cheney was no ordinary man. He was indebted to his own labor and perseverance more than to advantages for his rise to an honorable and useful station. He possessed strong common sense, ready insight into character, firmness of purpose, and a happy mode of communicating instruction, without rising above or falling below those whom he addressed. The main counsellor of wisdom to him was the word of God. He was thoroughly versed in the scriptures; not seeking to enlighten them, as the manner of some is, but gathering from them what he sincerely believed to be the truth, making them the point of departure and the place of return in all his ministrations. His manifest sincerity and depth of conviction opened to him the hearts of other men. In seeking to draw others to the ways of everlasting life, he manifested himself as one who himself was apprehended of Jesus Christ.

He was deeply earnest, solemn and impressive in all his efforts in his Master's service. He made no compromises with the infirmities and sins of men, but directed them to the one oblation for sin by which the pardon and the repose of the soul have been purchased for a fallen and dying world. His labors were owned and blessed, and he became an instrument of much good. He went about seeking to do good. In the house of want, sorrow, affliction and bereavement, he was a kind, sympathizing counsellor and friend. At the bed of sickness and of death he was searching and faithful, removing all false refuges, and pointing to the only, unfailing hope. He was very frequently called upon to perform funeral services, which furnished to him the occasion of making lasting impressions. Many of us can recollect him as he stood in the primitive New England mode, with the coffin for a pulpit, and the word of God upon it, discoursing of the realities of life and death, and acting as interpreter between the living and the dead. Under his moving words the latter seemed again to speak to the former of the vanity of all things beneath the sun, and of the only durable riches of the soul.

Mr. Cheney comes up to our minds to-day as the friend of the cause of our liberty in 1842, as the friend of the prisoner and the captive. He was an able advocate of the cause of temperance, and looked forward to a day of universal freedom.

For some years past, warned by the inroads of disease, he has seemed to serve at the portals of the temple, waiting for them to open before him, and disclose the way to a house not made with hands, eternal in the heavens. He did not feel himself to be living in his own, but in God's time; and when called he was prepared to depart with joy and not with grief; willing for his family and for duty, to live on here; happy in the thought of entering upon the employment and glories of the higher sanctuary. He has fallen in the vigor of his talents, and when he was never more useful to others.

[From the (Providence) New-England Diadem, Jan. 17th, 1852.]

ELDER MARTIN CHENEY.

This well known and much loved minister of Jesus, died at his residence in Olneyville, the 4th instant, in the 60th year of his age.

Elder Cheney has for some thirty years preached the gospel of Christ, and faithfully applied its principles to all the various sins of the age.

As a Preacher and Pastor, he has been successful in winning many souls to Christ, and in gathering and sustaining an efficient Church and Society.

He was among the first in our State to plead the cause of Temperence. When nearly all were silent, his voice was heard, and in his own pulpit, in behalf of total abstinence, and his interest and efforts in this cause continued to the close of his life.

He was also a pioneer in the cause of Freedom. Elder Cheney preached against slavery when but very few opened their mouths for the oppressed. The principles of universal liberty were so in harmony with the spirit of his Master, and with his own liberty-loving soul, that he could not but preach against slavery everywhere.

For several years he has advocated the principles of Peace. Years before the pledge of universal brotherhood was written he cherished its principles, and preached against "all the spirit and all the manifestations of war."

He was ready to meet any person, whatever might be his position in society, on any subject, on a perfect level. His pulpit could never with truth be called a "coward's castle."

Elder Cheney was an honest man; always preaching and acting according to his convictions and professions.

He was not a party man; for he would follow truth, let it lead from or to whom it might.

In preaching, he was earnest, logical and convincing.

He was a great man, naturally great, and well educated for his work; he was well acquainted with the Gospel and with the conditions and wants of men; he was a self-made man, not having a classical education; his knowledge was of a practical character.

As a neighbor and friend, he was social; ready to converse on all practical questions with freeness, and thus endeared himself to many.

Elder Cheney was a Christian, and not only prepared for this life but Heaven; and, although he has passed away in the midst of his labors and usefulness, he has, during his ministry, accomplished more for the world than most of those who live many more years.

We hope his mantle will fall on some one who shall, in his spirit, with some good share of his ability, enter into his labors as a Christian reformer in our midst.

D.

MARTIN CHENEY.

From the same paper.

[Extract from a speech of Hon. Nathan Porter, of the Rhode-Island Senate, at a meeting of the State Temperance Society, held January 13, 1852.]

Mr. Porter took occasion during his address, to speak of the life and services of the late Martin Cheney, and his connection with our cause, in a manner gratifying to the many friends of that faithful apostle in the Temperance reformation. The following are in substance a portion of his remarks :

Our cause is one which will live through the mutations of time and circumstances; the day which gave it birth, was a day the records of which will live upon the pages of our national history, as long as virtue holds a place in the nation's heart, as long as goodness will add to our greatness, or our present deeds give greater lustre to the friends which our fathers bequeathed to us.

Though times and circumstances may change, the nature of our cause can never change. Though the men who are the stoutest warriors of to-day, may be cut down by the common leveller, death,—on the morrow, in their places, will rise up other soldiers, who, girding on the armor of those who " have fought the good fight," will enter with fresh vigor into the cause of our just war. And thus shall man follow man, and army follow army, until our malignant and hated foe shall be entirely exterminated, and driven from the earth ; and man shall every where rejoice in our great deliverance.

We have been recently called upon to mourn the loss of one who, for many years in evil and in good report, has stood by our side and battled in our cause. One to whom we have looked for the strength of his arm, and the wisdom of his counsel. One whose heart, when *any* good object was to be accomplished, was ever in the work. Yet who made this, our cause, only secondary to the immediate cause of his Divine Master. I have known many men in my day, and I have sometimes studied character, and when I find sterling virtue and manly worth—where I find practice following precept, when I find the mouth speaking from the heart, and the heart filled with a love of the attributes of heaven, and all these qualities combined in a single man, I feel that God has indeed made man but a little lower than the angels. And sometimes such men do walk the earth to guide and direct us.

Such a man was Martin Cheney!—We may indeed say of him: "His life was gentle, and the elements so mixed in him, that nature might stand up and say to all the world, 'This is a man.'"

Martin Cheney gave the best proof of his moral greatness by conquering himself, and having gained the mastery of his worst enemy, he enlisted for the benefit of the world. He was, in his youth, addicted somewhat to the use of ardent spirits, but in the early days of the Temperance reformation, he was committed to its principles, and has ever since labored manfully to save his fellow men from the disgrace and ruin which so surely follow a life of intemperance. His own experience had been told, and retold, long before the association of Washingtonians was known, and his mild, though zealous entreaties led many hearts from dissipation to sobriety.

Mr. Cheney was, for some years, the President of the State Temperance Society, and in that capacity he served the cause faithfully and with much satisfaction to the people of the State. But affairs did not suit him. It was in the lonely walks of life that he loved to labor, it was in the elevation of his fellow men he found his chief pleasure. The great delight of his life was in following the precepts of Him whose cause he served, *"in going about doing good."* Hence his great anxiety for the spread of the principles of Temperance.

May his mantle fall on the form of one as faithful, and a like zeal for our noble cause animate the hearts of the many friends, whom he has left to mourn his great loss.

[From the (Pawtucket, R. I.) Business Directory of Jan. 17.]

CHARACTER OF MARTIN CHENEY.

The following is a substantially correct report of the remarks of the Pastor of the Freewill Baptist Church in this place, last Sabbath morning, in relation to the recent death of Mr. Cheney:—

"Help, Lord; for the godly man ceaseth; for the faithful fail from among the children of men."—Psalms xii: 1.

Mr. Williams remarked that probably the text originally referred to the apostasy of those who were or were supposed to be godly. But as the loss of salutary influences is in that case similar to the loss when godly men die, there is an appropriateness in using it in relation to the death of the godly. In this sense it is peculiarly appropriate in respect to the recent decease of Martin Cheney.

1. He was eminently godly in the purity of his private life. As a man, a friend, a father, a Christian, his private character was unstained. Though the earlier part of his life was somewhat recklessly devoted to sinful indulgences; yet from the moment that he became a Christian, he was a pattern of private and personal virtues. Many were ardently and often bitterly opposed to his sentiments, and some would gladly have availed themselves of almost any means to overthrow his influence, still his private character was never assailed. All who *knew* him in his private life were constrained to feel that few men ever possessed a greater share of that purity which is so prominent an element of godliness.

2. Godliness was eminently manifested in his devotion to principle. To him religion and the religious life were not the results of impulse, but the practical developments of truth. He was devout, not from the selfish motive of the pleasure of devotion, but because devotion was right—because it ennobled the heart and character, by bringing them into harmony with righteousness and the divine will. Hence his religious conduct never depended upon the caprice of feeling. However his sensibilities might have been for the time affected, his constant aim was to do, and do only, what was demanded by principle. There was therefore only one way to affect his life. Convince him that he was wrong, and from that moment his conduct was changed. In him there was nothing of approving the right and still pursuing the wrong. Hence,

3. He was eminently godly in exemplifying Christian principle. His independence and boldness in maintaining and practicing what he deemed to be right are proverbial. No matter how contrary to his own former convictions or practice, no matter how utterly opposed to the convictions or practice of society and those around him, so soon as he deemed any sentiment to be right, he at once proclaimed his adherence to it. Nor did it matter how much personal sacrifice might be demanded of him, in consequence. If he appeared likely to lose place and even influence thereby, it still failed to affect him. He had much of the spirit of Luther when he would go to Worms, "though there were as many devils there as tiles on the houses."

There was moreover little or nothing of pride of opinion in his character. He never seemed to be at all hindered from embracing a new opinion because he might have already committed himself to the expression of a different sentiment. Hence he was among the first to listen to the arguments in favor of the inviolability of human life; and when he thought them to be sound, he did not hesitate to disavow his former sentiments, and repudiate everything—even civil government itself—so far as it involved the taking of human life. And so of other things. However firmly we may be convinced that in some respects he was wrong; yet we cannot but respect the godly integrity that shuns no necessary sacrifices in order to uphold what it deems to be right. It is an element of godliness that few possess in so eminent a degree as did he whom we mourn to-day.

4. Godliness was strikingly manifested in the singleness and earnestness of his purpose. Conscientiousness was a prominent feature in his character, and a ruling principle in his life. It always governed his other faculties, and led him sternly to question the propriety of every step he proposed to take. However solicitous he might be for the success of any favorite measure, he never indulged in sly, underhanded dealing. Possessing a shrewdness and tact that would be likely to betray him into the arts of management, still he invariably spurned every advantage that was not gained by the dint of straight-forward effort. But that effort was always in earnest. Whatsoever his hand found to do he did with his might. His was no indolent or wavering disposition. His sentiments never lay dormant in his mind. They were living, acting, earnest things; and hence he seldom failed of accomplishing his purpose. His language, his voice, his gestures, his eyes, his countenance, all told that he spake from deep, honest and earnest conviction; and such speech is seldom ineffectual. He repudiated all seeming that was not also real; and when Martin Cheney spoke we all knew that it was the sincere, undisguised and straight-forward sentiment of his head and heart.

5. Added to all this was the light and glow of an uncommon intellectual ability. Self-educated he indeed was; and yet he was an intellectual giant. No one ever came in contact with him without finding a demand for his mightiest energies. His perceptive and analytical powers perhaps predominated; and hence

he was quick to detect and ready to expose a fallacy in an opponent. Hence, too, he was impatient of the pen. His perceptions would not wait its toilsome motion. He studied closely and scrutinizingly; but left behind him little of his pulpit thoughts—save in the form of brief skeletons. We remember one of his analytical efforts in this house. His theme was the "Beauty of Christ." We were somewhat familiar with the best definitions of beauty, given by Burke and others; but so far did he, to our conceptions, surpass them all, that we felt as if we had never heard a fitting definition of it before.

But he is gone. The world, the church, the denomination with which he was connected, have suffered a great loss. At our approaching Quarterly Meeting there will be a place vacant that none of us can fill. We never failed of seeing him at our quarterly gatherings—but he has attended for the last time. We shall see him no more, until we meet him at the judgment seat of the Eternal. How appropriate now to turn to the mercy seat and say:—"Help Lord; for the godly man ceaseth; for the faithful fail from among the children of men."

The speaker concluded with some remarks in relation to the necessity of the divine assistance, and the manner in which it should be sought to compensate us and the world for his loss.

[Extracts from a Discourse preached in the Roger Williams Church, Providence, January 11th, 1852, entitled the "Elements of Greatness:" By Eli Noyes, D. D.]

"Know ye not that there is a prince and a great man fallen this day in Israel?"—II. *Sam.* iii.: 38.

* * * * * *

A HUMAN MIND, possessing many elements of greatness, has just left us for the spirit world. That mind was great; for it did, in many of its attributes, bear a faint image of the Infinite mind. No one who was at all familiar with MARTIN CHENEY can refrain from saying that, in his death, a great man has fallen in our modern Israel.

* * * * * *

Many of my hearers have been acquainted with Mr. Cheney much longer than myself,—have seen much more of him, and have more frequently listened to his valuable instructions than it has been my privilege to do. But during the time of our acquaintance I have tried to study his character; and the more I examined it the more I respected it, till, at length, my respect almost amounted to a kind of adoration. Though, from motives of prudence, sparing of my praise to his face and to his intimate friends, yet I felt that I had his confidence and love—I know that he had mine. I love to speak of him; a recollection of his excellences awakens in my soul higher and holier motives; and while I refer to some of the elements of greatness which made up his character, I shall speak from my own personal acquaintance with the man.

Do not suppose that I intend to pay him a tribute of unmingled worship. Were the good man himself present, he would be the first to rebuke me for such a spirit of servility. He had his errors in judgment and in practice, or at least I thought so; but when we disagreed we soon came to a mutual understanding of the fact, and it did not mar our christian feeling toward each other.

* * * * * *

In recounting some of the elements of greatness in his character, I shall first of all notice his *Individuality. Mr. Cheney was himself, and no one else.* Some men entirely lose their personal identity in the society to which they belong; and the most of persons receive such a denominational stamp, that their peculiarities as individuals are in part lost;—what *one* is in his sentiments, habits of thought, tastes, tones of voice, and even physiognomy, so, to a great extent, are all the rest. So distinct is the impression made by the respective sects, that we can almost always detect a man by his address, and not unfrequently by the very expression of his countenance.

There are, however, men who have no particular family likeness to any denomination. There is nothing in their features, gesticulation, tones of voice, habits of thought, or any thing else, that would lead you to rank them with one sect rather than with another. Such were Robert Hall, John Foster, Chalmers, Channing, and Olin, and such, in the Freewill Baptist denomination, was Martin Cheney. I do not mean to say that he had no doctrines which gave him a stronger affinity for one denomination than for another. He had. I do not mean to say that he had no denominational preferences. He had; and they were strong. I have often heard him remark that he thought his views accorded more fully with those of the Freewill Baptists than with those of any other sect; and I believe his church has as marked a denominational character, and their denominational preferences are as strong, as those of any church in the land; but as far as appearance and habits were concerned, Mr. Cheney had no denominational tinge. He looked, he talked, and he acted in the main like other men; but the moment you strike upon any thing that specially appertained to his character, you will find it emphatically his own. . . . . . Mr. Cheney was himself without either effort or resistance. He never seemed to pride himself in being unlike his associates, and yet he, unconsciously to himself I think, maintained a personal identity that rendered him as acceptable to one class as to another.

* * * * * *

Mr. Cheney was not a man of liberal education. He made no pretensions to literary or classic lore; but, after all, he was educated. He was a close student of books, men and things; though he prosecuted his studies under his own guidance. His thoughts were to a great extent of his own manufacture, and he kept the mould in which they had been run for future use. . . . . . . A large share of his information he received from conversation. Not from borrowing the ideas of others, but from analyzing them and recasting them in his own mould, in connection with his own thoughts.

After a long discussion in a Ministers' Meeting or a Quarterly Meeting, I have often known him to balance the arguments, gathering the good and casting the bad away, with a keenness of perception and discrimination which I have seldom known to be equalled.

To him belonged great independence of thought. He claimed liberty of thought and of speech in a very high degree, both for himself and for others. He was often heard to say that one might as well eat for him as to think for him. This trait of character led to great candor in the discussion of opposing sentiments. I shall never forget the time when I came to give a missionary discourse in his church. It was just after some serious difficulties, which had existed between the two Quarterly Meetings with which we were respectively connected. The battle had been fought with too much asperity on both sides. Mr. Cheney's feelings were strongly enlisted on one side, and mine were as intensely enkindled on the other. But when I came under his roof he exhibited a noble-spiritedness, and an affability and kindness not to be met with in every opponent. He was not only kind but really congenial. Being requested to give an Anti-Slavery discourse in the evening, I took occasion to say to him that I should be under the necessity of giving utterance to sentiments which would be opposed to his views; believing as I did in the propriety of swearing to protect the Constitution of the United States, and the duty of maintaining human government though at the expense of human life. Never shall I forget the dignified look and the heartfelt earnestness with which he said,—"Brother Noyes, you can feel just as much at home in the expression of your honest convictions of truth in my pulpit as you feel in your own." The expression evidently came from the heart, and I enjoyed the most unrestrained liberty in giving the freest expression to my views; while he, at the close, with great cordiality, assented to the general sentiments of the discourse, and, in relation to the points to which he took exception, simply remarked that the people well knew that his views differed from mine, but he was nevertheless glad that the opposite side of the question had been so fairly represented. This was one of the incidents in my history which I thought worth remembering.

* * * * * *

He had all confidence in the truth, and believed it safe to follow it wherever it might lead.

In debate he asked nothing for dignity of office, superior abilities, or for gray hairs. If any respect was yielded for these things, he evidently regarded it as a mark of good breeding in his opponent, though he disdained to lay claim to such respect. He acted on the principle that, if his office, knowledge, or age gave him the advantage over his opponent, that advantage consisted solely in enabling him the more effectually to exhibit the truth. We seldom meet with a man who has a stronger antipathy against opposing dignity of office to talent or to truth.

Though he placed but little value upon appearances, and never *aimed* to be dignified, yet he *was* dignified without effort. No man could ever lay his hand upon the shoulder of Martin Cheney unless he intended to do a mean act. There was something in his very aspect which seemed to say,—"Approach me not with low and vulgar familiarity." He received strangers with proper courtesy and cordiality, but with no vulgar fondness. It was in the Spring of 1842, that I first became acquainted with Mr. Cheney, which was at his own home. I called upon him as a Foreign Mission Agent, and his dignified though perfectly affable deportment made a deep impression upon my mind; and I then received a high opinion of his talents and his piety, which I have had no cause to change. Since that time we have been more or less intimately associated, but never have I discovered any of that familiarity which would have led him to trust any part of his reputation in my hands. I was never such a confidant with him, and I doubt whether he had any such confidants.

Another distinguishing trait in the character of Mr. Cheney, and which, in a peculiar manner, exhibited greatness of soul, was his strenuous adherence to and advocacy of the cause of liberty. Oppression in all its forms he detested, whether it consisted in the irresponsible authority maintained by the master over the down trodden slave, the unjust usurpation of government over the individual conscience, or the self constituted authority of Quarterly Meetings to dictate to churches or to annul their action. * * * * * *

Christian firmness was a distinguishing trait in his character. From the time when he first embraced the truth, he continued steadfast unto the end. Some, indeed, were ready to predict he would not hold out a month; but years passed away and found him steady to his christian purpose, until, at length, every enemy despaired of his halting. The truth as it is in Jesus fed and fired his soul, and buoyed up his spirit against all opposition. No obstacles could dishearten him, gold could not buy him, flattery could not inveigle him, honor could not bedazzle him, and hell could not intimidate him.

> "From strength to strength, from grace to grace,
> Swiftest and foremost in the race,
> He carried victory in his face,
> He triumphed as he ran."

His worst enemies whom he has often beaten, if possessed of a spark of generosity, will honor the memory of so noble a specimen of humanity, who was so uncompromising in his principles, and who so rigidly adhered to what he believed to be right.

The benevolence of our honored friend was large. It was seen in his sympathy for the slave, the heathen, the poor, and all the distressed; and though his face was set against all sin, yet he never manifested any inclination to crush the erring, or to hedge up the way to prevent the vilest sinner from returning to the path of rectitude.

* * * * * *

But caution was the most prominent trait in Mr. Cheney's character. True, many thought him rash and hasty, but never was there a greater mistake. He was the very incarnation of cautiousness. His being the only preacher in Olneyville for so many years, he owed in a great measure to his cautiousness. True, he was accustomed to make some tremendous bounds, but he always struck right side up on *terra firma*. He would examine with candor and patience every subject that came up, whether good or bad ; and sometimes I have thought he would spend more time in the examination of a subject than it was really worth ; but he was one of the very slowest of men to commit himself that I ever saw. Sometimes he has been seen in a position where it seemed that he would be obliged to commit himself to what would very likely prove to be error, but he has always escaped the rocks and the breakers.

* * * * *

He continued steadfastly to the end in the christian faith. . . . . . . A few weeks before his death, he spoke to me as a dying man. To my question, if he found the gospel which he had preached while in health to be his support on the sick bed, he replied substantially as follows. " I have no fears. I doubt not God will take care of me. True, I do not believe in all respects just as I did when I commenced preaching. I think I have been receiving light all the way along, yet I am firm in the belief that God so loved the world that he gave his Son to save all who will believe. I do not profess however to know all about God or Christ, or to have a full understanding of what Christ has done for the salvation of the world. But this much I do fully believe, that all who from their own free will make Christ their trust, will be saved, and I see no chance for the rest. Some believe Calvinism, and others believe Universalism. I believe neither, but think we must be saved, if saved at all, through voluntarily trusting in Christ.

When I remarked that I wished I could do something for him, he replied :—" It would gratify you, no doubt, but you cannot. Pray for me—that is all you can do. I would like to get rid of this sickness if it is the Lord's will ; but I have no anxiety."

* * * * * *

All things considered, MARTIN CHENEY was the noblest specimen of humanity we have yet lost from our ministry. His loss will be deeply felt in the denomination, and through this whole State where his influence was so extensive. We, as a church and congregation, shall greatly miss his instructions and friendship. But more especially will his loss be felt by that church which has been witness to his entire christian life, and to which he has sustained the relation of an affectionate pastor from the time of its organization. May God give them grace to bear their affliction, and send them a pastor after his own heart.

His presence will no more honor our Quarterly Conference, where we were accustomed to join with him in prayer and in friendly debate. Some of us did, it is true, disagree with him on certain points, and our discussions have from time to time been warm ; but in respect to them and to him I would adopt the language of another, uttered in relation to the late venerable Professor Stuart, who fell on the self same day with our lamented Cheney.

" The ardor of discussion pauses solemnly before the grave. Those heats of feeling which controversy may have generated, melt into a milder and more refulgent tenderness, as we meditate on the excellence which death renders lustrous. And it may well make heaven more lovely to us, as we remember how many are yearly and monthly passing thither ; to lose all errors beneath the blaze of God's truth ; to drop every temptation with the body which is dissolved ; to be purged from all frailty in the fulness of the manifestation of the divine love ; to unfold every grace and to perfect all knowledge in the serene and perfect glory which spreads forever overhead. To that great company may God bring us in his good time."

[Resolutions passed by the Rhode Island Quarterly Meeting Conference, at its session in Providence, January, 1852.]

Resolved, That this Quarterly Meeting Conference most sincerely and deeply feel the loss of our highly esteemed friend and brother, the Reverend Martin Cheney, whose presence animated, whose counsels directed, whose sympathy cheered, and whose bold advocacy of the truth so often encouraged us in these our Quarterly Sessions; and we unite in thanksgiving to the great Giver of all good, that we have so long enjoyed the inestimable aid of so valuable a helper in the gospel—for whose memory we shall ever cherish the highest Christian regards.

Resolved, That the whole Christian church, but more especially the body with which he was immediately connected, together with the community in general, have sustained a great loss in the death of this eminent servant of Christ.

Resolved, That we tender to his afflicted family, and to the church of which he was pastor, our heartfelt sympathy, and our earnest prayer for Divine support in this, their sad bereavement.

Resolved, That we appropriate some time during the present session for prayer and conference, with special reference to this serious affliction; and that a sermon be preached at the next session of the Quarterly Meeting, commemorative of the character of our departed brother.

[In conformity to one of the above Resolutions, Rev. James A. McKenzie was appointed to deliver a discourse on the Life and Character of Mr. Cheney, before the Quarterly Meeting, at its session in May following. Circumstances preventing his attendance at that time, the discourse was delivered at its session in Foster, R. I., August 18, 1852. The following are extracts from that discourse.]

"That ye be not slothful, but followers of them who through faith and patience inherit the promises.—*Heb* vi. : 12.

* * * * * *

My first personal acquaintance with Brother Cheney was in North Providence, at the Quarterly Meeting, in January, 1832. He had just buried his second wife, but, with his heart torn, he was at the Quarterly Meeting to preach Christ Jesus the Lord, and fill his place as a member of that body. Unknown to each other, three ministers in succession preached from the same text at this meeting. Unknown to each other I say; for when the first preached, the other two were absent; when the second preached the third was absent; and it was only when the third preached that the whole three were present. I was the first, Brother Cheney the second, and Thomas Williams the third. The text was; " For the love of Christ constraineth us ;" and we all felt as the text saith. From that time Cheney and myself became intimate, and our regard was mutual, dear, and strong.

He was a man of christian hospitality. The best he had, all that came to him in the name of the Lord were welcome to; and they were made to feel so. He was never ashamed of his poverty in the first part of his ministry, nor ever made it an excuse for turning any away. . . . . He has told me that he felt thankful to God when he had a coat the worse for wear, and other clothes of the same description, given him. As poor as he then was, he devised liberal things; and if the loaves were of barley and the fishes little and few, he used what he had as the Lord's steward. . . . .

The first time I went to his house, his little motherless babe, wasted to a skeleton, lay in the cradle; our venerable and beloved sister—Mother Kelley—(now dead) whom he had engaged as housekeeper, with a countenance like Stephen's when it appeared as an angel's, sat by the sick; and Brother Cheney, with a hopeful sadness, as if faith pierced the dark cloud that hung over him, and saw beyond a clear sky and perpetual sunshine, received and welcomed me to his home. He has often said to me, "You live in the past as well as the future—I live only in the future." Hope was ever with him.

He early saw and felt the deficiency in the system and operations of the Connexion and the Quarterly Meeting as to the rights and dues of the ministry. He took up the subject, and wrote and published a circular letter or tract on the support of the ministry, urging it as the due of the minister as the servant of God and of the church. And this he did at a time when the naming of such a thing exposed the minister to the cry of, " hireling, hireling; a wolf in sheep's clothing;

seeking the fleece and not the flock; after dollars and cents and not after souls!"

* * * * * *

It was enough for Brother Cheney to see a thing wrong for him to throw himself in the front of danger, hostility, and power, to oppose it; and see a thing right for him to adopt it and identify himself with it, never hesitating, halting, or turning back in view of the sacrifices which such a course would call him to make, or privations it would call him to endure. "If it is right I am in for it, with all its consequences; If it is wrong I am against it, cost me what it may in opposing it," were the declarations of his heart, tongue, and conduct.

Intellectually he was great, comprehensive, and fruitful. . . . . . . Among the attendants upon his ministry for years, were found some of the most vigorous minds—lawyers, senators, and statesmen, who always listened to him with reverence and satisfaction. . . . .

He seized upon truths clearly, rationally, and decisively; he prepared himself by observation, reading, and reflection to exhibit and defend and press home what he judged to be true on every subject connected with the religious interest of the church and of the world. And religious interest, in his judgment, included everything affecting man mentally, morally, physically, and socially. With him, four R's went as other three R's went with John Ryland; who said a sermon was not a gospel sermon unless it had the three R's——Ruin by sin, Redemption by Christ, and Renewal by the Holy Ghost. So Brother Cheney seemed to think no sermon was complete, unless it embraced as topics, inferences, or consequences, temperance Reform, anti-slavery Reform, moral Reform, and Reform from war, violence, and all wickedness. When he gave his mind to a subject he seemed to lay hold upon it and master it at once; as has appeared on various subjects of local or general interest, on many points of doctrine and practice, and questions of morals. Whether in sermons, lectures, conversations, or discussions, he ever seemed perfectly at home. Whoever was his opponent in discussion, whether the scholar of high literary grade, or the divine of high titular distinction, or the man of ordinary sense and attainment, they, without exception, acknowledged his ability by their subsequent friendship or malignity. . . . . . .

With all the readiness with which Brother Cheney seized upon truths, he would look about and over and under and through a subject before he declared himself; but when he did so, you and all others knew where to find him. There were no inuendoes, no double entendres, no statements or observations that might be taken either way; when he spoke he could be taken but one way, and that was just the way he meant.

. . . . . He was never obstinate or dishonest in a mistake, and never did a thing, right or wrong, only as he thought it right and that so he ought to do. Convince him it was wrong, and he was ready to recall it.

He had the heart, the mind, the spirit of a true christian and servant of Jesus Christ. He never took state from the greatness of his ability, his prominency before the public, or the superiority accorded him by the voice of friend and foe. He ever felt that he was a brother among equals, and that their rights were as sacred as his own—they were one and the same. This was his doctrine—this he designed should mark his conduct. But his temper was hot. In the heat of discussion, keen, harsh, or perverse argument in opposition to his position, would send the purple flashing to his whitening locks. And I have found in him what seemed a lingering dislike of the person exhibiting such tact or opposition to him; and I used to talk with him about it when we would be together by ourselves, walking or in bed. I would tell him that he plead for freedom of thought and expression for himself and others, and for him to come down like a thunderbolt on a brother who differed as honestly from his position as he stuck to it, and think less favorably of an opponent because of this honest difference, was not doing as he taught, or as he would be done by; and with all the meekness of a loving, gentle, little child, would he acknowledge the wrong, and say he would try to guard against it. And at the close or returning from a Quarterly Meeting, he would say to me, "I watched myself and guarded my feelings; don't you think I am improving?" I would tell him, "Yes; but go on to perfection, and not lay again the foundation of repentance from dead works." And thus did we confer together.

* * * * *

He was a devout man; a man of prayer, family, social, and secret. It was not lip work without the heart; but it was heart's desire and prayer. He loved to pray, to hear prayer, and join in it. And in it, when his last

sickness depressed and held him down, he told me he found great liftings up to God and joy. . . . . .
He said to me, "I feel that I am in the hands of God; if it is his will that I recover, it is my choice; but if it his will that I should die, I am resigned. His will be done."

He was laborious in his ministry. He fulfilled his engagements in his own pulpit and church with diligence and zeal. He preached often at funerals, lectured often at home and abroad on religious and moral questions, and was often and unwearied on the platform in the meetings for the discussion of great moral topics, in Providence, Boston and elsewhere; and seldom failed to attend the Ministers' and Quarterly and Yearly Meetings in this State and in Massachusetts; and, when there, whoever excused himself from labor, Brother Cheney never did it. Not but that he delighted to listen to others, but he had no heart to sit still because others had no heart to bestir themselves. Of him in truth it may be said, "In labors more abundant." He never excused himself from any needful work, however thankless, and there was a good deal of that which he was called to do, and he did it. He never let ease, recreations, excursions, or secular considerations take him from his work; but every thing succumbed to his duty to God and man, as a disciple and minister of Jesus Christ.

* * * * *

Cheney, like Abel, brought the best and all he had—which was himself—and, through faith, offered it a living sacrifice, holy and acceptable to God; like Enoch he walked with God, and had the testimony that he pleased him; like Noah, moved by God, he built an ark for the saving of his house and hundreds more, and so proved himself an heir of the righteousness of faith; like Abraham, Isaac and Jacob, he acknowledged himself a sojourner on earth, and shone as a light in the world; like Moses he forsook Egypt, and sought to bring the church with him, not fearing the wrath of Rumsellers, Slaveholders, Lickspittles, or Aristocrats; like Gideon, Samson, Jepthah, and David, he was ready to meet and battle the enemies of God and the truth in every way which God directed; and like Samuel and all the prophets and the apostles, he shunned not to declare all the counsel of God, nor kept back any thing that was profitable to men—saints or sinners. He believed what they believed, and like them through faith and patience now inherits the promises.

A year ago and he was with us in Quarterly Meeting; but he has gone. We have seen his face and heard his voice for the last time on earth. His death has made a great breach among us. God gave him in goodness and took him in mercy. A great, good man has passed away from us, and we are bereaved. But he served his generation; and having done that by the will of God, he fell asleep. He has been useful; the good he has done will live and be increasing when his name shall have faded from human recollection. Blessed are the dead who die in the Lord; they rest from their labors, and their works do follow them. Thanks to God who gave us such a brother, friend and yoke-fellow, and continued him so long; and though he is now absent from us, he is present with the Lord, both ours and his.

[Letter from the Church at Olneyville, to the Rhode Island Quarterly Meeting, held in Providence, January, 1852.]

JANUARY, 20, 1852.

DEAR BRETHREN:—We come before you with sadness: for we are in deep affliction, on account of the death of our much loved pastor—who departed this life on the 4th instant.

Elder Martin Cheney has been with us from the commencement of his ministerial work, and from the organization of our church, which was in the year 1828. During all this time he has been steadily laboring for our interest and the good of this community.

We have ever found him faithful to his mission, as a servant of Christ, and always ready to defend the right at whatever hazard.

He has grown old in our midst, and we found him wise in counsel, prompt in action, and had learned to regard him as *really* a Father in Israel.

He lived not alone for us, but for all the human race: for he recognized the doctrine of the Fatherhood of God, and the Brotherhood of Man.

He has ever preached to us the *whole* gospel; applying its principles, as he understood them, to all the practices of men.

But he has gone. We shall hear his voice no more.

We must go to the house of worship, and not find him in our pulpit, to preach to us the precious words of Christ's gospel. We shall attend our church and covenant meetings as before, but he will not be with us, to give that counsel and encouragement which he was accustomed to do. When we attend your meetings, as we do by our delegates to-day, we shall not behold him as we have been wont to, engaging with so much interest in your proceedings.

But although he is gone, and we most deeply feel our loss, we are not in despair. But by the grace of God, we will go forward in our work, until we, like him, shall have honorably run our race and finished our work.

In behalf of the Olneyville church,
   Yours in affliction,
     D. R. WHITTEMORE,
     C. S. SWEETLAND,
       Committee.

[Extract from a letter sent by the Olneyville Church to the Quarterly Meeting, held at Scituate, in May, 1852.]

*   *   *   *   *   *

But while we address you, our minds dwell with special interest on our great affliction. It is known to you all that our Pastor has left us for a home with his divine Master and Savior in the spirit world.

We loved our Pastor, for he first loved us. He, as the friend and servant of Christ, and as our friend, had been with us for many years. Yes, during all the ever changing scenes of our lives, in health and sickness, prosperity and adversity, joy and sorrow, in early youth, at the bridal altar, and when death has taken our parents, brothers, sisters, companions, and children from us, our Pastor has been with us. He pointed us to the Lamb of God that taketh away the sins of the world; and told us that God so loved the world that he gave his only begotten Son, that whosoever believeth in him should not perish, but have everlasting life. He bowed with us when we prayed for mercy, and rejoiced with us when we submitted to God and found Christ precious to the soul. He led us into the baptismal waters, and gave us the hand of fellowship when we covenanted with God and the Church to live and die Christians. We partook of the symbols of Jesus' broken body and poured out blood—broken and poured out by his hands which are now cold in the grave. He always sympathized with us, and was ever anxious to promote our interests,—physical, mental, moral, temporal, and eternal.

We knew not his worth nor how much we loved him until he was taken from us. But the remembrance of him is dear to us. With the deepest interest shall we remember him and his labors of love, so long as these hearts shall throb with life. We shall think of him in our Sabbath services, in our recreations and pleasures; but especially at the house of mourning, in times of sickness and death.

We remember with peculiar pleasure the moral purity of his life. From his first profession of the Christian faith he never faltered—was never convicted of a crime. He was ever honest, upright, and pure in all the walks of life; and for years none attempted to oppose him by even hinting at anything immoral in his conduct toward his fellow-men. The whole people, virtuous and vicious, join in the acknowledgement that he was an honest man and a christian, if there was ever one.

We remember with high satisfaction his true independence of character. He was emphatically the servant of God, and recognized his direct responsibility to him; and therefore acknowledged no rightful power in man, the Church or State, to repeal, suspend, or modify the law of love—the law of Christ. In all his preaching and acting he refused to flatter or succumb to popular opinion; yea, even in his own church; for he was always in advance of the church as well as of the community in the reforms of the age. We followed after him in the Temperance struggle, and in opposition to War, and the great conflict with Slavery.

We fondly cherish the memory of his frankness and honesty; for we never found him speaking different things to different men. All knew his opinions and positions by his words. He was just what he appeared to be, and always meant just what he said.

His doctrines were just what he preached and argued at home and abroad.

We cherish the remembrance of his principles, which we consider the real doctrines of the gospel; and especially his opposition to Slavery, Intemperance and War, and his advocacy of honesty and benevolence in all the walks of life—all founded upon the higher law—the law of God.

We hope that the principles of freedom which he advocated will triumph, until all, like him, shall believe in free soil, free men, free speech, free trade, free will, free communion and free salvation. . . . . .

In behalf of the Church,

C. S. SWEETLAND, Clerk.

To the surprise of almost every one, Mr. Cheney's Will revealed the fact that, though his salary had always been moderate, he had so economized as to leave nearly three thousand dollars for the use of his family— a provision which reflects credit on himself, and affords them a relief whose absence it would be a hardship to endure.

Soon after Mr. Cheney's death, a meeting of all who felt an interest in the object was called to consider the propriety of erecting a suitable monument at his grave. Such a testimonial was unanimously voted of the value of one hundred and twenty-five dollars; and a Committee was appointed to superintend the erection; and, in a short time, it was standing above his dust. The design is simple, chaste and peculiar. Including the base, the whole height is about six feet. The shaft is of fine marble, and, at the base, is about two feet square. The shaft is surmounted by a plain capital, forming a small tablet, and on this—crowning the whole—rests a BIBLE. The shaft is inscribed as follows:

LIFE OF

[EAST SIDE.]

"I HAVE FOUGHT A GOOD FIGHT;
I HAVE FINISHED MY COURSE;
I HAVE KEPT THE FAITH."
2D TIM. IV. : 7.

[SOUTH SIDE.]

HE WAS A WARM PERSONAL FRIEND;
A KIND HUSBAND;
AN AFFECTIONATE FATHER;
A STRONG ADVOCATE FOR LIBERTY AND HUMANITY;
AND A FAITHFUL SERVANT OF GOD.

[WEST SIDE.]

ELDER
MARTIN CHENEY.
BORN IN DOVER, MASS., AUG. 29, 1792;
ORDAINED TO PREACH
APRIL 28, 1825;
WAS INSTALLED PASTOR OVER THE
FIRST FREE WILL BAPTIST CHURCH AND SOCIETY,
IN OLNEYVILLE,
AT THEIR ORGANIZATION,
NOV. 7, 1828;
AND CONTINUED SUCH UNTIL HIS DEATH,
JAN. 4, 1852.
HIS LAST WORDS WERE, "I HAVE A HOPE THAT
ENDURETH UNTO THE END."

The Society also voted an appropriation of twenty-five dollars, to procure and erect a slab to his memory in the pulpit which he had so long occupied. The form of the slab is that of a shield, the lettering is of gilt, and the inscription is the same as that on the west side of the monument.

Mr. Cheney's pilgrimage is closed. The wearied body rests; the freed spirit soars in diviner air, where every breath is an inspiration, and where it never tires in its climbings toward the mount of God. Yet long and deeply shall we and the world feel the pressure of his influence. And well shall it be, if these records of his life are allowed to act as a cord to draw us along the strait and narrow path which he trod in the flesh, and which terminates in the excellent glory where he walks and sings in white.

Check Out More Titles From HardPress Classics Series In this collection we are offering thousands of classic and hard to find books. This series spans a vast array of subjects – so you are bound to find something of interest to enjoy reading and learning about.

Subjects:
Architecture
Art
Biography & Autobiography
Body, Mind &Spirit
Children & Young Adult
Dramas
Education
Fiction
History
Language Arts & Disciplines
Law
Literary Collections
Music
Poetry
Psychology
Science
…and many more.

Visit us at www.hardpress.net

I'm The Story
personalised classic books

"Beautiful gift.. lovely finish.
My Niece loves it, so precious!"

Helen R Brumfieldon

★★★★★

UNIQUE GIFT

FOR KIDS, PARTNERS AND FRIENDS

Timeless books such as:

Alice in Wonderland · The Jungle Book · The Wonderful Wizard of Oz
Peter and Wendy · Robin Hood · The Prince and The Pauper
The Railway Children · Treasure Island · A Christmas Carol

Romeo and Juliet · Dracula

Visit
ImTheStory.com
and order yours today!

CPSIA information can be obtained
at www.ICGtesting.com
Printed in the USA
BVHW081617220819
556561BV00018B/3882/P